Transformational Public Policy

Transformational Public Policy examines how governments can more effectively handle uncertainty and risk in an uncertain and changing world. Unpredictable and changing circumstances often bring nasty surprises that can increase waste in governance and public debt. This book illustrates how new methods derived from signal processing techniques can improve the practice of public policy by transforming it through rapid learning and adaptation. Interventions are processes of discovery, not compliance.

Transformational Public Policy shows readers how the power of hypothesis testing in governance can be deployed. The book argues that public policy can be framed as tests of competing hypotheses subject to diagnostic errors. The aim is to learn how to reduce these diagnostic errors through cumulative experience. This approach can reduce the impact of negative unintended consequences – a topic of great interest to policymakers and academics alike.

Mark Matthews is a public policy specialist who has worked closely with different governments from both private sector and academic bases. He has a background in science and innovation policy and is particularly interested in the consequences of shortcomings in the ways in which governments approach uncertainty and risk – and what could be done to address these problems.

Routledge Studies in Governance and Public Policy

For a full list of titles in this series, please visit www.routledge.com/series/GPP

18 **Inclusive Growth, Development and Welfare Policy**
A critical assessment
Edited by Reza Hasmath

19 **The New and Changing Transatlanticism**
Politics and policy perspectives
Edited by Laurie Buonanno, Natalia Cuglesan and Keith Henderson

20 **Childhood Citizenship, Governance and Policy**
The politics of becoming adult
Sana Nakata

21 **The Idea of Good Governance and the Politics of the Global South**
An analysis of its effects
Haroon A. Khan

22 **Interpreting Governance, High Politics and Public Policy**
Essays commemorating Interpreting British Governance
Edited by Nick Turnbull

23 **Political Engagement of the Young in Europe**
Youth in the crucible
*Edited by Peter Thijssen, Jessy Siongers, Jeroen Van Laer, Jacques Haers
and Sara Mels*

24 **Rethinking Governance**
Ruling, rationalities and resistance
Edited by Mark Bevir and R. A. W. Rhodes

25 **Governmentality after Neoliberalism**
Edited by Mark Bevir

26 **Transformational Public Policy**
A new strategy for coping with uncertainty and risk
Mark Matthews

Transformational Public Policy

A new strategy for coping with uncertainty and risk

Mark Matthews

LONDON AND NEW YORK

First published 2017 by Routledge

2 Park Square, Milton Park, Abingdon, Oxfordshire OX14 4RN
711 Third Avenue, New York, NY 10017

Routledge is an imprint of the Taylor & Francis Group, an informa business

First issued in paperback 2018

Copyright © 2017 Mark Matthews

The right of Mark Matthews to be identified as author of this work has been asserted by him in accordance with sections 77 and 78 of the Copyright, Designs and Patents Act 1988.

All rights reserved. No part of this book may be reprinted or reproduced or utilised in any form or by any electronic, mechanical, or other means, now known or hereafter invented, including photocopying and recording, or in any information storage or retrieval system, without permission in writing from the publishers.

Notice:
Product or corporate names may be trademarks or registered trademarks, and are used only for identification and explanation without intent to infringe.

British Library Cataloguing in Publication Data
A catalogue record for this book is available from the British Library

Library of Congress Cataloging-in-Publication Data
Names: Matthews, Mark, 1950– author.
Title: Transformational public policy : a new strategy for coping with uncertainty and risk / by Mark Matthews.
Description: Abingdon, Oxon ; New York, NY : Routledge is an imprint of the Taylor & Francis Group, an informa business, [2017] | Series: Routledge studies in governance and public policy ; 26 | Includes bibliographical references and index.
Identifiers: LCCN 2016004562 | ISBN 9781138824041 (hbk) | ISBN 9781315741710 (ebk)
Subjects: LCSH: Political planning. | Administrative agencies—Management. | Risk assessment—Government policy. | Risk management—Government policy. | Uncertainty—Government policy.
Classification: LCC JF1525.P6 M335 2017 | DDC 320.6—dc23
LC record available at https://lccn.loc.gov/2016004562

ISBN: 978-1-138-82404-1 (hbk)
ISBN: 978-1-138-31787-1 (pbk)

Typeset in Galliard
by Apex CoVantage, LLC

For Katherine, Daniel and Luke

Contents

List of figures	x
Preface	xii
Acknowledgements	xx
List of abbreviations	xxii

1 Introduction: governance and entropy — 1

Innovation and austerity 4
Governance, uncertainty and signal processing 13
The potential for surprise 15
What seems to be wrong? 17
The relationship between the practice of public policy and
    the study of public policy 20
The risk amplification ratio 21
Specific propositions to be tested 25
Outline of the book 25

2 The limitations of uncertainty and risk-averse public policy — 30

Governance paradigms 32
Experimentalist governance 37
Risk management and governance 42
The relevance of subjectivist economics (and its self-imposed
    limitations) 46
The relevance of information theory 47
Framing the long-term challenge 49
The learning deficit in governance 52
The public sector innovation agenda 54
A formal model of investment risk in the innovation process 58
The growing chasm between robotic learning and
    learning in governance 61
Conclusions 62

viii   *Contents*

3   Government as uncertainty and risk manager of last resort   66

Science and innovation policy and the transformation of substantive uncertainty into quantifiable risk 68
Research and experimental development 69
Public science and the grey area between risk and uncertainty 75
Theoretical power and investment risk: lessons from business and innovation 77
Prescience as an outcome class 84
Prescience and protecting the value of national balance sheets 86
Policy implications 86
Lessons from attempts to implement prescience as a research outcome 90
Conclusions 91

4   Concepts for facilitating the transition   95

The intriguing history of Bayesian inference 97
The evolution of signal processing and machine learning methods from their Bayesian roots 105
Applying signal processing methods to governance 112
Mapping substantive uncertainty, stochastic risk and controllable risk 120
Conclusions 124

5   Implementing the transition   127

The limitations currently faced 127
Re-formulating risk management 131
Achieving transformational public policy: 'brownfield' versus 'greenfield' sites 134
Interventions as hypothesis tests 135
Value-for-money measures 140
A practical method for assigning odds in hypothesis tests 140
Calculating odds-based hypotheses test results 147
Implementing a Bayesian expression of the policy learning cycle 156
A dynamic approach to diagnostic errors 158
Implications for cross-sectoral collaboration over public policy 160
Conclusions 161

6   Conclusions: lower entropy governance   163

The core argument 163
Implications for developing economies 167
Conclusions on the set of propositions tested 168
Scope for enhanced international cooperation 171

Adopting an open innovation approach 172
Towards a compromise-based solution to tests of statistical significance 175
Next steps 179

Glossary	186
Afterword	190
Appendix	194
Index	205

Figures

1.1	Framing the potential for the interoperability of appraisal, evaluation and risk management using learning cycle interdependencies	6
2.1	Asymmetric uncertainty and the differences between evidence-based policymaking and intelligence-based policymaking	33
2.2	An expected value representation of the innovation process	59
3.1	Design capabilities as confidence curves	72
3.2	Reduced *beta* as the research outcome: understanding the value of research outcomes using the Capital Asset Pricing Model	78
3.3	The links between academic research and achieving bankable feasibility for investments	80
3.4	How simulation modelling pushes 'First of a Kind' along the learning curve	81
4.1	A Bayesian learning loop	100
4.2	The conditional probability formula for Bayes rule	101
4.3	Shannon entropy	105
4.4	Shannon error correction model framed in a public policy context	106
4.5	The Confusion Matrix	107
4.6	A Natural Frequency expression of Bayes Rule	108
4.7	Conditional probability expression of Bayes Rule	109
4.8	The simplified Bayes Rule	109
4.9	The Receiver Operating Characteristic	110
4.10	Measuring diagnostic capability in organisations	111
4.11	A Ternary representation of knowledge acquisition phases	121
4.12	A Ternary representation of knowledge domains	122
4.13	A Ternary representation of the disjuncture between theory and practice in risk management	123
5.1	Diagrammatic representation of the UK ROAMEF policy learning framework	129
5.2	Diagrammatic illustration of the Maryland Scientific Methods Scale	131

Figures xi

5.3	Different perspectives on risk management	132
5.4	The scope for integrating different perspectives on risk management	133
5.5	Exploiting synergies in risk management	133
5.6	Odds-based hypothesis tests in appraisal and evaluation	141
5.7	Using updated odds to integrate appraisal and evaluation	143
5.8	Visualising uncertainty and risk in return-on-investment calculations	145
5.9	Aligning the risk curve and defence intelligence categories	150
5.10	The Boolean approach to evidence assessment	154
5.11	Analysis of competing hypotheses in security intelligence analysis	155
5.12	Competing hypotheses in the policy learning cycle	157
5.13	A Bayesian expression of the policy learning cycle	158
5.14	Possible pathways when linking appraisal to evaluation	159
6.1	Potential shifts between target-delivery and discovery mode	177
6.2	Using Diagnostic Capability Plots to inform capability maturity assessments	182
6.3	System of synergies to be exploited	183
A1	An biosecurity illustration of natural sampling	195
A2	How test sensitivity thresholds relate to statistical (and assumption) distributions	199
A3	ROC curves as diagnostic capability measures	200
A4	The expected value equation used to inform test sensitivity choices	201

Preface

The discussion of how well governments cope with uncertainty and risk in this book stems from my experiences as an academic, a management consultant specialising in public policy, and as the inaugural director of a government-funded policy think tank based in a university. The more familiar I became with the reality of how governments operate, the clearer it became that there was a fundamental problem with how uncertainty and risk were handled – or rather mishandled. The symptoms were powerful and pervasive and suggestive of an underlying pathology that revolved around a risk-averse preference for evidence, data, rules and procedures over the types of judgement and flexible and adaptive operating practices required of the uncertainty and risk manager of 'last resort'. This pathology often appeared to be driven by an assumption that the public sector could operate more effectively if 'hard' evidence were used rather than subjective judgement – with the recourse to judgement being treated as a problem to be eliminated rather than something upon which circumstances dictate that we must rely. This preference for quantification also extends to how substantive uncertainties and risks are handled, resulting in an avoidance of substantive uncertainty and an aversion to risk that is not well aligned with governments' role as uncertainty and risk managers of last resort. The result appeared to be an ideal type for governance being conjured up that was divorced from the reality of what governments must be able to do.

This ideal type reflected the 'deficit' perspective: that the public sector was less effective than the private sector (and the non-profit sector) and must therefore be reformed via the combination of shifting some public services into the private sector (privatisation), the adoption of private sector–influenced performance metrics and hard targets (managerialism), assertions that the public sector should emulate private sector innovation practices (innovation), and various kinds of contractual partnerships between the public sector and the private sector and the non-profit sector (partnerships). As manifestations of an underlying pathology, these deficit-framed characteristics of modern governance pointed to a severe loss of confidence in governance that, to me, appeared to stem from neglecting governments' role in dealing with all the truly nasty things that markets and the businesses that shape these markets, civil society and the general community as a whole cannot cope with. These nasty things will happen irrespective of whether we have evidence on them. Consequently, insisting on robust evidence tends to deflect the attention (and capabilities) within governments to those areas that are most remote from the most important core functions of governance. The result is a tendency to dwell on details of the past rather than the complex, ambiguous and often confusing prospects in the future – to follow access to 'evidence' gleaned from what has happened so far rather than do what really matters as regards trying to cope with the future.

The deficit assumption only stacked-up if one assumes that governments' role as uncertainty and risk manager of 'last resort' is not particularly important. The deficit assumption focuses attention on the prevalence of inefficiencies in governance but does not counter-balance this scrutiny with an adequate recognition that there are other things governments must do that markets and business *cannot do*. We seemed to lack an appropriate conceptual and theoretical framework for articulating what is distinctively different and vitally important about governance when it comes to coping with uncertainty and risk. Whilst there is widespread recognition, and especially at the politically conservative end of the political spectrum, of the core responsibilities of government (national security etc.) this recognition did not translate effectively into a framework that would avoid the numerous pitfalls of trying to govern in a 'business-like' manner. This may be because those at the conservative end of the political spectrum were predisposed to argue for a combination of focusing on the core things that only governments can do whilst also advocating market solutions to much that governments do but that the private sector can also do. This conflation seems to have caused some confusion – confusion that has directed attention away from considering how to get better at the core functions of governance in ways that simply emulating private sector approaches will not suffice.

I therefore set out first to draw attention to the links between the flaws in the deficit perspective and the under-recognition of the distinctive role of governments in regards to uncertainty and risk and, second, to start to explore the practical concepts, methods and tools that would help to re-balance the situation. These methods would need to be able to frame governance *directly* as a matter of handling information relating to substantive uncertainties and quantifiable risks.

I had already had some success as a policy consultant in recommending that the ways in which public science helped us to better understand the uncertainties and risks that we may face in the future should be treated as a distinct outcome class (which I labelled 'preparedness' at that time and refer to as 'prescience' in this book). That outcome class provided a counter-balance to the dominating concept of research commercialisation as the intended outcome from public science – an imbalance that had been distorting notions of how funding for public science yields a return-on-investment. The challenge I was left with was how to measure these preparedness outcomes within the strictures of modern governance.

xiv *Preface*

As thoughts and ideas on to how to move forward and do things differently emerged I was encouraged by these practitioners to sit down and pull a range of material together into what amounts to a manifesto or prospectus for rethinking how we handle uncertainty and risk in governance. For these practitioners, the ways in which 'best practice' is framed in public policy creates as many impediments to effective governance as it solves. These impediments tend in the main to be expressed in dysfunctional aspects of how governments attempt to cope with the unavoidable reality of substantive uncertainty and quantifiable risk. In a nutshell, the problem boils down to a public management ethos that has a strong preference for aversion to both uncertainty and risk. This creates an ethos at odds with the distinctive role that governments must play in coping with the uncertainties and risks that markets (in particular) are unable or ill equipped to deal with.

The key step in examining these issues, which stemmed from this search for ways of measuring preparedness outcomes, was the growing awareness that one of the ways in which the concept of entropy is used in the physical sciences (framed in relation to the concept of information) had direct relevance to governance – and beyond that of simply a metaphor. When entropy is defined (as in Claude Shannon's seminal work on the mathematics of information) as the statistical potential for surprise in a signal then we have the theoretical foundation for looking at governance from this signal processing perspective. From this angle, entropy is greatest when there is the maximum potential for surprise in receiving signals in the future. As this potential for surprise (i.e. entropy) drops the ability to assign higher odds to receiving particular symbols in the future increases – in other words information content increases and entropy decreases. This suggests that the technical means may be at hand to articulate the ways in which administrative practices and procedures can increase the potential for surprise above the levels that are set externally by the real world. This gives concrete expression to the anecdotal sense, familiar to many people who work in government or who must deal with government: the sense that risk-averse practices increase entropy and therefore push up costs and reduce productivity (and increase rather than decrease risk exposure).

Governments base their work on information collection, communication and information processing (often by committee) in order to make decisions. Frequently, these decisions must be made when information is sparse, ambiguous and therefore confusing. This is where effective judgement really matters – not so much in the sense of somehow conjuring up a 'right' decision in highly confusing circumstances but in the sense that confidence in judgement will tend to result in reduced paralysis in decision-making. It is often better to make *any* decision in a timely manner rather than dither – and especially the case if there are opportunities to learn and adapt at a later stage. Consequently, the parallels between governance and the code-breaking work that stimulated the formulation of the mathematics of information are strong. This book reflects an initial attempt to develop an approach to doing public policy and governance grounded in what is now know as information theory – an approach intended to make it easier to govern effectively and efficiently by revealing the shortcomings of the current ways of doing things. It is more useful to offer practical solutions alongside a critique.

The book is in many respects 'translational' in the sense that it sets out to integrate a diverse range of disciplinary perspectives with the primary aim of assisting practitioners working in government, and those who need to work or liaise with governments. However, the arguments and ideas developed may also be of interest to those seeking to understand, from a more distant perspective, how governments could improve the effectiveness with which they operate. The structure of the book, and the wide range of disciplines and research foci covered, reflects this pragmatic intention. Whilst some technical matters are covered, wherever possible the details are dealt with 'offline' to the main thrust of the arguments in order to allow those less comfortable with the mathematical concepts and tools to proceed without the speed bumps caused by that dimension of the case being developed. In line with this ethos, diagrams are used wherever possible to get the technical messages across.

Whilst running a public policy collaboration between government and academia I frequently encountered one manifestation of this divergence between academic work and governance challenges. Senior government officials expressed a strong interest in dialogues with academics over things that they should be worrying about – but are not. That ethos is re-assuring for obvious reasons (reducing the potential for surprise is very important). However, the majority of academics were uncomfortable about speculating beyond the data and analyses at hand – and tended to repeat the need for 'more data and research' before such questions could be answered. The issues highlighted on the academic side tended to be those that would support the next cycle of funding requirements for research careers. This became an issue of frustration and disappointment for the government officials – and rightly so.

An additional frustration stemmed from the reluctance on the academic side (though specific to academics who had self-selected as interested in engaging with government) to discuss *theory*. When the importance of theory as a basis for developing useful hypotheses was raised, the academic response tended to be that 'ideology' should be avoided and that government officials were not interested in ideology or abstract concepts. The propensity to conflate theory with ideology reinforced a reluctance to think explicitly about evidence as a matter of testing hypotheses.

One wonders whether the same level of frustration would have been encountered thirty years or so ago. It has become easier (faster and cheaper to access data) and the sheer size of the higher education sector has increased (as government policy settings seek to drive up numbers entering universities). As a result, the likelihood of coming across academics operating in areas relevant to public policy willing and able to engage in conceptual thinking, discuss theoretical issues and generally speculate intellectually may have decreased. Public policy is increasingly framed as a matter of obtaining better empirical evidence – not of seeking to make advances in conceptual thinking that can shape how we approach using evidence from the past to help us grapple with the future.

xvi *Preface*

In my own experience in running a joint government–academic research programme commissioning policy-relevant research there was a marked reluctance for academics to formulate theoretically relevant and robust hypotheses to be tested. When pressed on this matter, the response was that theory and hypotheses were high-level academic concerns unsuited to collaborative work with government. The emphasis tended to be on seeking funding for collecting data as an end in itself, justified on the basis that it was 'building the evidence base'. This too became a matter of frustration on the government side (where novel conceptual perspectives can be highly valued, especially if they help to reduce the potential for nasty surprises).

The book fuses aspects of economics (both neo-classical and subjectivist/Austrian approaches), the philosophy of science and science policy, innovation management and competitive strategy, aspects of physics, information technology, engineering management, statistics, history, political science, sociology and work on public policy and public administration (particularly public sector risk management). All of these disciplines and subjects share common ground in a concern with the relationships between uncertainty (both substantive and statistical), information and risk. These inter-relationships can be succinctly expressed in the simple notion of reducing the potential for nasty surprises in an uncertain and risky world. Particular attention is paid to using these diverse disciplinary perspectives to examine how the potential for nasty surprises can, inadvertently, be increased rather than decreased by the design choices made over how best to administer and govern.

The main contribution of the book is to draw the attention of practitioners to the importance of these issues, foster better awareness of the shortcomings to current risk-averse modes of governance (which are actually risk amplifiers according to the perspective developed) and to go on to suggest practical solutions. Indeed, many of the ideas in this book have been developed from, and will in the future contribute to, executive education courses for government officials. On the basis of these interactions there is a strong appetite within governments to explore new ways of thinking about uncertainty and risk – an appetite that values conceptual clarity over the rather muddled and compliance-oriented status quo.

When I started work on the manuscript the main focus was on the potential to design and deliver collaboration between government and academia in such a way that it made a significant (positive) difference to the effectiveness of governance. The first step in this direction had been to work with my private sector colleague Geoff White (with whom I had a long-standing shared interest in these matters), to design and test a hypothesis-based approach to programme evaluation in collaboration with a state government in Australia. This approach encouraged government to frame its interventions explicitly as hypothesis tests. Rather than drawing up funding agreements that specified how contractual compliance would be demonstrated (via various measures) the funding agreements drawn up after this pilot exercise simply specified the hypotheses to be tested and left it to the funding recipient to decide which data would provide the most effective test of the hypotheses. Whilst conceptually elegant, cost-effective and implementable this approach still required a formal basis for assessing the relative degrees of support for these hypotheses given available evidence. It became clear that assessing the relative degrees of support for these hypotheses would most easily be done if these hypothesis tests were framed in binary (true or false) terms along the lines of clinical diagnosis.

This binary approach would be well aligned with the other key aspect of governance that I was keen to promote: treating public policy as a process of investing in trying to obtain lower odds of bad things happening and higher odds of good things happening. This 'odds-based' perspective, in which uncertainty and risk are integral to, indeed the foundation of, the intervention rationale contrasts markedly with the dominant risk-averse stance in modern governance – based on well-defined objectives that are either met (successful interventions) or not met (failed interventions) – irrespective of the uncertainties over whether or not these interventions actually make a useful difference. It seemed to be much better to approach policy in this odds-based way.

The critical juncture that framed the way the book has ended up came from starting to explore the various ways in which Bayesian inference had been used in the Second World War to deal with a range of situations in which life-and-death decisions had to be made with sparse and ambiguous information. Like many people, I had been wary of Bayesian inference because it seemed to be hard to grasp even though the basic principles made sense intuitively. I was only provoked into engaging with the Bayesian world when a peer reviewer for a chapter I had written in an edited book that drew upon aspects of the work in this monograph commented that I was exploring ideas relating to uncertainty and risk that were better handled within a Bayesian framework. Once I started to read this literature it was clear that it was of great relevance but also clear (as I had always assumed from the sidelines) that it was so mathematically complex in implementation that it was unlikely to contribute to transforming how public policy is designed and delivered. Consequently, I used a revision of the edited book chapter to argue for the development of a simplified and standardised Bayesian expression of the policy learning cycle that could be used on a day-to-day level within the public sector to guide and inform learning and adaptation. I also added some initial thoughts on what such a standardised framework might look like to that chapter.

The problem I faced was that I could see how to design a standardised Bayesian expression of the policy learning cycle, but not a *simplified* expression. The standard textbook definition of Bayes Rule is based on conditional probability, and if one is not expert in conditional probability, it is a complex and slippery thing to understand. The breakthrough in researching this book was when I came across a reference to Gerd Gigerenzer's work on a technical website and, as a result, became aware of the use of 'natural frequencies' in clinical uses of Bayesian inference. These are simply the use of the raw data on disease prevalence combined with the estimated incidences of true positive, false positive, true negative and false negative test results. When these natural frequencies xviii *Preface*

are used Bayes Rule becomes very simple to apply: it is simply the ratio of true positive test results divided by the sum of true positive and false positive test results. In other words, the likelihood that a positive test result for a condition actually means the condition is present (an estimate that is heavily influenced by the combination of the overall prevalence of the condition and the accuracy of the test result based on experience to date).

This natural frequency approach therefore provided the formal basis for the simplified version of Bayesian inference required to produce a practical standardised diagnostic method for use in the public sector. This line of investigation took me to the signal processing and machine learning methods that revolve around two by two (usefully named) 'confusion matrices' created by true positive, false positive, true negative and false negative test results. Framing policy analysis, and the monitoring and evaluation of policy implementation, in confusion matrix terms seemed to be clearly relevant to the real conditions under which governments have to act – not least in the sense that accumulating evidence can strengthen not just weaken the degree of confusion faced.

These methods, which rely on framing public policy as binary (true versus false) tests of competing hypotheses, therefore held out the promise of framing an approach to governance far better aligned with the distinctive role of uncertainty and risk manager of 'last resort'. The natural frequency expression of Bayes Rule provides a solution to the challenge I had set myself: *how to contribute to more effective governance by developing a conceptually elegant, robust and implementable framework for framing all government interventions as testable hypotheses – testable via implementation and able to learn and adapt effectively.*

From this perspective, the contribution of science to public policy is not simply a matter of using the best available scientific evidence to inform policy (as the challenge is so often framed) but of exploiting the methodological essence of science (contested knowledge based on the robust empirical tests of theories) at the core of the policy process. From this perspective, states of 'confusion', as reflected in biased and usually ambiguous test results, are the most plausible conditions to find ourselves in – *but* can be addressed using a diagnostic framework that has been explicitly designed to accept the unavoidable reality of these confusing signals.

The final step towards achieving the objectives I had set myself was when I came across the technical work in signal processing and machine learning that stemmed from efforts in the Second World War to test and select radar operators for their accuracy in interpreting blips on radar screens. The 'receiver operating' assessment framework developed from those roots in the Second World War, which is now being used widely in signal processing, machine learning and also in clinical diagnosis, plots test accuracy in a comprehensive and conceptually clear manner. Perhaps most interestingly, this diagnostic tool emphasised situations in which diagnostic results were either effectively random, or, worse than random in the sense that results were negatively correlated with reality (inverted conclusions). This framework consequently provided a potentially useful means of contributing to diagnostic capability in public policy using simplified and standardised Bayesian methods.

The bottom line I articulate in this book is that public policy and governance stands to gain substantially by approaching what governments do explicitly as signal processing and adaptive learning challenges – as the 'information state'. In short, by approaching the governance challenge as Claude Shannon and Alan Turing approached code breaking and signal processing in the Second World War: as sparse, ambiguous and often confusing signals relating to major risks and existential threats. Consequently, what started out as a book on government–academic collaboration in public policy ended up becoming a book with the broader and more ambitious remit of contributing to debates on practical ways of reforming governance by considering novel theoretical angles on the challenges faced.

Acknowledgements

This book would not have been possible without the financial support provided by the Australian Government for the HC Coombs Policy Forum under the *Enhancing Public Policy Initiative* delivered via the Commonwealth-Australian National University Strategic relationship. The partnership work in public policy carried out via the Forum provided the impetus for exploring the issues covered in this monograph. Additional support was subsequently also provided by the *Australian Centre for Biosecurity and Environmental Economics* (ACBEE) via a small consultancy contract. Both sources of funding are gratefully acknowledged.

The bulk of the arguments and associated ideas presented in this book were developed via numerous talks given to government officials (mainly in Australia) and associated discussions, together with some pilot applications of some of these ideas carried out in partnership with governments. All of these discussions and the pilot projects were invaluable in focusing attention on the potential for a book focused on issues of interest to practitioners. I am therefore very grateful for the time and attention provided by this large number of government officials.

I am especially grateful to the officials in one government department (that must, at their request, remain anonymous) for being willing to issue a contract variation that allowed a key piece of an emerging analytical approach to be tested in a real-world context. It was the opportunity to carry out that experimental test of a hypothesis testing based evaluation methodology that provided the initial impetus and confidence to proceed in developing the ideas reflected in this book.

Feedback from participants in the following talks deserve special mention: *Australian Government Department of Human Services* on 24 September 2013, a keynote address at a workshop on government–academic collaboration organised by the *Australian Government Department of Prime Minister and Cabinet* on 13 June 2014, the inaugural *Policy Reflections Forum* address at the *Australian Government Department of Communications* on 5 March 2014, and also at a seminar organised by the *Queensland Government* on 25 June 2014. Useful comments were also provided at a talk given at an *Australia New Zealand School of Government* (ANZSOG) workshop on Experimentalist Governance on 11 and

12 February 2014 and also at a seminar given to the Masters of Public Policy students at the *Blavatnik School of Government*, University of Oxford, on 19 April 2014.

Once those discussions were over, and it became time to prepare the book manuscript it became clear to me that it was essential to move beyond a critique of current uncertainty and risk-averse governance stances.

I decided to test the Bayesian aspects of the arguments I was developing in writing the book via some spin-off publications. Consequently, parts of chapters one, two and five draw upon a chapter by the author published in *Designing and Implementing Public Policy: Cross-sectoral Debates*, edited by G. Carey, K. Landvogt and J. Barraket (London: Routledge, pp. 75–89). These three chapters also draw upon a more technical article on risk management in the public sector jointly written with Tom Kompas and published in *Asia and the Pacific Policy Studies* (Vol 2, no. 3) together with a forthcoming article by myself to be published in *Asia and the Pacific Policy Studies* later in 2016.

Chapter two draws upon a brief discussion of UK government experience in fostering innovation in the public sector originally presented in a chapter of mine in the book *Critical Perspectives on Australian Public Policy: Selected Essays*, edited by John Wanna (Australia and New Zealand School of Government, ANU E-Press). The discussion of the relevance of Austrian (subjectivist) economics in chapter two also draws upon arguments in the ANZSOG book.

Chapter three draws on two pieces of policy advocacy work by myself on preparedness as an outcome class in science and innovation policy. These think pieces were commissioned by (the then named) *Federation of Australian Scientific and Technological Societies* (FASTS), now known as *Science and Technology Australia* (STA).

In terms of individuals, I would like to give particular thanks to: Gemma Carey, Michael Cooney, Katherine Daniell, Edward DeSeve, Jenny Gordon, Paul Harris, Peter Høj, Tom Kompas, Marie McCauliff, Aaron Maniam, Ian Marsh, Tarik Meziani, Katherine Morton, Martyn Pearce, Robert Picciotto, Simon Pringle, Dennis Rank, Sue Regan, Ben Reilly, Jon Stern, Geoff White and Grant Woollett. All of these people at different times either encouraged me to develop the ideas in this book or provided useful feedback and suggestions as the ideas were being developed. Thanks also to my local café in Sheffield, Remo's in Broomhill, who graciously put up with my completing the book over several strong coffees every morning. A special thanks goes to Sung Lee for suggesting that I draw together and integrate assorted contributions delivered via talks and seminars given the practitioners into a book – and for helping to arrange the subsequent publishing contract. Finally, and most importantly, I would like to thank my editor at Routledge, Yong Ling Lam, and her editorial assistant on this book, Samantha Phua, and Kate Fornadel who copy edited the manuscript for their patience and support in bringing this project to fruition.

Abbreviations

CAPM	Capital Asset Pricing Model
CFD	Computational Fluid Dynamics
DCP	Diagnostic Capability Plot
EV	Expected Value
FDA	Food and Drug Administration
IFRS	International Financial Reporting Standards
ISO	International Standards Organisation
KPI	Key Performance Indicator
MEL	Monitoring, Evaluation and Learning
NASA	National Aeronautics and Space Administration
NPV	Net Present Value
QCA	Qualitative Causal Analysis
R&D	Research and Experimental Development
RCT	Randomised Control Trial
ROC	Receiver Operating Characteristic
RSD	Rapid Spiral Development
SME	Small or Medium Sized Enterprise

1 Introduction
Governance and entropy

> It is a small section only of natural phenomena that one gets from direct experience. It is only through refined measurements and careful experimentation that we can have a wider vision. And then we see unexpected things: we see things that are far from what we would guess – far from what we would have imagined. Our imagination is stretched to the utmost, not, as in fiction, to imagine things which are not really there, but just to comprehend those things which *are* there.
>
> Feynman (1967, pp. 127–8)

In *The Discourses*, Niccolò Machiavelli refers to Xenophon and stresses the importance of learning how to quickly recognise patterns in landscapes (Machiavelli, 2003).[1] As he remarks, 'For all countries and all their parts have about them a certain uniformity, so that from the knowledge of one it is easy to pass to the knowledge of another'.[2] It is useful to treat this as a metaphor for the roles of evidence and conjecture about the unknown in public policy – about handling the known *and* the unknown. If we take the time to consider the terrain that can be seen (the known) and to try to identify general patterns in the landscape, then that can help us to visualise what (for example) the unseen valley to one side might look like (the unknown). If one makes a habit of visualising the unseen valley on the basis of the known valley and then bothers to take a look into the next valley in order to see how accurate the conjecture was, one learns how to get better over time at this process of inferring the unknown from the known, although this is a learning process never free from the surprises created by the inherently unpredictable, see Taleb (2010).

As Machiavelli hints, learning how to identify patterns in landscapes that allow us to improve conjectures about what unseen terrain might look like can be critically important in a skirmish or battle. In those frantic situations it may be necessary to visualise what the terrain in an adjacent unknown valley may look like in order to give orders to troops during a battle – with no time to scout out that valley (i.e. gather more evidence). The decision must be made on the basis of conjecture not robust evidence.

Machiavelli's advice on constantly searching for general patterns in terrain is an important one for public policy in general. As this book will demonstrate,

2 *Introduction*

leadership can be enhanced by making use of concepts from information theory. Governments must constantly learn-by-doing in improving their ability to conjecture about the unknown on the basis of the known. The unseen valley is a metaphor for what we now call 'horizon scanning' – but we only see the ridge defined by current evidence not what lies beyond it. The unseen valley beyond the observed ridge is information we don't yet have – and can surprise us. Our conjectures about what is as yet unseen can be valued in inverse proportion to the assumed likelihood of receiving unexpected information in the future – this is a key insight in information theory and a point to be explored throughout this book.

This book is concerned with how we might translate our well-meaning intentions to govern effectively by getting better at learning and adaptation in an uncertain and changing world into the practical tools and techniques that will help us to do this. The focus is upon the ways in which current approaches to handling uncertainties and risk act as an impediment to governing effectively – and on designing a strategy for removing this impediment. As such, this contribution builds upon existing work advocating a transition to more 'experimentalist' modes of governing based on learning and adaptation, see Sabel and Zeitlin (2012).

The ideas in the book are the fruits of constructive engagement with practitioners in government, primarily over the years 1997 to 2014. This engagement took place as a management consultant specialising in public policy work and also as an academic researcher working in public policy. A pattern emerged from this practice of various aspects of public policy: when things went wrong (as they often did) the reasons often appeared to relate to how substantive uncertainty and quantifiable risks had been handled – or rather mishandled. Managing these uncertainties and risks, which are central to what governments are trying to achieve, were usually treated as 'add-ons' to core activities. The uncertainty and risk dimensions of interventions were bundled together on the sidelines, as 'bolted on' risk assessment exercises aimed in the main at compliance with standards and guidelines. This growing awareness of the patterns in what engineers call 'failure modes' stimulated a sustained exploration of better ways of handling uncertainty and risk in the policy process.

The quote from Richard Feynman's (1967) lectures at the start of this introduction is used in recognition of his point that the ways in which we express technical concepts can have an impact on how creatively we act when searching for solutions, a point highlighted by Gigerenzer and Hoffrage (1995). In this context, the widespread use of decimal probability coefficients in public policy (and other areas such as medicine) is itself an issue. As work in psychology has revealed, in cognitive terms decimal probabilities don't align with how our minds judge opportunities and risks on the basis of accumulated experience. Our minds work with relative frequency counts, for example the number of times we have succeeded in trying to do something and the number of times we did not succeed. These 'natural frequencies' used in cognition lend themselves to odds-based expressions of opportunities and risks, Gigerenzer and Hoffrage op. cit. and also Gigerenzer (2000) and Gigerenzer (2002).

Introduction 3

This reliance on decimal probability coefficients to express risks is a consequence of the French Revolution, which led to the introduction of percentages to calculate tax and interest rates – these percentages then, in turn, being translated into a decimal representation of likelihoods, Gigerenzer and Hoffrage op. cit. Laplace used these decimal probabilities to operationalise Bayesian inference, and also to express uncertainty as even odds a probability of 0.5. This is a stance that, arguably, placed limitations on how substantive uncertainty is framed: there is a big difference between assuming a probability of 0.5 for an as-yet-unmeasured variable and recognising simply that we don't know something, i.e. are in a state of ignorance – not simply even odds; see Bammer and Smithson (2008) and in particular Smithson (2008) for a discussion of different aspects of uncertainty and risk. We have traded off mathematical convenience against a recognition of the value of discovering what we don't (yet) know – or may never know. This is an issue to which we return at various points in the book.

Picking up on Richard Feynman's point again, if our minds find it hard to conceptualise risk when it is expressed in decimal probabilities rather than natural frequencies, then it is plausible to conjecture that our creativity and innovation in striving for better ways of coping with both substantive uncertainty and quantifiable risk has been constrained by moving away from odds-based ways of expressing risk – an unintended consequence of the French Revolution. Interestingly, as covered later in the book, Alan Turing opted to use odds-based methods in the path-breaking decryption work carried out at Bletchley Park during the Second World War because this provided a more intuitive link with the data (Good, 1979). In recognition of these issues, there is a strong emphasis in this book on proposing new ways of expressing risk in a public policy environment – methods explicitly designed to foster creativity and innovation in governance.

In response to this challenge, the emphasis in the book is on combining some conceptual thinking on the nature and implications of uncertainty and risk for the practice of public policy with the translation of this thinking into practical suggestions for how to implement these ideas. This unpacking of the relationships between substantive uncertainty and quantifiable risk and the implications for public policy aligns well with the main thrust of the arguments in Helga Nowotny's recent book that was published at the same time as this manuscript was being finalised (Nowotny, 2015). However this book attempts to explore these issues in more detail as regards the day-to-day practice of public policy in an administrative sense and with a stronger focus in practical ways of moving forward without conflating substantive uncertainty and quantifiable risk.

In some areas, notably the notion that intended intervention objectives can, and should, be framed explicitly as tests of hypotheses, government departments have piloted and subsequently adopted forms of this experimental approach focused on discovery rather than compliance. This amounts to a 'proof of principle'. In other areas, the suggestions still await these experimental and pilot activities. Given the developing nature of these experimental pilots conducted

4   *Introduction*

with government departments aimed at testing and improving this new strategy for handling uncertainty and risk in the public sector, up-to-date information is provided online rather than in appendices to the book.[3]

One caveat to stress at the outset is that references to 'adaptive governance' in what follows are focused on governments' ability to learn and adapt from the perspective of self-imposed constraints created by adherence to rules, guidelines and procedures designed around an aversion to uncertainty and risk and geared towards compliance rather than focusing on creativity and innovation. Whilst this focus can recognise the networked nature of governance associated with the use of the term 'adaptive governance' in the economic, political science and environmental literatures, this collaborative dimension is only explored in relation to opportunities for reform in how governments approach appraisal, monitoring and evaluation and risk management functions.[4] The strategy for handling uncertainty and risk covered in this book is compatible with the broader 'adaptive governance' literature stemming, in particular, from Elinor Ostrom's work on the effective and equitable management of 'common pool resources' but this inter-connect is not developed here (Ostrom, 1999). The problem framing used in this book aligns more closely with Michel Crozier's work in the 1960s on the consequences of hierarchical modes of organisation in government which limits learning and adaptation until the need for change reaches crisis levels at which point top-down changes can take place (Crozier, 1964). Adaptive governance must, somehow, reconcile the potential for innovation in policy that stems from networked collaboration between a range of entities and communities with the rigidities stressed by Crozier – which are still with us and manifested in how governments manage uncertainty and risk in the policy cycle. The deliberate, and it will be argued damaging, fragmentation of how interventions are appraised, how they are then monitored and evaluated and how uncertainties and risks are handled represents an impediment to any transition to adaptive governance in the networked sense.

Innovation and austerity

It is timely to consider how to deliver stronger learning and adaptation in governance because we live in an era of austerity in the public sector. Government departments are trying to cope with doing a lot but with greatly reduced resources. These are, in some areas of government (e.g. health care, social security, and in some respects potentially in national security), crisis conditions. These crisis conditions tend to come home to roost in the uncertainty and risk domains. Indeed, this austerity is to a large part a result of shortcomings in how uncertainty and risk have been handled and still are handled. Notably in relation to approaches to regulatory functions applied to banking and finance, which made (and sanctioned) specific assumptions about risks and statistical distributions that increased the potential for nasty surprises to occur (an issue covered in chapter two).

The 'Obamacare' experience, i.e. the Patient Protection and Affordable Care Act (ACA) of 2010, reflects this aspect. There is little evidence (in the public domain at least) of effective risk management in the design phase in the face of the great complexity and inherent risks in such a major intervention. In particular, many of the problems experienced stemmed from the all-too-familiar symptom of current risk management practices (in this context reflected passively rather than actively): locking-in key design parameters of the intervention when there is still high substantive uncertainty over how the intervention will actually work (Deloitte, 2014). The persistence of this problem, which stems from the ways in which public management 'best practices' require firm targets and mechanistic means of reaching these targets, is all the more striking given the long-standing recognition that when there is substantive uncertainty the best approach is to plan to keep design options open for as long as possible and avoid premature lock-in (Klein and Meckling, 1958). The persistence of such problems tells us that compliance with rigid target-driven approaches to public management still trumps the 'discovery' ethos set out by the likes of Klein and Meckling.

On a more positive note, experience tells us that advances in the public sector tend to occur during crises. However, these advances tend to take place when there is the political vision and leadership to question long-standing assumptions about how things should be done, to encourage the search for innovative solutions and to act to reduce the strength of the various impediments to change that can characterise a bureaucracy.

If austerity is handled simply by down-sizing what government departments attempt to do (by reducing the rate of work – which in turn pushes up waiting times) without attempting the radical (disruptive) changes that have the potential to increase productive capacity with fixed budgets, then this austerity will be both painful and a wasted opportunity. An opportunity will have been missed to create the conditions for a more fundamental improvement in how things are done within the machinery of government. This lost opportunity means that as times of austerity ease, as government departments have more to spend, then the old ways expand in scale – bringing with them the scaled-up waste that characterises the unchanged status quo. This scaled-up waste is currently expressed in the United Kingdom in a tendency to dispense with the formal evaluation of interventions (the function that in principle tells us how to do better in the future) – a stance that reflects the (disposable) 'compliance ritual' dimension to evaluation studies in the sense that they are too rarely a source of learning and adaptation, to a large part because uncertainty and risk are handled as bolted-on considerations.

If, on the other hand, these austere times are used as a catalyst for creativity and innovation, then when the austerity eases any increase in the scale of the public sector is also associated with an increase in how effectively these activities are carried out – there is innovation.

The current status quo as regards how potential policy interventions are designed and appraised, monitored and evaluated and risks managed is one of 'balkanisation'. Whilst, in principle each function should consist of an effective

6 Introduction

learning and adaptation cycle, which is usefully characterised using Edwards Deming's terminology as the plan-do-check-adjust cycle, the reality is very different. The appraisal function, which assesses benefits and costs in some way or other, emphasises how this should be planned and executed. There are guidelines, often very detailed, as to how to go about this. However, there is a much lower emphasis on closing the implicit learning loop in appraisal by examining, on a regular basis, how effective the recent appraisals carried out have been. The result is a weak learning cycle in appraisal.

Similarly, the evaluation function, which can also be characterised in an identical fashion using Deming's terminology, emphasises planning and doing (execution) but with a lower emphasis on closing the learning loop by considering how effective the evaluation cycle is. In both cases, the dominating ethos is one of compliance with rules and guidelines. The risk management function also exhibits similar limitations as regards learning and adaptation.

The following diagram (figure 1.1) illustrates one of the key explanations as to why each of these learning cycles do not operate effectively: *they take place independently of each other and with little scope to exploit the synergies between them.* They are rather like the cogs in a gearbox that cannot transmit force because they don't mesh with each other properly. Closing the learning loop in appraisal relies on interoperability with the evaluation function (information on actual outcomes with a clear link to initial expectations). From this

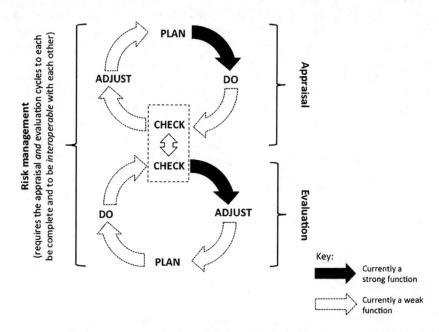

Figure 1.1 Framing the potential for the interoperability of appraisal, evaluation and risk management using learning cycle interdependencies

perspective, effective learning in risk management regarding interventions relies upon the interoperability of appraisal and evaluation (risk management involves the same plan-do-check-adjust cycle). The ability to relate the 'check' function in appraisal and evaluation in a seamless manner is the key to getting these 'cogs' to work together – each assisting the other.

The main challenge at present is that the methodologies, and often the teams that carry out appraisal and evaluation, are both different and separated in time. Evaluations follow appraisals after significant lags, information is lost in the interim. Appraisals may have been outsourced and/or intervention rationales only loosely specified in the first place. Appraisal, evaluation and risk management are all treated as discrete functions with little effort paid to simplifying and integrating them to produce a more coherent system.

From a learning and adaptation perspective austere times are an opportunity to re-think the overall functional effectiveness of how we appraise, monitor and evaluate government interventions and how we cope with the inherent uncertainties and risks faced in attempting these interventions. In practical terms, as the above characterisation suggests, this means developing new and better ways of seamlessly integrating appraisal, evaluation and risk management in the public sector – addressing the shortcomings illustrated in figure 1.1. Just as engineers seek to reduce the risk of a machine failing by simplifying the design of that machine as much as possible, including sequential re-designs over time – each of which simplifies things – so too should our efforts to produce a seamlessly integrated, and therefore more effective, approach to appraisal, evaluation and risk management. This will require that the currently distinct functions of the appraisal of interventions, the monitoring and evaluation of their consequences and the management of risk are forced to transition from separate compliance rituals to a unified framework that is useful because it is less prone to errors – not because its use is required by rules and standards.

This book is an exploration of how a clearer and analytically robust focus on public policy as an information-based process might drive such a transformation – a transformation with the potential to lift the cost-effectiveness of governance through reduced waste, in turn enabled by a transition away from compliance rituals in appraisal, evaluation and risk management and towards more integrated processes better able to generate actionable information that facilitates learning and adaptation. If, as in engineering, aiming for simplicity is the key, then we must search for solutions able to give us this simplicity – solutions able to integrate appraisal, evaluation and risk management in ways that do not currently happen. This means that the same teams should be responsible for all three key functions (which rarely happens at present) and that these teams should have the right tools for this job – practical tools that get to the heart of how interventions are designed and delivered.

One aspect of such practical tools that warrants particular attention are diagnostic errors: cases in which it turns out that a finding is reversed (something thought to be true is not true or something thought not to be true is in

8   Introduction

fact true). In a governance context, this means that appraisals are error-prone, accumulating experience in implementation can reveal such errors, and that evaluation and risk management methods can also generate diagnostic errors. These errors can compound each other. Diagnostic errors in framing and appraising a potential intervention can be missed in subsequent evaluation studies. Critically, however, such errors are best grasped statistically by considering their general prevalence – not just specific cases. This is the same principle that the likely accuracy of a medical blood test is best judged on the basis of broader statistical understanding of false positive and false negative error rates in that blood test. The information value is extrinsic to specific cases. This assessment of specific results against the general incidence of errors in results of that type is not currently a feature of either appraisal or evaluation studies in the public sector – though it can be a feature of some approaches to risk management. Appraisal studies tend to stick tightly to the specifics of a case and pay little attention to the extent to which other similar appraisals have turned out to be wrong in various respects – a cautionary dimension. Similarly, evaluations also tend to stick to the specifics and don't calibrate likely error rates against those derived from sets of similar evaluations, i.e. conduct pattern recognition studies.

Given that diagnostic errors are the main focus in the signal processing techniques that underpin information and communication technology it makes sense to examine the extent to which those methods could be used in a seamless framework for integrating appraisal, evaluation and risk management. In practice, moving towards a more seamless approach to appraisal, evaluation and risk management faces the impediment that different people and teams tend carry out each of the three activities. Each activity has developed distinctive technical frameworks and terminology – approaches which can get very complex and hard to grasp in full by generalists – generalists who at a senior level will make the key decisions in response to these studies. This disconnect can reinforce the compliance ritual problem. It is also worth noting that this focus on diagnostic error rates also provides one basis for measuring value for money – lower rates of diagnostic error are useful, reduce wasted spending – but also come at a cost.

To what extent can collaboration between government and academia, and policy think tanks assist here? Government officials who attend university seminars on policy-relevant issues tend to come away dissatisfied because so much of the discussion has focused on debates over the adequacy of data sources and the analytical methods used. On the other hand, academics who have participated in meetings and workshops within government tend to come away concerned by the lack of attention paid to potential biases in data sources and the analytical methods used (methods frequently viewed as over-simplistic). Government, academia and policy think tanks do tend to get something useful from each others' activities as regards useful, perhaps surprising, information and insights.

What tends to be missing are the compromises (technical trade-offs made) in the methodologies used to make sense of this information. The division of labour between practitioners, researchers/educators and advocates of particular policy solutions (often now found in policy think tanks) results in pressures to specialise rather than integrate. Hence, policy think tanks will tend to focus on producing easily accessible and insightful analysis of data coupled with interesting suggestions for government on what to do. Innovative methodological advances are rare. Academia will tend to focus on striving for the most robust evidence-based analysis of a situation – a rigorous process that can take a long time (and more often than not throws up new puzzles and uncertainties that highlight the need for more research).

The dominant 'classical' basis for determining formal statistical significance in these studies is the probability that the data observed could have been generated by random processes. The lower this probability the more 'statistically significant' the result. A significance threshold of a less than 5 per cent chance of random factors producing the observed results is usually used. This approach to determining statistical significance is derived from sampling theory: the data we actually get to observe is treated as a random sample from a fixed but unobserved set of parameters. Hence, the larger and/or more frequent these samples the more reliable the assertions we are able to make about reality (there is lower risk that we are wrong in these assertions). Hypotheses are tested in comparison to a null hypothesis of no treatment effect (including any placebo effect). This sampling theory approach does not pay much attention to the strength of the causal impact observed. This means that sampling strategies and sample characteristics have a strong influence on whether or not statistical significance is attained, see Meehl (1978), and that some powerful interventions are not available because they don't achieve statistical significance when evaluated whilst other interventions do attain statistical significance but only yield low (or even harmful) treatment effects (Ziliak and McCloskey, 2014). The resulting association between the dominance of these 'frequentist' sampling theory–based tests for statistical significance and firm target-based approaches to designing and delivering public policy is striking – and, arguably, under-explored relative to the importance of the issue for the effectiveness of governance.

On face value it is logical, from a sampling theory perspective, to treat public policy as a matter of setting rigid and objectively measurable performance targets (e.g. to set a specific cap on numbers of economic immigrants as has been done in the United Kingdom) even though the decision on the level to set such a target is not aligned with access to the policy mechanisms to actually influence the risk of not meeting that target. Whether or not the specific target is met becomes in effect a randomised sampling exercise – actual outcomes will or will not meet the target based, in effect, on the 'luck of the draw'. As with frequentist statistical significance, the assessment of whether or not the intervention is effective is based on the data we actually get to observe being treated as a random sample from a fixed but unobserved set of parameters that we cannot adjust through experience. The current prevailing policy ethos appears to prioritise the apparent decisive and firm, objective, nature of governing by target-setting on the basis that it focuses collective behaviour on attempting to improve performance but in a manner that, from a risk management angle, is only loosely

10 *Introduction*

connected to the actual ability to set and meet realistic targets. The target becomes a bet in an uncertain world and, consequently, we would expect to find a strong element of random effects when examining statistical data on whether or not these targets are met. Whilst the 'pressure' on behaviour that results from this target-setting can be effective (in effect we get lucky) the randomised disconnect between cause and effect restricts the ability to learn and adapt: when we do meet a target it can be hard to extract useful information on how to set future targets in such a way that the likelihood of meeting them has increased as a result of learning-by-doing. If we set targets rather randomly (as arbitrary choices that will spin well *now* as decisive leadership in the media), then the information we gain from policy implementation is constrained by this randomness in setting objectives. In effect, this ethos drives up the discount rate in the public sector because it places a low value on ways in which the choices we make now can lead to better or worse outcomes in the future. This 'random-pick' approach to target-setting reinforces the functional disconnects between appraisal, evaluation and risk management.

A striking illustration of this issue of how substantive uncertainty and random factors can be handled better or worse can be found in commercial aviation (a sector well-regarded for the ways in which it uses anonymous reporting by pilots to highlight risks and drive risk mitigation).[5] Wide-bodied passenger aircraft on long-haul flights face a major productivity challenge relating to the decision over how much contingency fuel to carry. The significance of this challenge is easily grasped if one considers the fact that by the time an aircraft has flown one of the longest journeys (such as London to Sydney) it may have to burn 10 litres of fuel for each litre of fuel being carried on arrival. This is an obvious cost burden (and environmental impact factor). It means that the decision as to how much contingency fuel to carry on each journey must seek not to carry too much spare fuel but must also factor in a wide range of considerations over risks – most with uncertainties over whether they will eventuate and what will happen if they do eventuate. Bad weather, long times being 'stacked' waiting to land at the destination, and other factors all come into place. There is also the choice to be made over how fast to fly given prevailing conditions – fuel burn increases exponentially with air speed. Pilots fly to a 'cost index' that is a proprietary trade secret of each airline – an algorithm that reflects accumulated experience in managing these risk margins. The linked targets for travel time and contingency fuel reserves minimise costs when they are frequently updated with the latest and most accurate information on actual experiences. The various uncertainties over weather, possible routing changes etc. faced leading up to departure must be considered.

Once the aircraft has taken off with the set fuel reserve a fixed target is in place – the aircraft must do whatever it can not to run out of fuel. The greater the uncertainties on that day and prior to departure the greater the fuel reserve will have to be. On some days decisions may need to be made only with reference to quantifiable risks based on data collected from experience – usually because there are no hints of the unexpected. On other days, security intelligence may be passed on to suggest that there may be hard-to-predict problems in countries on or near the intended flight path – these may be novel problems (they have never happened before) but the pilot under guidance from the airline's security staff may decide to reflect that increased substantive uncertainty in an unusually large contingency fuel reserve for that journey (in case a major re-routing or diversion is required).

Consequently, airlines pay great attention to trying to optimise this decision in the face of these uncertainties – which means learning-by-doing in managing these risks but in a cautious manner. A particular pilot who is unusually cautious in regularly carrying a larger contingency fuel load than colleagues will face questions over his or her judgement and performance in delivering productivity contributions to the airline.

As is clear in this air transport example, cost-effectiveness stems from the ability to link *appraisal* (in this case the fuel contingency level decision given past experience and prevailing future circumstances) with *evaluation* (learning how effective that appraisal was) with the distinction between substantive uncertainty and quantifiable risk placed centrally in these appraisal and evaluation activities. The value of evaluation lies mainly in how it helps the appraisal function to cope with uncertainty and risk in the future.

Clearly in this illustration both data and judgement matter – and so do approaches to uncertainty. The target (the contingency fuel load) is set in an evidence-based manner but strenuous efforts are made to whittle down uncertainties through learning-by-doing. The process works as a rational and effective basis for making risky decisions because each day's flights set their contingency fuel reserves on the basis of algorithms that use the latest data on these risks from the past whilst also allowing for judgement over what the future may have in store for that particular flight (judgement that may include risks associated with political turmoil as well as weather forecasts). This is the essence of the Bayesian approach. If airlines went about these decisions in the way that target-driven public policy tends to do at present, then they would pay much less attention to making sense of all available data on uncertainties and risks and would most likely reduce their productivity by carrying excessively large contingency fuel loads simply because they have put themselves into a situation in which by not making sense of all available data they face a higher ratio of substantive uncertainty to quantifiable risk than would otherwise be the case. The greater this ratio the greater the potential for nasty surprises to occur (like running out of fuel).

From a public policy perspective the above illustration highlights the ways in which analytical failings stemming from a failure to seamlessly integrate appraisal, evaluation and risk management can drive up wasted expenditure and, as a result, increase the cost of governance for taxpayers (including the cost of servicing sovereign debt to be borne by future generations). Setting performance targets in a manner that is analytically disconnected from how uncertainties and risks are handled in problem diagnosis makes it hard to learn and adapt and

12 Introduction

hence perpetuates public sector inefficiencies. In other words, what may appear to be philosophical niceties revolving around how well or badly governments handle substantive uncertainties relative to quantifiable risks have tangible costs for us all. Every cancelled intervention, cost overrun or failure to quickly learn and adapt in the face of the unexpected when implementing policy represents an avoidable cost burden driven, to a tangible extent, by poor choices over how to handle substantive uncertainty relative to quantifiable risks. The frequency with which these inefficiencies are reported tells us that this problem in governance is non-trivial.

Hence, for governments this issue of methodologies, of the philosophical links between how statistical significance is judged and how we approach governance in an uncertain world is important. In frequentist statistics the parameters are fixed and the data we get to observe is treated as being extracted from other potential sets of data that we cannot observe. This means that *changes* in these fixed parameters (e.g. an assumed statistical distribution that we cannot observe directly) are not factored into the analysis. Consequently, frequentist approaches are not good at dealing with situations in which these parameters are changing – which in the social, political and military domains can be as a direct result of people and organisations observing what governments do and changing their own behaviour in response (Giddens, 1984). This reflexivity (which Giddens calls the 'double hermeneutic') is particularly important in the regulatory domain. This type of response, and its implication for the effectiveness of public policy, can be referred to as 'learning-by-undoing'. Governments try to learn-by-doing in formulating and delivering policy and those whom they seek to change the behaviours of respond by learning-by-undoing in the implementation these interventions.

In such circumstances, the results from a Randomised Control Trial (RCT) are subject to this behavioural 'double hermeneutic'/learning-by-undoing. Findings gleaned by any point in time *if published and understood* by the subjects in ways that modify relevant behaviour can be falsified in subsequent years. In short, frequentist underpinnings to public policy, underpinnings currently being strengthened by the emphasis in RCTs in evidence-based policymaking, perpetuate impediments to learning and adaptation. Learning-by-undoing decreases the shelf life of any intervention – even if based on the 'gold standard' of robust scientific evidence (RCTs).

Given the diverse interests and incentives in each of these three domains (appraisal, evaluation and risk management), and the problems for learning and adaptation posed by a strong reliance on frequentist statistical analysis, it makes sense from a practical perspective to explore ways of overcoming these problems. This requires a framework within which design choices in the methodologies used in appraisal, evaluation and risk management can be made by considering ease of use and timeliness from a practitioner's perspective. Such a framework has to correspond *just enough* with the reality of uncertain and changing conditions that it is practicable. This means recognising substantive uncertainty as a reality and not attempting to assume it away in order to get a firm target with loose justification. It means avoiding complex mathematical and modelling approaches wherever possible. It means that speed to results is vital and that transparency in how these results were arrived at is also very important. All too often, complex analytical methods can appear themselves as a form of noise to decision-makers because they are unable to quickly grasp how data inputs relate to the analytical conclusions. Complex benefit-costs analyses involving risk factors, real options models and a range of advanced statistical approaches also suffer from this problem. This complexity causes a disconnect between analysis and decisions – a disconnect that restricts learning and adaptation. The resulting need to greatly simplify a representation of complex circumstances to non-specialists is incredibly challenging.

The logical starting point is to focus on the core issues of information and noise (i.e. randomness) in the policy cycle. Appraisal, evaluation and risk management (the three functions it could be useful to turn into a seamless activity) are all processes that have to grapple with this balance between information and noise. In appraisal, if the signal-to-noise ratio is low (a lot of randomness is anticipated) then it is preferable to be honest about this at the outset and to strive to put in place ways of learning and adapting in ways that can improve this signal-to-noise ratio as implementation proceeds. In evaluation, it is useful to focus on how effective these efforts to improve the signal-to-noise ratio have been – and are likely to be. For obvious reasons risk management is a central part of this approach to appraisal and evaluation.

These trade-offs are likely to have roles for frequentist analytical and target-driven policy stances when circumstances indicate that this is the best approach. However, the trade-offs will also need to involve finding a place for non-frequentist analytical methods (such as Bayesian inference) and more discovery-oriented policy stances when circumstances warrant this. In other words, the pathway to re-formulating how governments cope with uncertainty and risk in appraisal, evaluation, learning and adaptation plausibly lies in finding a better way of choosing the most suitable analytical method to match the most suitable policy stance. This creates a space for negotiated compromises in the links between the choice of statistical method and the choice between target-driven and discovery-based intervention designs.

Governance, uncertainty and signal processing

With these practical objectives in mind, the main focus in the book is on a fairly detailed and methodologically oriented look at what it means to govern in an uncertain and risky world – a world especially well configured to throw up nasty surprises. Within this broad theme, particular attention is paid to the ways in which the choices we make over how to govern can increase rather than decrease this potential to face these nasty surprises. Investigating these issues involves placing an emphasis on some of the underpinning conceptual assumptions that are used in governance – and could be used in governance. These conceptual concerns revolve around governance as an information process. As noted earlier, this perspective provides an opportunity to explore the extent to which the formal diagnostic tools used in information theory, tools that have driven the

14 *Introduction*

radical and disruptive changes of the information age, could be usefully applied to help us govern in a more adaptive manner better able to cope with the realities of substantive uncertainty and quantifiable risk.

From this angle, what governments do, and how well they do it, can be approached as a matter of identifying, interpreting and reacting to observed patterns. A key issue as regards these patterns is the extent to which the external environment with which governments must interact *and* the ways in which decisions are made as to how to react are effectively random.

What distinguishes aspects of this book is, however, an explicit recognition of the practical reality of uncertainty about the future – a reality that reduces the practical utility of 'evidence' gleaned from the past as a basis for avoiding nasty surprises in the future. From this perspective, beliefs and judgement, much maligned in the current emphasis on 'evidence-based policymaking' can, and should, play a key role in avoiding nasty surprises – not least in providing a conceptual bridge between what we understand about the past and what we may expect in the future.

The use of concepts from information theory is intended to stimulate thinking about how we can best approach these challenges. This is because the mathematics of information provide an analytically coherent framework for thinking about uncertainty, noise and information – issues usefully summarised in the notion of information entropy (in essence a measure of the potential to be surprised by information that we might receive in the future). It is this link between information and entropy that provides us with a means of thinking about governance as a process with the potential to both decrease and (if we get it wrong) increase entropy. This contrasts with the mechanistic tendencies in current approaches to public management.

However, unlike much contemporary discourse in the social sciences, some aspects of which favour an emphasis on modernity as a complex, fluid and hard-to-pin-down set of conditions,[6] the use of the concept of entropy here is more precise and more pragmatic. If we are to recognise the shortcomings in how we currently choose to govern as a basis for developing strategies for change, then we need to appropriate concepts to draw attention to these shortcomings. The notion of entropy, and the associated notion that the potential for nasty surprises provides a useful basis for thinking about the advantages and the disadvantages of different ways of governing, is proposed as a practical method for driving useful change in governance. The ways in which we define a problem have a strong influence on how we think about solutions to that problem.

These arguments have been informed, in part, by experience in conducting a range of evaluations of public sector funding (particularly in relation to support for innovation of various types). The lessons from that experience must necessarily be couched in general non-specific terms as to do otherwise would breach confidentiality constraints. Thus, when examples and illustrations are used to reinforce some points in the argument these are framed in such a way that it is not possible to identify the country or specific entities or funding programmes involved.

The potential for surprise

In a general sense, the metaphor of the seen and unseen valley with which this chapter opened, and the role of tests of conjectures in learning how to improve the ability to use the patterns observed to infer likely patterns that *may be* observed, points to the importance of minimising the potential for surprise as a characteristic of effective governance. This is an important issue to which we will return. From this perspective, a key principle of governance is to reduce the potential for nasty surprises, not just within governance but in the economy, society and natural environment as a whole. One just has to consider the nasty surprises that arose in 2008 and 2009 as the global financial crisis kicked in to grasp the importance of improving the articulation between substantive uncertainty and quantifiable risk in regulatory stances.

As the mantra that 'we need more evidence-based policy' is repeated there is a risk that this will focus attention too closely on the valleys of evidence we are in and away from the critically important conjectures relating the as-yet-unseen valleys. As Andrew Stirling observes: '*Since contemplating the unknown necessarily requires imaginings beyond the available evidence, it is treated as unscientific in conventional risk regulation. What is truly unscientific, however, is this effective denial of the unknown*' (Stirling, 2009). The more we frame success in analysing evidence around the legalistic notion of 'proof' of 'facts' and cause and effect the greater the risk that the efforts (and costs) expended will fail to help governments to handle uncertainties and risks. This, in turn, increases the potential for nasty surprises. Unlike academic research, effective governance is about reducing the potential for surprise in an uncertain and risky future – not simply a matter of reaching peer review–based consensus over the reasons why things happened in the past. Contemporary academic peer review is uncomfortable with the conjectures and speculative thinking that is central to reducing the potential for surprise. Policy think tanks are, as a result, better positioned to conjecture and speculate in this manner – but tend to avoid exploring methodological issues that could strengthen their ability to conjecture and speculate beyond the currently available evidence. If we had a better conceptual framework for leveraging these distinctive competencies, then perhaps we could govern better than we do.

There is a more general issue here, however, relating to the concepts of 'proof' in using evidence (the valley we are currently in) and intelligence relating to the as-yet-unseen valley. In a commentary published by the *Washington Post* in 2013 just before Colin Powell delivered 'evidence' to the UN that the Saddam Hussein administration in Iraq had developed weapons of mass destruction ex CIA officer Bruce Berkowitz addressed the distinction between intelligence work and detective work.

> *Detective work and intelligence collection may resemble each other, but they are really completely different. Detectives aim at meeting a specific legal standard – "probable cause," for example, or "beyond a reasonable doubt" or "preponderance of evidence." It depends on whether you want to start an*

16 *Introduction*

investigation, put a suspect in jail or win a civil suit. Intelligence, on the other hand, rarely tries to prove anything; its main purpose is to inform officials and military commanders. The clock runs differently for detectives and intelligence analysts, too. Intelligence analysts – one hopes – go to work before a crisis; detectives usually go to work after a crime. Law enforcement agencies take their time and doggedly pursue as many leads as they can. Intelligence analysts usually operate against the clock. There is a critical point in time where officials have to "go with what they've got," ambiguous or not. But the biggest difference – important in all the current controversies – is that intelligence agencies have to deal with opponents who take countermeasures. Indeed, usually the longer one collects information against a target, the better the target becomes at evasion. So do other potential targets, who are free to watch.

Berkowitz (2003)

Berkowitz went on to stress how intelligence analysis has been influenced by (nuclear) arms limitation treaties. The requirement to obtain 'proof' of treaty violation has tended to shift intelligence analysis towards *ex post* detective work and away from *ex ante* anticipation of possible future risks (given uncertainties and ambiguities).

We see a similar process taking place as the notion of evidence-based policy-making has taken hold. Evidence is treated as engendering 'proof' of cause and effect for things that have happened in the past – proof arrived at in the main only after lengthy and costly research activities. As evidence of the Iraqi weapons of mass destruction episode illustrates, when the search for 'proof' is combined with an excessive emphasis on using the media as a component of the policy process then the potential for nasty surprises (in this case an exaggerated threat that sanctioned an inappropriate response) can increase.

From this perspective, the extent to which evidence-based analyses are able to inform *future* policy interventions rests upon the combined impact of the rate of change in pertinent conditions together with the degree of uncertainty and risk faced over potential future states of the world. In general, the greater the combined impact of the rate of change in pertinent conditions together with the degree of uncertainty and risk the less useful, and indeed even dangerous, a reliance on evidence-based policymaking alone becomes. Evidence-based approaches (as currently formulated) also suffer from long time lags that reduce their utility to policymakers.

We are wise therefore to be cautious in how we apply 'hierarchies of evidence' in a public policy context.[7] The notion of these hierarchies (there are several schema used but they tend to place meta-reviews of randomised control trials at the top and expert opinion and judgement at the bottom) is useful. However, as the arguments above suggest this utility is high for academic research but lower for real policy decision-making that must take place on a timeline without the ability to delay and with only sparse and potentially ambiguous information at hand. In effect, the need to base decisions on conjectures about the future derived from, but not limited to, a general assessment of the available evidence creates a link between the bottom and the top of a hierarchy of evidence. Expert judgement is part of a learning loop via which uncertainties and risks are handled – not simply the bottom rung of a fixed ladder. Leadership involves making assumptions about the unseen valley on the basis of the valley of evidence that we have – but not limited to that valley of evidence. This leadership may involve initiating RCTs to test innovative concepts but these RCTs are themselves an outcome from expert opinion and the creativity associated with it. Hence, whilst from a static standpoint a hierarchy of evidence makes great sense as a quality assurance mechanism, from a dynamic standpoint that hierarchy takes the form of a segment of a broader learning cycle in which the creativity and innovation that drives what will be tested (we hope rigorously) in the future will in part be a fruit of human ingenuity not simply a more mechanical consequence of robust statistical tests of pilots or rolled-out initiatives.

From a signal processing angle, the utility of a hierarchy of evidence lies in the ways in which it is able to reduce diagnostic errors. A well-done RCT is simply a particularly effective means of minimising diagnostic errors (i.e. the likelihood of a false positive or a false negative test result). Consequently, if we are to maximise the effectiveness of this dynamic learning–based aspect of the hierarchy of evidence then the key issue becomes that of measuring empirically, via accumulating experience, the prevalence of these diagnostic errors. If that evidence were to tell us that, in fact, expert judgement performed relatively well compared to other items on the hierarchy (taking the need to conjecture about *future* states of the worlds into account) then the hierarchy would need to be re-ranked. In other words, where different types of evidence sit relative to each other in the hierarchy of evidence should be evidence-based and that evidence can be provided by using signal processing methods that measure the incidence of diagnostic errors. This incidence of diagnostic errors can only be measured with hindsight by identifying cases in which subsequent tests revealed previous diagnostic tests to be wrong.

What seems to be wrong?

To summarise, there is a troubling syndrome at work within the public sector that can be characterised as follows.

First, governments face persisting problems in being cost-effective, in part, because of the ways in which they choose to approach uncertainty, ambiguity and risk on the one hand and demonstrate transparency and accountability on the other. The result is that governments tend to be averse to uncertainty, ambiguity and risk whilst seeking to demonstrate their legitimacy, framed as efficient and effective governance – but in a manner that downplays governments' distinctive role in handling the uncertainties and risks that markets cannot cope with. This stance makes it particularly difficult for governments to deliver a key aspect of public value (i.e. what the electorate values) – acting as the uncertainty and risk manager of last resort, i.e. handling the problems that

18   *Introduction*

markets, businesses and civil society can't cope with, see Moore (1995) on the concept of public value.

Second, the emphasis on evidence-based policymaking is encouraging unrealistic expectations within government over the potential to benefit from academic research, whilst at the same time encouraging academics to justify funding for empirical research, and delineate the useful public outcomes from their research, either as contributions to the 'evidence base', or for science funding, innovation and research commercialisation outcomes. The assumption, held in both government and universities (and many policy think tanks), is that more effective public policy can, and will, be deduced from better quality, and greater volumes of, data and the use of classical tests for statistical significance that are ill suited to forward-looking challenges.

Third, there is a reluctance to recognise the relevance and utility of using tests of hypotheses both to analyse evidence and as a learning and adaptation method – despite the well-known importance of this aspect of the scientific method. This issue was brought home to me in an inter-governmental workshop a few years ago at which I gave a talk on how the time and cost of monitoring and evaluating public sector programmes could be reduced by boiling the evaluation process down to conventional scientific tests of hypotheses – the relative support for which could be assessed at any time using the available data and information. Whilst this notion attracted positive interest by most government officials the suggestion was effectively vetoed by one national representative on the basis that the preferable basis of effective policymaking should be randomised control trials (RCTs) rather than tests of hypotheses. The problem with that view is, of course, that RCTs are simply a means of testing hypotheses in the first place. RCTs allow the influences of independent variables to be discerned more readily. The issue lying behind that sort of attitude within government is one of form over substance: a failure to grasp why RCTs are used in health and medical research (in particular) and a tendency, manifested in the flurry of work on public sector innovation, to emphasise what is perceived to be new and trendy over the underlying challenges of governing wisely. Innovation is a means to an end not an end in itself. The current belief that RCTs are 'innovative' neglects why RCTs can be so powerful on a methodological level – as a means of testing hypotheses in a particularly robust manner.

Whilst there are a range of problematic aspects of this sort of assumption about what evidence is (to be addressed in this book), a fundamental objection is that setting up evidence-based policymaking as an ideal type for effective public policy, a stance increasingly linked to defining randomised control trials (RCTs) as the (to use a too-often-repeated phrase) 'gold standard' of evidence, overlooks the importance of governments' role as uncertainty and risk manager of last resort – and the tremendous politically important public value that stems from this role. Robust evidence has its greatest utility when it has been collected and analysed and this value will decay in the future *unless* the future looks very much like the present *and* the people and organisations whose behaviour a policy intervention seeks to modify fail to factor their new understanding of what government is trying to do (to them) into their decision-making. As noted earlier, this is a public policy dimension of the double hermeneutic stressed by Anthony Giddens: if I let you know the theories I have about you, you may change your behaviour in response and cause that theory to become untrue (Giddens, 1984) – resulting in learning-by-undoing.

The combination of these discount rate and learning-by-undoing dimensions can be a powerful reason why evidence-based policymaking has greater limitations than many assume. However, the even greater problem is that empirical evidence from the past may not be able to inform critically important decision-making over risky, uncertain and ambiguous issues that *may* be faced in the future. Political leadership, after all, is the art (not the science) of decision-making under great uncertainty and as such is fit for purpose when decisions with high downside risk (or upside opportunity) cannot be delayed until enough evidence is accumulated to comply with evidence-based policy norms (French, 2014).

The issues stressed above mean that there is more potential for improving the cost-effectiveness of governance (partly by making mistakes less frequent and less costly but also by coping with uncertainty and risk better) stemming from focusing government–academic (and think tank) collaboration on the *methods* used in public policy rather than in accumulating more empirical evidence. Simply accumulating more empirical evidence faces decreasing marginal returns to investment. On the other hand, advances in the methods used to make sense of data and information in the context of substantive uncertainty, ambiguity and risk address the key problem faced in governance: driving down the cost of governance in a changing, uncertain and risky world.

This approach is by intention highly conceptual in the sense that it attempts to lay out a roadmap for developing the sort of approaches to public policy that are better able to cope with uncertainty, ambiguity and risk. One cannot be cautious and risk averse in such a mission – it is necessary (and useful) to move beyond carefully analysed data and evidence and, instead, to offer conjectures and ideas that *may* prove to be useful in the future *if* they can be implemented effectively as tools and techniques. What we require is, simply put, tractable methods for making and testing these conjectures via hypothesis-based approaches to governance.

Bayesian inference features in these arguments – but framed, and informed by, the use of such methods in the Second World War and Cold War code breaking and other national security work in the US and the UK. These were advances that were made to inform decision-making under conditions of great uncertainty and risk (the Second World War and the Cold War), deployed in an iterative learning-oriented manner and in which practical expediency trumped the methodological controversies that have dogged much of the post-war era. Bayesian approaches are drawn upon not in order to engage with methodological debates in academia (where pro- and anti-Bayesian stances are still evident) but in order to raise awareness within government of the potential of these methods to form the basis for a more effective implementation of policy learning cycles.

20 *Introduction*

Use of Bayesian methods allows the development of an analytical framework for use in public policy based on making, and then using, the distinctions between substantive uncertainty, statistical uncertainty and actionable information. The latter is defined as information for which the levels of statistical uncertainty are sufficiently low that it forms a reliable basis for decision-making. What results is a three-dimensional framework that can help to clarify, assess and communicate the ways in which advances in knowledge and understanding involve a mix of translating substantive uncertainty into statistical uncertainty and then (if possible) squeezing down statistical uncertainty to the point(s) at which it can become actionable information.

It is worth noting that the use of such a framework is still compatible with the argument that many government decisions must be made even if there is no or very little actionable information – it is just that it helps to be clearer about the mix between substantive uncertainty, statistical uncertainty and actionable information – and how that mix is changing over time, to a large part as a result of investment. Indeed, as the book will demonstrate, the ability to track transitions between substantive uncertainty, statistical uncertainty and actionable information provides one basis for measuring and communicating the return on investment from research, learning-by-doing, regulatory frameworks and other government-funded activities.

The relationship between the practice of public policy and the study of public policy

The academic study of governance, public administration/management and public policy are not unusual in the ways in which actual practice relates (and does not relate) to the *study of* that practice. For example the research carried out in business schools tends to focus on grasping, characterising and explaining what practitioners are doing (e.g. as regards innovative practices, competitive strategies etc.). This emphasis on emerging patterns and the explanation of these patterns is, in turn, useful to the practitioners who – collectively – drive these changes because the academic work brings greater clarity and coherence to practice. The result is that actual practice and the study of that practice co-evolve – each feeds off the insights obtained from the other. It is not usually the case that advances in actual practice are driven by a linear translation and adoption of new ideas generated in the academic domain – although this can happen and the ramifications can be profound.

Similarly, the relationship between what practitioners do and what those who study what practitioners do adopts this co-evolution dynamic. For example practitioners were exploring a range of significant changes to how governments operate prior to these changes being analysed in academia and referred to as 'the new public management' (Hood, 1991). A similar process is now underway associated with academic research over 'the new public governance' (Osborne, 2006, 2010). However, unlike the co-evolution relationship in the practice of business and the *study of* the practice of business, the relationship here appears to be less productive. Some practitioners dismiss the relevance of the academic study of what they do, objecting to a perceived element of critique and questioning the practical relevance – to them – of the work being produced by academia. The result is that there is a discourse between academic observers of actual practice that only connects weakly (if at all) to what practitioners actually do. This is, of course, a familiar problem in academic–practitioner relationships.

If we wish to transition towards a more productive co-evolution relationship then one solution could lie in placing a greater priority (on the academic side) on suggesting advances in methods and procedures of potential use to real practice and (on the practitioner side) being willing and able to collaborate in testing and refining these new methods. Such collaboration should, ideally, include a stronger emphasis on defining the problems that these new methods could usefully address. This sort of relationship would be better placed to produce a stronger and more useful co-evolution dynamic that (as currently happens) draws attention to shortcomings in practice *and* (as happens far less) strives to come up with potentially useful solutions to these shortcomings – i.e. moving beyond critique as an end in itself.

For this reason, most of this book focuses on exploring how insights from analytical work across a broad range of academic disciplines might be used to develop useful practical tools and techniques for practitioners in the public sector. This pragmatic emphasis is reflected in the following discussion of a metric intended to summarise the problems associated with the ways in which we govern can *themselves* amplify the potential for nasty surprises to occur.

The risk amplification ratio

Whilst a detailed explanation of how the core organising proposition tested in this book follows in chapter four, it is useful to introduce this proposition up front in order to help to organise and braid together the various strands of argument.

The core proposition to be explored is reflected in the following ratio:

$$\text{Risk amplification} = \frac{\text{Achieved potential for surprise}}{\text{Unavoidable potential for surprise}}$$

This simple ratio tells us that governments face a range of complex and unavoidable factors that can surprise them. Risk is defined in a manner aligned with the most recent incarnation of the international risk management standard ISO31000: 2009 as 'uncertainty over objectives'.

This simple equation also provides another potentially useful concept and measure:

$$\text{Governance entropy} = \text{Actually achieved potential for surprise} \\ - \text{Unavoidable potential for surprise}$$

This expression of the relationship highlights the ways in which the amplification of risk stemming from the mind-sets, practices and procedures of governance

22 Introduction

can be viewed as a decrease in the capacity to anticipate events, resulting in an increased potential for surprise. In this sense, governance entropy is an expression of the well-understood tendency for bureaucracies to self-organise around internal interests and incentives rather than generate public value outside of governance. In this case, the result is an increased potential for nasty surprises.

Consequently, this risk amplification ratio provides a high-level measure of both current capability challenges in governance and provides a basis for planning future improvements in capability and assessing the progress made. The simplicity of a bird's-eye-view metric of this type is important because one can easily get lost in the complexity and detail of real governance processes and procedures – approaches that can amplify rather than simplify complexity.

The 'risk registers' commonly used by governments that list risk factors and risk mitigation actions can, in fact, amplify rather than reduce risks. These registers usually avoid considering interactions between these risks and do not provide an overall measure of risk either. These risk registers are compliance-oriented rituals that do little to actually assess and manage risk. As a result, insufficient attention can be directed at signs that risks are a problem – the emphasis is on having complied with a risk management standard and then setting that assessment aside in order to get on with policy delivery.

In contrast, the risk amplification ratio based on the potential for surprise does provide such an overall measure of risk exposure. Perhaps most usefully, it is able to encompass administrative procedures and guidelines by providing a framework for analysing how those procedures can increase or decrease the amplification of risk in specific circumstances. In line with the arguments flagged so far and to be addressed in greater detail in the rest of the book, a mechanistic stance towards objectives is avoided in preference for a more realistic and pragmatic stance.

The level of actually achieved potential for surprise, and hence the risk amplification factor, decreases with effective learning and adaptation. Crucially, however, this decrease in risk amplification is best achieved because conjectures (hypotheses) are made about what it is plausible to find in the unseen valley. By implication, if the machinery of government is poorly equipped to develop and test forward-looking hypotheses it is poorly equipped to minimise the amplification of risk. From this dynamic perspective, the effectiveness of risk management rests on a hypothesis generation and testing dynamic. This is currently not a well-developed aspect of risk management outside of the security intelligence community.

Given that modernity is assumed by many commentators (in effect) to involve an increased potential for surprise, any tendency to further increase this problem is a matter of concern. Building on this point, the sort of paradigm shift in governance explored in this book revolves around finding new and better ways of driving down the amplification of risk by converging the *actually achieved potential for surprise* with the *unavoidable potential for surprise*. It is hard to learn how to reduce the potential for surprise if one is not realistic about both

Introduction 23

the unavoidable potential for surprise and the actually achieved potential for surprise prevailing at the present time.

As noted earlier, information theory provides us with a useful tool for operationalising this proposition because it (literally) is able to calculate the potential for surprise (via the concept of *Shannon Entropy*, which will be used on a practical level in the form known as *Metric Entropy*, see Shannon (1948) for the seminal paper articulating information theory).[8] This measure calculates the likelihood that information that might be received in the future (on the basis of what has been experienced to date) can be predicted. It yields a number between 0 and 1.0 in which 1.0 tells us that the data are an equally distributed random string (i.e. has maximum potential for surprise) and 0 when there is no potential for surprise. Whilst the concept of entropy can be confusing, and has multiple interpretations (such as measuring the degree of 'disorder' or usefulness of energy in a system), in this context it is sufficient simply to treat the concept in the terms in which it is measured – as an observed pattern that can be characterised on the basis of how predictable each permutation of the data is. There are well-established analytical methods for calculating the potential for surprise in sequences of information; the challenge, which is not trivial, is to implement this approach in a governance context. The sequencing dimension is particularly important because of the importance of identifying signs of changes in the behaviour of a flow of data.

Metric entropy also expresses in a succinct and powerful manner the point that new information is most interesting and useful when it is least expected. This perspective emerged from security encryption work because it is important to be able to calculate the amount of information required in a signal in order to conceal (or reveal) a hidden message. That challenge relates to the ways in which signals containing information and apparently random signals ('noise') are mixed together. In encryption work, and the wide range of information and communication technology applications that have exploited these fundamental principles, the ability to distinguish between signals and noise, manifested in the ability to calculate the potential for surprise, is of critical importance. For example the approach allows the minimum amount of information to encode a signal and transmit and receive it intact to be calculated given the lexicon (range of symbols) used to convey the message. If we transpose this analytical perspective to governance then the signal-to-noise ratio becomes more than a metaphor for aspects of governance – it becomes a means of calculating measures of how well governance is performing in the face of uncertainties and risks. The notion that we can assess the degree of governance entropy stands to contribute to the formulation of effective strategies for reforming governance.

By framing the issues in this analytical manner, the ground is prepared to examine governance from a novel and potentially useful perspective. Most importantly, this perspective is not simply that of critique – rather it is one that seeks to develop and apply practical insights and tools with the potential to reform governance by improving the capability to cope with uncertainty and risk and to reduce (rather than increase) the potential for surprise. From this

24 *Introduction*

angle it is logical to have drawn upon the techniques used in encryption and decryption (methods that reduce the potential for surprise) in order to start to craft a more generalised approach to governance.

Given the importance of changing circumstances, the concept of 'weak signals' is of particular significance in developing this approach to effective governance. Change does not always happen gradually, there can be jumps and discontinuities – surprises that can be particularly de-stabilising. Consequently, the ability to spot what are termed 'weak signals' of potential jumps and discontinuities is of particular importance in governance. This too is an area in which work done within the national security community has a more general relevance to public policy. If these weak signals are to be spotted (and reacted to) then the ways in which interventions are managed must, by design, be sensitive to the importance of this aspect of learning-by-doing.

Disease outbreaks are, arguably, the most widely recognised example of the importance of spotting weak signals. When an infection can grow exponentially the cost-effectiveness of efforts to limit or eliminate the infection decreases exponentially. In other words, the earlier we act the (much) better that is. Whilst governments have well-established surveillance mechanisms for areas like biosecurity that include processes for reporting surprises (i.e. unexpected observations given usual statistically predicted incidences, such as a 'notifiable disease'), this ethos is less well developed in other areas of public services. The current rigidities are not well suited to spotting, let alone reacting to, weak signals. Current methods focus attention on relatively inflexible programme milestones and KPIs (compliance) rather than a more forensic examination of the lessons being learned as the intervention is implemented and, in particular, *any indications of looming surprises.*

This is why a transition to an over-arching emphasis on minimising the potential for surprise can create an environment in which the likelihood of missing weak signals of potential rapid and/or dramatic changes in circumstances is reduced (though this is never something that can be eliminated). Chapter five examines practical ways of improving the capacity to handle weak signals based on the principles of information theory. The approach advocated rests upon the use of competing hypotheses specifically developed (and evolved through practice) to identify the types of surprises that could indicate an increased likelihood of a pending rapid change in circumstances. Signal detection methods using Bayesian inference are useful in this respect because they focus on signals in sparse and ambiguous data rather than statistical significance in a sampling sense – though as chapter five will consider, both approaches are useful complements to each other rather than substitutes. The key function is to be able to spot a surprise (anomaly) in information and data with lower numbers of observations than are required for sampling theory–based definitions of statistical significance.[9]

These issues are important because taxpayers bear the costs of governance entropy, i.e. the amplification of risk. In this respect, the case developed in this book contributes to an understanding of both the tendency to privatise profits but socialise risks, see for example O'Connor (2001) and also Harvey (2010), but also aligns with aspects of the critical perspective towards governance expressed in public choice theory. Examining governance entropy is the way to bridge such different perspectives and helps to focus attention on the ways in which the self-interests within governance, coupled with successful efforts by businesses and elements of civil society to socialise risks via governance, results in increased inter-generational inequities – as future generations are forced to bear the costs of the amplification of risks today. From this perspective, austerity measures that are de-coupled from efforts to reduce governance entropy are missing an important opportunity to drive long-term advances in how we govern. If we persist in governing without learning effectively *whilst governing* then public debt will continue to be shaped by the amplification of risk.

Specific propositions to be tested

The specific propositions to be explored and tested in this book are as follows:

1 It is useful to analyse the effectiveness of governance from the perspective of attempts to minimise the potential for surprise.
2 An equation linking the amplification of risk to the ratio of *actually achieved* potential for surprise over the *unavoidable* potential for surprise provides a practical and conceptually robust method for implementing this focus on the potential for surprise.
3 The concept of governance entropy, defined as the extent to which the unavoidable potential for surprise is increased by mind-sets, practices and procedures (resulting in amplified risk) provides a useful analytical contribution to the public sector reform process.
4 A simplified and standardised Bayesian expression of the policy learning process has the potential to support efforts to minimise the potential for surprise.
5 Testing competing hypotheses using the simplified and standardised Bayesian decision-support framework expression provides a practical and conceptually robust means of minimising the potential for surprise by creating a seamless integration of the currently distinct appraisal, monitoring and evaluation and risk management functions.

The conclusions reached over the nature and extent of support for these propositions are presented in the concluding chapter.

Outline of the book

The approach taken in this book has been strongly influenced by recent experience in engaging with government from an academic base – a process in which the importance of using visualisation methods to express policy challenges and

26   Introduction

to help to analyse evidence became clear. Visualisation, if done clearly and effectively, can provide decision-makers in government with a stronger 'bridge' to the analytical work carried out in academia and policy think tanks, see Lindquist (2011) for a review of policy visualisation work.

Chapter two examines the limitations of uncertainty and risk-averse public policy. It considers how governance is re-constituted for fast learning when existential threats such as major wars are faced and the main lessons from studies of public sector cost overruns and from programme audits, reviews and evaluations under normal conditions. The strengths and weaknesses of the current public management ethos are assessed, as is the public sector innovation agenda and efforts to encourage experimentalist governance. Chapter three focuses on governments' distinctive role as uncertainty and risk manager of 'last resort'. This covers science and innovation policy, the use of 'prescience' as a distinct outcome class. The chapter also considers the relevance of subjectivist Austrian economics to public policy in this context.

Chapter four considers the conceptual framing and formal analytical tools necessary to deliver stronger learning and adaptation using Bayesian approaches. Chapter five focuses on the practical methods for implementing the conceptual framework defined in chapter four. The main emphasis is on structured hypothesis testing using the simplified Bayesian approach and using odds (for and against) rather than probability expressed test results. Finally, chapter six concludes the book by discussing the implications for government–academic collaboration and engagement and the scope for improved international cooperation in public policy capacity-building. It ends by setting out five next steps in this transformational pathway.

The first half of the book (chapters one, two and three) are diagnostic in the sense that the focus is on what is not working as well as it should in public policy. The second half of the book (chapters four, five and six) is speculative – the focus is on how we might innovate in response to these shortcomings. The diagnostic half of the book deliberately avoids a lengthy rehearsal of the wide range of evidence on the dysfunctional aspects of public policy that are consequences of failures to learn and adapt and other problems associated with difficulties in coping with substantive uncertainties. There would be little additional gain from running through all these familiar problems, whilst making the book much longer and the issues more cumbersome to grapple with. Rather, the emphasis is placed on developing some, it is hoped, useful novel perspectives on these problems – perspectives that can then be used to frame an agenda for the innovative response covered in the second half of the book. The second half of the book attempts to frame some foundational principles (based on signal processing concepts) via which we can develop innovative solutions. These are more akin to sign-posts in a work-in-progress than to completed work in which solutions to the gaps and technical challenges have been fully articulated. As such, this second half of the book is a 'manifesto' that lays out an agenda for moving forward. The decision to publish at this early exploratory stage in the efforts to develop these concepts for use in public policy was made in recognition of the power of adopting an 'open innovation' approach – fostering collective and collaborative responses via experimentation and pursuing multiple ideas in parallel with the potential for cross-fertilisation. The transition to modes of governance that are better able to learn and adapt in the face of substantive uncertainties and nasty surprises will be a collective effort with no definitive solution.

Notes

1 The initial discussion of Machiavelli in this chapter is based upon a keynote address by the author at a workshop on government–academic collaboration in Canberra organised by the Australian Government's *Department of Prime Minister and Cabinet* on 13 June 2014.
2 The passage is taken from 'That a General ought to be equated with the lie of the land' in The Discourses.
3 Accessed at: http://marklmatthews.com/transformational-public-policy/
4 See Hatfield-Dodds et al. (2007) for a useful discussion of adaptive governance from a public policy perspective.
5 This illustration of the value of distinguishing between substantive uncertainty and quantifiable risk when setting targets stems from interviews conducted by the author with aerospace industry executives in relation to opportunities for business–academic collaboration.
6 The sociological and political science literature focuses on these interconnections between uncertainty, risk and modernity, notably Beck's work on the risk society (Beck, 1992), Przeworski's idea of democracy as organised uncertainty (Przeworski, 1991) and Giddens's work on modernity and risk (Giddens, 1999).
7 See Leigh (2009) for an influential discussion of the utility of hierarchies or evidence from a public policy angle.
8 This is Shannon entropy divided by the length of the string, i.e. number of items of evidence.
9 This is an important issue in clinical medical diagnosis because useful and potentially life-saving findings may require the use of methods, such as Shannon entropy, that do not require conventional sampling theory–based thresholds of statistical significance to be met. See for example Wessel et al. (2000) for a discussion of the use of Shannon entropy in predicting risks in cardiac data. This is a context in which it is useful to be able to identify any tendency for heart rate variability to become simple (reduced potential for surprise) rather than complex (increased potential for surprise). In general, the more simplistic the patterns in the detailed variability of heart beats the greater the risk of heart failure – this insight reversed the traditional assumption that a healthy heart would have a more regular beat pattern. It is easier to identify symptoms using Shannon entropy than via conventional tests of statistical significance.

References

Bammer, G and Smithson, M (eds.) 2008, *Uncertainty and Risk: Multidisciplinary Perspectives*. Routledge, London.
Beck, U 1992, *Risk Society: Towards a New Modernity*. Sage, New Delhi.
Berkowitz, B 2003, *The Big Difference between Intelligence and Evidence*. Commentary in the Washington Post. Re-published by the RAND Corporation, Santa Monica, CA.

28 *Introduction*

Crozier, M 1964, *The Bureaucratic Phenomenon*. University of Chicago Press, Chicago.

Deloitte 2014, *Risk Management for Health Care Reform Programs: A Health Plan Perspective*. Deloitte Consulting LLP Paper. Risk Management Institute, Virtual Library.

Feynman, R 1967, *The Character of a Physical Law*. MIT Press, Cambridge, MA.

French, R 2014, How do we judge policies? *The Political Quarterly*. vol. 85, no. 1, pp. 29–36.

Giddens, A 1984, *The Constitution of Society*. Polity, Cambridge, UK.

Giddens, A 1999, Risk and responsibility. *Modern Law Review*. vol. 62, no. 1, pp. 1–10.

Gigerenzer, G 2000, *Adaptive Thinking: Rationality in the Real World*. Oxford University Press, New York.

Gigerenzer, G 2002, *Reckoning with Risk: Learning to Live with Uncertainty*. Penguin, London.

Gigerenzer, G and Hoffrage, U 1995, How to improve Bayesian reasoning without instruction: Frequency formats. *Psychological Review*. vol. 102, no. 4, pp. 684–704.

Good, I J 1979, Turing's statistical work in World War II. *Biometrika*. vol. 66, no. 2, pp. 393–396.

Harvey, D 2010, *The Enigma of Capital and the Crises of Capitalism*. Profile Books, London.

Hatfield-Dodds, S, Nelson, R and Cook, D 2007, *Adaptive Governance: An Introduction and Implications for Public Policy*. Paper Presented at the 51st Annual Conference of the Australian Agricultural and Resource Economics Society, Queenstown, New Zealand, 13–16 February.

Hood, C 1991, A public management for all seasons? *Public Administration*. vol. 69, pp. 3–19.

Klein, B and Meckling, W 1958, Application of operations research to development decisions. *Operations Research*. vol. 6, no. 3, pp. 352–363.

Leigh, A 2009, What evidence should social policymakers use? *Australian Treasury Economic Roundup*. vol. 1, pp. 27–43. Canberra.

Lindquist, E 2011, *Grappling with Complex Policy Challenges: Exploring the Potential of Visualization for Analysis, Advising and Engagement*. Discussion Paper. HC Coombs Policy Forum, The Australian National University, Canberra.

Machiavelli, N 2003, *The Discourses*. Penguin Classics, London.

Meehl, P E 1978, Theoretical risks and tabular asterisks: Sir Karl, Sir Ronald, and the slow progress of soft psychology. *Journal of Consulting and Clinical Psychology*. vol. 46, pp. 806–834.

Moore, M 1995, *Creating Public Value*. Harvard University Press, Cambridge, MA.

Nowotny, H 2015, *The Cunning of Uncertainty*. Policy Press, Cambridge.

O'Connor, J 2001, *The Fiscal Crisis of the State*. Transaction Publishers, New Jersey.

Osborne, S P 2006, The new public Governance? *Public Management Review*. vol. 8, pp. 377–387.

Osborne, S P (ed.) 2010, *The New Public Governance*. Routledge, New York.

Ostrom, E 1999, Coping with the tragedy of the commons. *Annual Review of Political Science*. vol. 2, pp. 493–535.

Przeworski, A 1991, *Democracy and the Market*. Cambridge University Press, Cambridge, UK.

Sabel, C and Zeitlin, J 2012, Experimentalist governance, in D Levi-Faur (ed.), *The Oxford Handbook of Governance*, Oxford University Press, Oxford, pp. 169–183.

Shannon, C E 1948, A mathematical theory of communication. *The Bell System Technical Journal.* vol. XXVII (July), pp. 379–423.

Smithson, M 2008, The many faces and masks of uncertainty, in G Bammer & M Smithson (eds.), *Uncertainty and Risk: Multidisciplinary Perspectives*, Earthscan Publications Ltd, London, pp. 13–25.

Stirling, A 2009, Risk, uncertainty and power. *Seminar Magazine.* vol. 597, pp. 33–39.

Taleb, N N 2010, *The Black Swan: The Impact of the Highly Improbable*, 2nd edition. Penguin, London.

Wessel, N, Schumann, A, Schirdewan, A, Voss, A and Kurths, J 2000, *Entropy Measures in Heart Rate Variability Data.* Proceedings of the First International Symposium, ISMDA 2000 Frankfurt, Germany, September 29–30.

Ziliak, S T and McCloskey, D N 2014, *The Cult of Statistical Significance: How the Standard Error Costs Us Jobs, Justice and Lives.* The University of Michigan Press, Ann Arbor.

2 The limitations of uncertainty and risk-averse public policy

Contemporary notions of good governance reflect the confluence of three policy narratives that describe how efficiency and effectiveness can be achieved in the public sector. First, the 'new public management' ethos characterised by the privatisation of certain public services and a strong emphasis on the use of targets and performance measures to drive performance and demonstrate transparency and accountability (Hood, 1991). The genesis of this business-like approach goes back to Robert McNamara's tenure as Secretary of the United States Department of Defense in the early 1960s (Hayward, 2015). McNamara introduced the objectives-based budgeting ethos used in the Ford Motor Company (his previous employer) to the Pentagon. This approach to budgeting placed a strong emphasis on the activities, outputs and outcomes intended to achieve stated objectives and contrasted with traditional funding allocations based on existing organisational structures, see West (2011) and Hayward (2015). McNamara's subsequent tenure at the World Bank helped to establish this ethos more generally.

Second, the concept of evidence-based policymaking that places a high priority on the collection and analysis of data as a basis for making policy decisions and makes explicit claims about avoiding 'ideological' issues (Solesbury, 2001). Third, the strong and pervasive role of formal process compliance-based approaches to risk management reflected in various standards and guidelines, and especially in ISO: 31000: 2009. Uncertainty and risk are linked. In ISO 31000 risk is defined as uncertainty over objectives with little attention paid, reciprocally, to the effect of the choice of objectives on uncertainty – despite the reality that it is the objectives that we choose that define risk exposure, usually in the light of how much substantive uncertainty is associated with different objectives. This problem is compounded by profit-seeking innovations in the private sector that turn risk into a tradable commodity (Kay, 2015). From a philosophical perspective risk is reified (the complex evolving processes that create risk are treated as 'things' not relationships). This reification requires that substantive uncertainty and quantifiable risk are conflated with each other to create a tradable 'package' (most evident in modern investment finance). These tradable packages downplay the ways in which substantive uncertainties (what we don't know) impact upon the value of the package. Enough has been written about the role of traded bundles of high-risk mortgage debt in the 2008/9 financial crisis to make this point – together with the ways in which this crises revealed shortcomings in government regulatory methods (Kay, 2015; Stiglitz, 2010).

This commodification of risk engenders a spurious sense of security. We downplay the importance of investing in discovering things that reduce substantive uncertainties. This increases the potential for nasty surprises to occur. In an uncertain and changing world investing in discovery has a higher return on investment (in reducing the potential for nasty surprises) compared to investing in the 'sleights of hand' via which substantive uncertainties are re-framed and mis-represented as quantifiable risks.

The roots of this philosophical problem go back to Laplace's use of the mathematical convenience of treating uncertainty as even odds (a probability of 0.5). In contrast to framing substantive uncertainty as a zero (or perhaps miniscule) odds of various competing hypotheses being correct based on currently available evidence, a mathematical way of saying 'we don't yet know', this convenient sleights of hand allows mathematical formalism to advance but at the cost of diverging from reality. Treating uncertainty as even odds deflects attention from the return on investment to be achieved by discovering more about what is going on (and therefore may go on in the future). A discovery-based perspective is made clearer by making efforts to de-couple substantive uncertainty from quantifiable risk and by using alternative means of expressing that uncertainty that avoid the 0.5 probability assumption.

In combination, this mix of problems with current ways of handling uncertainty and risk in governance encourages decision-makers in the public sector to approach risk as:

- something that should be avoided and/or displaced into others (Power, 2004) – an aspect that can make it difficult to integrate risk into effective strategic plans;
- a compliance-based impediment to policy delivery rather than an integral component of what delivering policy in a prudent manner actually involves doing (Hanger, 2014);
- being treated as a failure to achieve clearly defined objectives and in a manner in which risk is defined as any uncertainty over objectives (ISO 31000: 2009);
- a matter of maintaining 'risk registers' based on the assumed likelihood of occurrence and severity of potential impact – but with no overall measure of resulting risk exposure, and;
- a tendency to overlook the implications for decision-making arising from the treatment of substantive uncertainty (incalculable risk) as if it is calculable risk and, as a result, missing opportunities to learn-by-doing in coping with the inherent risks of governing.

The result is a situation in which the management of real, and often unavoidable, uncertainties and risks by officials is hampered by a reluctance to speculate

32 *Limitations of risk-averse public policy*

and conjecture (as that goes beyond the available 'evidence'). Indeed, the concept of evidence used in the public sector tends to err towards a preference for 'facts', and especially simple 'killer' facts used to justify a desired and media-friendly intervention (Stevens, 2011).

Governance paradigms

Part of the impetus for privatising government services and state-run enterprises has been the perception, and in many cases the reality, that markets and businesses are able to be more efficient than the public sector. Whilst there are a number of reasons for this, the capacity to learn-by-doing in an adaptive manner is one important aspect: the discovery of more efficient and effective ways of doing things via the accumulation of practical experience. As Michel Crozier has stressed, there is a tendency for bureaucracies to resist the types of bottom-up evolutionary change that could potentially be driven by learning and adaptation and to only succumb to the imperative for widespread change when crisis ('tipping') points are reached – at which point the organisation traditionally responds at a systematic level driven by top-down imperatives (Crozier, 1964).

A range of other factors that can affect the relative effectiveness of public versus private service delivery, from incentives through to work place rigidities, can all impact upon the capacity to learn-by-doing. Given this, when considering ways of improving the cost-effectiveness of governance it is natural to examine how effective learning-by-doing is *in practice*. This can be a useful lens through which to examine governance because it is able to shed light on reasons why opportunities to learn-by-doing have been overlooked or, if recognised, not utilised as effectively as they might.

The standard approach adopted by modern governments revolves around tightly specified and often contractually defined performance measures. This 'invents' a theoretical future in which the intervention will operate rather than allowing that future to be discovered through learning-by-doing. The results are clearly defined targets and milestones, *Key Performance Indicators* (KPIs), outputs, outcomes and intended impacts. Deviations away from the plan are viewed as problems – 'variances' against plan – reflecting poor programme and contract management, and penalties may apply. The language, mind-sets and technical methods deployed are those of the factory production line – an environment in which statistical process control methods seek to assure quality levels via minimising variances against specifications and plans.

The result is that many (if not virtually all) government interventions construct a rigid edifice that is both a driver of overhead costs (in programme management and reporting) and rigid in the face of justifiable reasons for adapting on the basis of learning (including surprises – both nasty and fortuitous). It is extremely hard to get funding allocated (internally or externally) without constructing this edifice of false precision. Although government officials, in the main, are well aware of the major limitations of this approach it has proved hard to replace it with a different ethos able to demonstrate transparency and accountability. In effect, therefore, we govern in a manner that substitutes KPI and contract compliance–based demonstrations of transparency and accountability for actually doing useful things in as cost-effective a manner as we are able. The wasted expenditure associated with the current ethos (reflected in interventions that stick rigidly to outmoded or poorly defined rationales, fail to deliver useful benefits but are not stopped because monitoring and evaluation (M&E) processes and contract management are not fit for purpose etc.) is hard to estimate but is likely to be very high.

Of course, these rigidities associated with invented rather than discovered futures become more of an issue of concern when circumstances are changing more rapidly. The 'evidence' gleaned from past experiences is more likely to provide a useful basis for decision-making about the future if it is very similar to the past. This would be fine *if* public policy was (say) a criminal court hearing (which it is not – unless of course things go badly wrong). In general terms, the greater the combined impact of the rate of change in pertinent conditions together with the degree of uncertainty and risk the less useful, and indeed even dangerous, a reliance on evidence-based policymaking alone becomes. Evidence-based approaches (as currently formulated) also suffer from long time lags and relevance deficits that reduces their utility to policymakers.

Figure 2.1 (from Matthews, 2015) illustrates the principle that uncertainty over understanding both the future *and* past experiences should, ideally, be treated as a 'U'-shaped curve that reaches its lowest point in the immediate

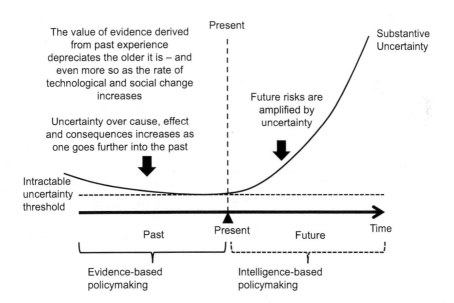

Figure 2.1 Asymmetric uncertainty and the differences between evidence-based policymaking and intelligence-based policymaking

34 *Limitations of risk-averse public policy*

past (lags in receiving and assessing information mean that there is always more uncertainty over the present than the immediate past). Although there is far greater uncertainty in regards to what the future may involve, we can never be certain about our understanding of the lessons from experience to date. All other things being equal, we are more uncertain the further we go into the past. In this diagram, a distinction is made between the evidence-based policy-making domain (historical experience) and an intelligence-based domain that looks forward into the future – and must grapple with the uncertainties and risks that this involves.

This approach to articulating the relationship between evidence-based policymaking and intelligence-based policymaking is based upon the notion of discount rate symmetry with regards to the future *and* the past. Just as we apply a discount rate to assumptions and estimates relating to the future we should also apply a discount rate to the past. The value of findings obtained from the analysis of the *past* (i.e. the evidence base) does not eliminate uncertainty and risk over what actually happened and what actually caused this. The greater the rate of change in the economic, social and technological conditions the greater the discount rate that should, in principle, be applied to evidence from the past. In the modern world the discount rate applied to the future will be much greater than that applied to the past – however the principle of symmetry is an important one.[1]

As will be discussed later on, the reflexive ability of those whose behaviour we seek to alter to understand and to react to government interventions – to learn-by-'undoing' – is a powerful rationale for recognising the utility of factoring these changing circumstances into our assessment of the value of evidence gleaned from the past. From a decision-making perspective, uncertainty, ambiguity and risk don't just relate to the future – they also relate to our understanding of history and the lessons for decisions that need to be made today about what to do in the future. Evidence alone is not a solution to the challenge of governing effectively.

The current public management ethos continues in part because there is no credible alternative. The approach proposed in chapter one may have merit because, in focusing on the potential for surprise, it provides a potential solution to the challenge of developing a credible alternative by explicitly recognising that the ability to minimise the potential for surprise when circumstances are changing is a very valuable over-arching goal for governance. This means that programme and contract management could start to transition to a dominant focus on minimising the potential for surprise – as an outcome that can in principle be tracked and used to assess the return-on-investment. In effect, this public investment attempts to buy more compelling odds in the future than would otherwise be the case. This stance is of particular relevance to funding for academic research because it explicitly recognises that useful outcomes and impacts do not just stem from the commercialisation of that knowledge, but from enhanced preparedness for understanding uncertainties and risks (Matthews, 2009) and is discussed in chapter three.

Limitations of risk-averse public policy 35

Persisting cost overruns, and in some cases failures to deliver the intended objectives, in government programmes and projects are, from a learning-by-doing perspective, symptoms worthy of examination. If public sector entities are consistently under-estimating what it will cost to deliver programmes and projects (and the time required to achieve these objectives) then this persisting problem deserves an analysis of what engineers call the 'root causes'. In other words, the indirect and fundamental drivers of the problem – drivers that may not be readily apparent without an analysis of the complex webs of cause and effect that may link symptoms to causes. Significantly, there is no shortage of data on persisting cost overruns, or of well-considered studies of the causes of cost overruns (especially as regards defence and projects but also for a wide range of other government-funded activities).

For instance, in 2006 the RAND Corporation (once again) concluded that there is a systemic and persisting tendency to under-estimate weapons system costs. When adjusted for factors such as inflation and the different system quantities produced the mean cost growth factor was 1.46, i.e. 46 per cent more than had been anticipated (Arena et al., 2006). More generally, whenever the media reports that a large and very costly public sector software project gets into trouble, or is abandoned it is unlikely that the general public will be surprised.

Consider the following aspects of what governments do and the ways in which these activities are carried out. Interventions are planned, sometimes in great detail, with firm targets, performance measures and milestones. There may be technical appraisals on the anticipated benefits and the costs of delivering these benefits – appraisals of varying quality and credibility. Politicians and the advisors will pay particular attention to being seen to act decisively by using engagement with the media to that end. Uncertainties and risks will tend to be viewed as unwelcome complicating factors that will get in the way of delivering. 'Risk management' will take place, but too often as a compliance ritual at some distance from the 'main game' of clearly defined interventions designed to reduce ambiguity over what will be achieved and how this will be achieved.

Once the intervention is underway any monitoring of progress will tend to involve the generation of data – but data that is rarely made use of in a regular analytical manner to track actual progress. Particular attention will be paid to whether concrete non-fudgeable milestones are being met. The intervention will usually receive one or more evaluations (depending on how large and long-lived it is), each of which usually results in some tweaking and evolution of what is being attempted and how it is being attempted. These interim and ex post evaluations will usually relate only loosely to the original ex ante appraisal of the intervention. Things may have moved on, perhaps in unexpected ways so the original appraisal is outdated and of limited use. The original appraisal may have been weak methodologically. It may have relied (if required) on benefit-cost estimates outsourced to consultants rather than use estimates developed and 'owned' in house. This outsourcing (displacing the problem) greatly restricts the ability to learn from experience – creating a break in the learning

36 *Limitations of risk-averse public policy*

cycle. It may not be clear why the intervention was implemented as it was, what the design trade-offs made were – and why. In some cases, not uncommon, it will be necessary for the evaluation(s) to devote much (costly effort) to retrospectively re-constructing the initial case for the intervention – and in some detail. This can be especially hard when understanding has advanced and events have unfolded because there will be an understandable tendency to try to, in effect, re-write history by retrospectively framing the original case for the intervention from a contemporary perspective. These retrospective efforts diminish the potential to learn-by-doing and, like risk management, tend to steer the evaluation process towards the characteristics of a compliance ritual.

One thing that characterises these stylised aspects of the policy process is an aversion to approaching uncertainties and risks via conjectures about possible future states of the world – conjectures that don't avoid the challenge that substantive uncertainty tends to be unavoidable and, hence, cannot be assumed away under the pretence that it is a component of quantified risk. The usual architecture of planned interventions uses firm targets and progress milestones in a manner that creates a 'siege mentality' in the face of any conjectures about what could go wrong or is insufficiently understood. At certain points these voices are marginalised because the conjectures question prematurely locked-in assumptions. These voices are treated as a threat to 'delivery' when, in reality, ignoring those voices is a threat to delivery.

It is not hard to see that the picture being painted is one of wasted expenditure and missed opportunities to learn. The greater the emphasis on appraisal, evaluation and risk management as compliance rituals the greater this potential for waste in the public sector. Indeed, efforts by governments to be transparent and accountable (in clearly demonstrating the value-for-money of what they are doing and have been doing) can itself be a source of waste if the dominating ethos is one of compliance rituals. These activities are performed but in ways that don't actually generate much public value (i.e. outcomes valued by the general community).

One major cause of these problems, problems that will be familiar to anyone who has worked in government or worked closely with government, is this disjuncture between what appraisal, evaluation, and risk management are supposed to achieve ideally and what they achieve in practice. In more concrete terms, this means asking what the information gain is from the spending on appraisal, evaluation and risk management. This information gain (what we now think we know that we did not know before) is a key dimension of the return-on-investment. If compliance rituals dominate appraisal, evaluation and risk management then this information gain is at best low – and, worse, can sometimes be negative – we know less than we used to know because we have missed out on opportunities to learn in a changing world.

The general assumption seems to be that the public sector is unusually likely to run into these sorts of problems – implicitly because it seems to be hard for government to learn from past experience. This stance aligns conveniently with the neoliberal view that markets are better at achieving objectives than bureaucracies. Whereas a company that failed to learn from past experience is unlikely to survive (unless, for example it is a large bank judged by government to be too big to fail) we cannot do without governance in the same way – all we can do is privatise some parts – but by no means all – of the public sector. Consequently, the severity of market-based tests of the capacity to learn does not apply in the same way in the public sector, except under conditions of war and other existential threats that governments are primarily responsible for handling.

Experimentalist governance

Whilst the importance of adaptive learning based on keeping options open in an uncertain and changing world is a well-established managerial principle, see Klein and Meckling (1958) for an influential contribution, after nearly sixty years, there are still pleas for governance to transition to a more adaptive learning-based and 'experimentalist' mode, see for example Sabel and Zeitlin (2012). Although the framing may be different (Klein and Meckling were concerned with weapons system development decision-making and Sabel and Zeitlin stress a multi-level governance context) the underlying principles, as reflected in governance, have been constant.

The challenge is to find practical ways for the public sector to operate in an adaptive learning-based and generally experimentalist manner whilst still being able to demonstrate value-for-money. The latter aspect is particularly important because the dominance of quantification under the new public management ethos means that any transition to a governance stance based on enhanced learning and adaptation will be most easily achieved if value-for-money can be demonstrated.

History has taught us that wars and other existential or major threats (including the 2008 global financial crisis) do tend to result in a dramatic increase in governments' capacity to learn-by-doing and adapt. However, as Michel Crozier highlights, it takes enormous threats to create the conditions in which governments can organise themselves to learn fast and effectively and to adapt in line with that learning. In such circumstances value-for-money considerations are trumped by the dire consequences of too many nasty surprises to allow for survival.

When the existential threats diminish, the capacity to learn tends to reduce and the status quo of cumbersome and risk-averse decision-making re-asserts itself. In short, historical responses to existential threats provide compelling evidence that the public sector is capable of fast and effective learning, but also provides evidence of a tendency to revert to type as soon as the opportunities arise.

One way of looking at this issue is to consider the consequences of being surprised. When existential threats are present the consequences of being surprised are so severe that governments deploy very powerful capabilities to reduce the potential for surprise. In wartime economies (the most extreme case) budget

38 *Limitations of risk-averse public policy*

allocations are strongly influenced by avoiding the costs of being surprised – reflected most obviously in ramped-up spending on intelligence and counter-intelligence activities and a generalised receptiveness to discovering more about the unknown. In contrast, in a peacetime context the costs of being surprised are far lower, hence less is spent on avoiding being surprised and budget allocations are both stricter and more managerialist in their implementation. This is suggestive of a form of equilibrium relationship between what governments spend on avoiding surprise and the costs of being surprised.

The interesting, and potentially significant, aspect to this behaviour is any correlation between the emphasis placed on avoiding surprise and the capacity to learn-by-doing. If these two issues are closely related though it is plausible that they don't need to be closely related in principle; this suggests that the machinery of government is not usually configured to learn-by-doing and can only achieve the necessary changes to that configuration when existential threats drive up the costs of being surprised. Why this might be the case is revealing. Experience tell us that the odds that a new public sector project will be delivered on time and to budget are lower than the odds that the project will be late and/or over-budget. Furthermore, these performance assessments also provide decision-makers with a range of useful insights into these risks. In the face of such odds, we would expect decision-makers to learn-by-doing: to adjust their forecasts and budgets on the basis of the accumulating evidence of risk drivers. An avoidance of that sort of learning and adaptation suggests that a greater priority is being placed on compliance with hierarchical procedures (the classic bureaucratic syndrome) than on discovering better ways of doing things in the future.

This is an especially salient issue from a risk management perspective because it suggests that risk management in governance is not a static (if evolving) capability, but moves between two distinctly different states with little or no scope for functioning in intermediate states – rather like the transition between a gas and a liquid. Mathematicians describe this sort of discontinuity-based behaviour as a jump diffusion process: a system moves rapidly from one distinctive state to another, with each state having distinctively different evolutionary characteristics.

In principle, this adaptive learning process should be aided by the formal frameworks and guidelines used to manage risk in the public sector. These risk management frameworks should help governments to learn-by-doing, yielding reduced risks of cost overruns and time delays via accumulating experience. Why then is this conceptually simple process of learning-by-doing in coping with risks (and associated uncertainties) such a problem in the public sector? Why do governments find it so difficult to govern cost-effectively by exploiting the advantages of learning-by-doing in general, and in risk management in particular?

As noted earlier, one theme throughout the analysis and arguments developed in this book is the importance of maintaining a clear and analytically robust distinction between substantive uncertainty and risk (where the latter is calculable and the former is not). The persisting cost escalation problem provides an illustration of the importance of this distinction. If risk is treated (either formally or in tacit practice) as subsuming substantive uncertainty then it can limit and distort learning-by-doing. This is because it is much easier to learn from calculable odds (likelihoods) of things happening than from situations in which likelihoods cannot be calculated. Starting with opening odds (before implementation) and ending the learning cycle with closing odds makes it much easier to analyse how understanding has changed. Where odds cannot be calculated it is better not to pretend that they can, unless methods are available that are able to incorporate that substantive uncertainty into the odds calculation and not by assuming even odds as a proxy for uncertainty. It follows from this that risk management frameworks that force substantive uncertainties (incalculable risk) to be treated as calculable risk will tend to 'contaminate' risk assessments by conflating calculable and incalculable factors. In statistical terms, this will be reflected in higher levels of statistical uncertainty than would otherwise be the case (i.e. if a clearer distinction were drawn between substantive uncertainty and calculable risk).

In the language of information theory, which as this book will seek to demonstrate can form a powerful basis for reducing the cost of governance by enhancing learning-by-doing, conflating substantive uncertainty and calculable risk decreases the signal-to-noise ratio (i.e. the conflation pushes up the noise we must tolerate when identifying useful information). In the cost overrun case, data on past cost overruns is the signal (upon the basis of which decision-makers can adjust their cost forecasts) whilst the substantive uncertainty is the noise (it is not actionable information). It follows that decision-makers would be wise to find better ways of distinguishing between signals and noise – maintaining an analytical distinction between substantive uncertainty and risk is a useful means of doing this.

In practical terms this means that drawing up budgets and plans for future projects should be informed by data from past experiences in a manner that avoids conflating substantive uncertainty and risk. This perspective is, in essence, Bayesian in the sense that the estimated odds of things happening in the future are updated whenever new information is received. However, as the previous argument suggests, a Bayesian approach to learning-by-doing in governance may be most effective when a distinction between substantive uncertainty and risk is maintained. In a Bayesian approach, substantive uncertainty is reflected in reduced odds that a hypothesis is true given available evidence. This is simply because this distinction allows for a clearer assessment of the signal-to-noise ratio. If we don't know something then we should avoid pretending that we do know it.

Adopting such a stance makes it easier to distinguish between the anticipated potential variances in factors that will affect the cost, timeline and success of a project and the factors over which we don't have sufficient information or understanding to even begin to quantify risks. Compliance with bureaucratic frameworks that force substantive uncertainty to be treated as a form of calculable risk can increase the potential for nasty surprises to occur.

40 *Limitations of risk-averse public policy*

Bayesian inference is also useful in a governance context because it can handle false positives in the analysis of data. There is also an explicit consideration of previous estimated likelihoods that a hypothesis is not correct. This is key to the cost escalation issue because experience tells us that previous estimated likelihoods that project budgets are accurate are, in statistical terms, low. This can be a particularly important benefit of applying such methods in the public sector – not least because the consequences of negative unintended consequences from a policy intervention can be so damaging. If an insufficient effort is made to distinguish between substantive uncertainty and statistical uncertainty (i.e. risk) then the likelihood of mis-specifying and miscalculating false positives and false negatives increases beyond the levels that could be obtained with a more accurate approach. Indeed, the persisting failure to address cost overruns by updating likelihoods using available data (in a Bayesian manner) can be thought of as a tendency to generate false positives (if we conceptualise a project plan and budget as a hypothesis test). The puzzle is: *why has it proven to be so difficult to develop a better capability to factor past experience into future plans and cost projects?*

One compelling avenue for developing testable hypotheses that may explain this puzzle is that the way in which governments operate in some way creates an impediment to learning from experience – in the sense that the evidence from the past is not used as effectively as it potentially could be in drawing up plans for addressing uncertainties faced in the future. There is circumstantial evidence (aligned with plausible assumptions) as to why it is so hard to use historical evidence to inform planning for the future. These points revolve around a combination of the following factors and issues.

First, neo-classical economics (which pervades thinking and analysis in the public sector) works with 'ideal world' assumptions of perfect information from which reality is treated as a degraded environment in the sense that imperfect information is assessed against the idealistic and unobtainable concept of 'perfect' information. This mind-set, in turn, encourages forecasts and predictions to be treated as mechanistic processes prone to 'errors' and biases of various kinds.

For example the Australian Treasury uses a forecast bias methodology based soundly upon neo-classical principles. This methodology encourages the view that divergences between what was forecasted or predicted and what actually happened are 'failures' that need to be addressed in the future. This stance, when the media comes into the loop (always on the lookout for a story about governance failures), encourages and perpetuates an unrealistic narrative about what it is theoretically possible for governments to achieve. As Hayek and fellow Austrian economists frame things: much of what the future has in store is unknowable and must be discovered not 'invented'. Or, as Keynes observed, 'The social object of skilled investment should be to defeat the dark forces of time and ignorance which envelop our future'.[2]

The more general philosophical point is that governments do need tools and methods for demonstrating (and communicating) the contention that rational decisions are being made and that neo-classical economics provides a workable basis for achieving this. It has not helped matters that the alternative 'subjectivist' or 'Austrian' strand in economics has, in the main, avoided empirical work and mathematical expressions of theoretical stances that can, in some circumstances, play an important role in public policy. Thus, whilst Austrian economists stress the importance of substantive (Knightian) uncertainty – a key issue given that governments can be thought of as the uncertainty and risk managers of last resort – they have put little effort into developing more formal methods for expressing the significance of this point, and for integrating substantive uncertainty into the sort of formally expressed analytical framework that can inform policy decisions (where transparency and accountability can make it difficult to rely on assertions of judgement and collective responsibility when relevant evidence is available). One thing this book tries to do is to re-frame this subjectivist economic perspective as a constructive contribution to ways of reforming governance – rather than (as it currently tends to be framed) solely as a libertarian 'free market' critique of some aspects of the public sector. There is no reason why the subjectivism in Austrian economics cannot be de-coupled from the methodological individualism and implicit (rarely explicit) downplaying of governments' distinctive role as uncertainty and risk manager of last resort associated with neoliberalism.

In comparison to subjectivist economics, the physicists and the mathematicians engaged in developing and using information theory (a key factor in the dramatic success of information and communication technology) have been far more active in developing analytical approaches to uncertainty – albeit with a string emphasis on statistical uncertainty. Aspects of these analytical techniques are directly relevant to implementing subjectivist approaches as practical tools within government. One just has to consider quantum mechanics, which is now exploiting aspects of uncertainty over the (particle spin) states of electrons to achieve a dramatic increase in computing speed (the problem has been turned into a solution).

This leads to the second point, which is that public policy would benefit from access to a formal analytical framework for handling the impact of substantive (rather than statistical) uncertainty on decision-making. This sort of formal analytical framework would need to be capable of distinguishing between substantive and statistical uncertainty – including the concept of information framed, as in information theory, in terms of the estimated likelihood of observing an event in the future. In information theory the less likely an event is assumed to be – the greater the information gain *if* it is observed. In short, a framework that avoids conflating what we don't (yet) know with the wide range of reasons why we observe statistical variations.

Third, the sort of framework outlined above will need to be based upon, and able to inform and enhance, the learning processes useful to governance and public policy. This means that the ways in which substantive uncertainty, statistical uncertainty and actionable information are treated should be approached as

42   *Limitations of risk-averse public policy*

a continuous learning process. As the earlier discussion of cost overruns highlights, there is little evidence that a learning cycle of this type, able to factor substantive uncertainty into deliberations, is currently being used. Put simply, we should not be surprised to find that we are not learning-by-doing as effectively as we might because the frameworks that we use to inform decision-making in the public sector don't allow us to distinguish between substantive and statistical uncertainty and, as a consequence, make it hard to draw attention to, even value, investments that have resulted in the translation of substantive uncertainty into statistical uncertainty, and the reduction of statistical uncertainty to the level at which it can be treated as actionable information.

The fourth point, which is covered in its own section below, is that the ways in which governments frame and handle risk may itself be an impediment to governing in a cost-effective manner.

Risk management and governance

There are presently two main ways in which risk is defined by governments:

- as the likelihood that something may happen and the magnitude/severity of the consequences if it does happen;
- as the effect that uncertainty has on the achievement of objectives (ISO 31000: 2009).

The combination of these perspectives towards risk and the extensive use of targets is especially important. Setting clear performance targets against which efforts are directed at minimising the difference between these targets and actual outcomes has become an accepted feature of modern governance. Policy settings are adjusted in an attempt to minimise the risk that targets are not met. Setting targets is assumed to make governments look decisive, serious and effective. As with cost overruns, the general community tends not to be surprised when these targets are not met – it would be foolish and naïve to believe that governments have sufficient control over enough variables to actually meet many targets.

As a result, risk management in the public sector becomes a matter of striving to meet these targets – which may be set arbitrarily and with an eye on how they present via the media. This aspect is highlighted in the way in which ISO 31000: 2009 defines risk in terms of uncertainty over objectives. If this definition is applied to contexts when objectives equate to targets (e.g. restricting annual immigration volumes to a specific value by a set date), then risk management takes on a compliance guise. A dominating focus on the risk of not meeting targets also restricts the capacity to learn-by-doing by creating an imbalance between the short-term fear (risks) of not meeting targets and the longer-term rewards of getting better at anticipating and dealing with unexpected problems.

When risk management becomes heavily skewed towards the risks of not meeting targets rather than minimising the broader potential to reduce nasty surprises, the outcome can be increased risk. This is because the focus on meeting targets displaces a focus on searching for signals of unexpected events – events that may not just make these targets irrelevant – they may dramatically increase exposure to risk in a more general sense.

However, there is nothing inherent in the definition of risk (as uncertainty over objectives) to prevent the adoption of a more enlightened stance – this is an issue to which we return when considering the objective of minimising the potential for surprise.

Current risk management standards and guidelines place a strong emphasis on the risks faced in achieving stated, usually target-based objectives – with these objectives treated as a given (in effect as an independent variable). Whilst there is a useful emphasis on continuous improvement in risk management practices, there is not a strong emphasis on the ways in which the decisions made in setting objectives will influence the nature and extent of the risks faced. This point can be summarised by inverting the ISO 31000: 2009 definition of risk to become: *the effect of objectives on uncertainty.* Clearly, the more ambitious the objectives the greater the uncertainty faced in achieving these objectives.

Engineers are familiar with the ways in which system complexity increases likelihoods of system failure due to complex interactions and cascading failure modes. This is why engineers prefer to simplify designs in order to reduce the likelihood of failures (and build in redundant/duplicated systems where failures are most likely). This relationship between objectives, uncertainty and risk forms the basis of well-developed design, development and demonstration in engineering systems (most evident in NASA and US Department of Defense structured programme management methods for complex engineering systems), see Morris (1994). In line with Klein and Meckling (1958) those methods explicitly focus on attempting to balance the uncertainty (hence risk) associated with attempts to achieve technical objectives with the benefits of actually achieving those technical objectives.[3] This results in a system design trade-off between aiming for the most technically demanding and potentially most useful objectives ('stretch targets') and the uncertainties and risks faced in attempting to meet those objectives.

In many circumstances (especially when major wars with technologically sophisticated adversaries are not happening) this trade-off results in less ambitious objectives being set in order to reduce the likelihood of failure to acceptable levels. Scrutiny of this trade-off between objectives and uncertainty/risk also results in efforts to develop more effective innovation pathways that minimise uncertainty and risk – notably in the re-adoption, over the last decade or so, of NASA Apollo Program–style incremental modular approaches to system evolution (known as Rapid Spiral Development).

Rapid Spiral Development (RSD) involves the deliberate prioritisation of modular system designs that allow incremental advances and testing of discrete system components whilst holding other module designs constant. The best example is the way in which the Apollo space program tested discrete system components and their use in several successive missions – an explicit risk

44 *Limitations of risk-averse public policy*

management technique. The phasing out of the Space Shuttle in preference for a return to the RSD approach, in the form of the Orion program currently being developed by NASA, reflects recognition that a modular system design allows functionality to evolve in each mission and for new technologies to be tested and adopted far more easily and cheaply than when using a fixed system such as the non-modular Space Shuttle (which was forced to operate with very outdated computer systems because it was so costly to update sub-systems within that rigid system design). Consequently, Rapid Spiral Development methods have the potential to inform innovation and risk management in the public sector precisely because they reduce the risks faced at a given level of uncertainty over objectives.

Sailing a ship whose journey is affected by winds and sea currents provides a useful metaphor for this link between uncertainty and risk and efforts to attain clearly defined objectives. The dominant managerialist model in public policy and public management reflects a situation in which we are forced to *assume* that we have reasonably accurate navigation charts upon which we can specify the objective that we seek to reach. Our actual progress towards that objective is, however, influenced by the uncertainties and risks caused by the combination of winds and ocean currents that we may encounter – factors that may throw us off course and may, if not addressed via course corrections that factor in these displacements, lead to us missing our objective. It is hard to find examples of plans and risk management approaches in governance that do not conform to this model of risk as a factor that throws things 'off course' from targets.

An alternative perspective on how the existence of uncertainty and risk can affect governance can also be expressed via a navigational metaphor. Consider a situation in which there is no reliable chart (or even no chart at all) and in which the objective is to explore the region, survey what is found and *create* a chart. In such exploratory activities, not only is the objective one of *discovery* (translating the unknown into the known), the winds, reefs and ocean currents encountered during the exploration are also findings in themselves – factors to be marked on the chart for the (risk-focused) guidance of those that follow.

In other words, where *exploration* is involved, uncertainties and risks are not disturbances to a planned pathway to a clearly defined objective, they are themselves factors that are discovered by research and learning-by-doing. In a public policy and public management context, the salient point is that many of the things that governments do (and fund others to do) are closer to the exploratory voyages that generate new maps of previously unknown places than they are to plotting a course to a clear destination on a navigational chart.

From this perspective, many of the problems encountered in policy and public management stem from attempts to treat situations in which no navigational chart exists (so a voyage needs to be undertaken to draw up the chart) as a situation in which the chart does exist – and the objective can be clearly marked on the chart. This is simply because governments have evolved practices and procedures for planning what they will try to do, and measuring and assessing what they do achieve, *as if* the navigational chart exists – even if it does not.

Hence, the response to an uncertain and risky situation is to make a range of (often) heroic speculative assumptions in order to be able to draw up a plan (navigational chart) without the benefit of anyone having made the journey to collect data. In such situations, it is not surprising that the assumed chart may not relate very much to what is actually discovered when the journey is made.

It is therefore no surprise that reviews and evaluations of government programmes tend to conclude that there were major shortcomings in plans and the assumptions made and, on that basis, make recommendations on how to limit these problems in the future. This cycle repeats itself over and over because practices and procedures require clear plans (akin the navigational charts) when there may be none that are backed by reliable observational data. It is not usually deemed to be acceptable for a government department to proceed with spending funds without a clear and detailed plan in place.

Part of the problem is that a more incremental and exploratory approach to addressing a challenge may find it hard to secure funding because the end-result cannot be clearly defined and justified in value-for-money terms. Competitive budget allocation processes force the generation (to continue to use the metaphor) of invented navigational charts in order to demonstrate the necessary level of paperwork to secure funding.[4] This problem can be compounded when high-level political pressure results in situations in which a project plan without an adequate sense of uncertainties and risks (because the venture is novel) must be delivered irrespective of risks and problems because a firm and public commitment has been made to do so. In these circumstances, risk management within governments becomes a game of demonstrating compliance with agreed procedures and guidelines. Risks (framed as likelihoods and consequences) are identified. Risk mitigation actions are specified designed to reduce risks to acceptable levels. This pretence that risks have been mitigated can diverge from reality. This amounts to a ritual: paying homage to risk management as a form of obligation and demonstration of respect. Indeed, this ritualistic approach to risk management has created a situation in which there are lengthy aspirational narratives concerned with 'best practices' in risk management – but a remarkable lack of succinct and implementable risk management tools able to assist in this difficult talk. The ratio of 'much aspirational talk to little constructive action' in risk management seems to have got worse decade by decade. More often than not, there is not even a consideration of possible interactive effects between different risks or an emphasis on looking for indications/early warning signs that these interactions are being encountered. Risk management (and associated uncertainties) are treated as a compliance ritual and not as something that will be discovered when trying to do something new.

The navigational metaphor used earlier provides a useful means of illustrating this core problem in governance (the difference between working with a navigational chart based on real and imagined data). It also provides a basis for developing a solution to this problem: *the need to develop concepts and tools that allow governments to manage public expenditure relating to innovative and*

46 *Limitations of risk-averse public policy*

exploratory activities without the unnecessary cost and spurious precision associated with the current risk-averse ethos.

The navigational metaphor also helps to draw out the key distinction between information and substantive uncertainty – and highlighted the risks and consequences when public management practices and procedures require, in effect, *assumed* information to be substituted for uncertainty (the spurious detail in a project plan relating to exploratory activities). Indeed, a paradox emerges from these managerialist attempts to force spurious precision into situations that are in essence exploratory. Whilst managerialism is focused on avoiding surprises (by focusing attention on targets, unambiguous objectives and concrete performance measures) that ethos can in practice increase rather than decrease the potential for nasty surprises. Spurious precision that invents an idealised target-based future rather than discovers a real future in a more open-ended manner creates a situation in which the assumed state of the world reflected in targets is far more likely to turn out to be incorrect than correct. Consequently, the potential for nasty surprises is increased rather than decreased. Anyone with hands-on familiarity with programme management and monitoring and evaluation practices in the public sector will be familiar with the consequences of this paradox.

Overall, these points highlight the opportunity to re-boot risk management in governance as a process of learning how to minimise the potential for surprise. Such an approach would still (broadly) align with the emphasis on risk as uncertainty over objectives but would re-configure concepts in such a way that the emphasis is on creating learning loops that focus on ways of reducing the risks caused by being surprised by unfolding events. Objectives would be transformed from precisely defined performance targets (achieve X by year t) to demonstrable reductions in the potential for surprise – measured and treated as an objective in itself. Chapter five runs through the technical aspects of how this type of objective can be defined and assessed (an approach based on Bayesian tests of competing hypotheses). In a nutshell, public sector performance and risk management can, and should, transition from framing risks in terms of a failure to meet performance targets (targets with a tendency to be arbitrary in any case) and towards a focus on learning how to reduce the potential for surprise. Reducing the potential for nasty surprises is, after all, an aspect of governance that is both readily grasped and highly valued by the general community.

The relevance of subjectivist economics (and its self-imposed limitations)

Rather than a world of quantitative uncertainty, the Austrian economic perspectives describes a human condition in which creativity is a necessary response to substantive uncertainty (effectively ignorance) over what the future has in store – both good and bad. In some circumstances there are no probabilities to assign to future states of the world, but rather the necessity to act *creatively* in order to generate parameters that can be assigned probabilities (and hence managed 'rationally'). The resulting competition is *inherently* a process of discovery and innovation, see O'Driscoll and Rizzo (1985). From this standpoint, markets are inherently *exploratory* and *innovative* collective endeavours that operate via selection.

If we think about markets in this more analytical way – as exploratory processes and selection mechanisms – then it is easier to understand their limitations and, hence, grasp why public sector innovation is so important in helping us to manage uncertainty. Markets can cope with risk (quantifiable likelihoods) but they cannot cope with uncertainty as easily.

It is worth noting that the uptake of Austrian economic perspectives within government has been relatively limited, to a large extent because Austrian economists have tended to avoid using formalism (mathematics and statistics) to express and implement their ideas. The strong ideological emphasis focused on the performance limits to governance compared with the powerful self-organising, exploratory and innovative aspects of market processes means that rather than contributing to better governance that perspective has tended to be manifested as an attack on governance. This is a shame because insights from Austrian economics are very useful as a means of articulating a tractable subjectivist approach via structured hypothesis testing.

The relevance of information theory

It is useful to consider the implications of Claude Shannon's seminal work on the mathematics of information in this context. In stark contrast to Austrian economics, information theory has taken similar insights relating to uncertainty and information but has expressed these formally and in a manner that has had profound impacts on economy and society (by providing the mathematical basis for information and communication technology writ large).

Writing shortly after the end of the Second World War, Shannon distinguished between information and uncertainty (defined as entropy) and expressed the value of new information that might be received in terms of the assumed likelihood of an event happening and being observed. In that framework, which has been incredibly useful in information technology, the less likely an event is assumed to be – the greater the information gain *if* it is observed (Shannon, 1948).[5]

Shannon's use of the concept of entropy in the Second World War had a very specific national security objective: the need to be able to calculate the minimum volume of information required to encrypt a message given the statistical frequencies with which different letters are expected to appear for linguistic reasons. Shannon entropy is therefore an expression of statistical uncertainty.

The analytical value of Shannon entropy (as this approach is now known) lies in maintaining and using this distinction between information and uncertainty. In information theory, this distinction allows for tractable calculations of highly complex things, especially error identification and correction and signal-to-noise

48   *Limitations of risk-averse public policy*

ratios and has provided an analytical framework that has assisted a range of technological advances to be made (including wi-fi).[6] Information entropy is also used now in medical diagnosis, notably in the diagnosis of cardiac problems. Heart rate variability can be too high and too low, with a healthy range between these extremes. Entropy measures are used to analyse the likelihood that observed variability is problematic, see Wessel et al. (2000).

If, as current public management practices in effect advocate, we fudge this key distinction between information and uncertainty by forcing government officials to pretend that the uncertainties they face are lower than they actually are (by requiring in effect that information is invented in order to *assume* reduced uncertainty), then it is not hard to see why things go wrong so often. As information theory shows us, clarity over the distinction between information and uncertainty, the ability to calculate likelihoods of receiving different signals in the future, and the identification and correction of errors and noise are key to coping with complex and changing circumstances (and especially in regards to distinguishing between signals and noise). Noise is defined as situations in which observed patterns appear to be random – hence contain little or no information. Noise is measured using Shannon's framework by the extent to which sequences of datum are random in occurrence.

In science this distinction between random noise and information has led to some fascinating investigations into processes that appear to be random (i.e. noise) but are actually the result of complex non-linear dynamics. For example the famous case of the apparently random distribution of time intervals between drips from a tap that, on closer examination, turn out to exhibit complex chaotic patterns due to feedback between the release of drips of water and the stock of water sitting waiting to drip, see Ambravaneswaran, Phillips and Basaran (2000).

This information theory perspective can be applied to missed opportunities to learn in public policy. In the author's experience in working in the real practice of public policy, the most useful way of examining the effectiveness of the policy learning process is to focus attention on missed opportunities to learn-by-doing in designing and delivering public policy. This is because a focus on missed opportunities to learn in the face of uncertainties and risks gets to the heart of what governments do. This realistic focus, in turn, encourages scrutiny of the reasons why governments overlook opportunities to learn. The underlying principle is that in an uncertain and risky world governments should seek to maximise the availability of decision-support information they have access to. If they do not, then there is a risk that a better decision could have been made – *given what is currently understood and assumed to be the case.*

Consequently, governments should aim to minimise the extent to which the assumptions they hold over the range of likelihoods and consequences of wanted and unwanted events (i.e. risks *and* opportunities) are distorted by failures to use all available information on those likelihoods and consequences. This is not to argue that this available information will always be adequate from the perspective of idealised models and frameworks (not least the neo-classical economic thinking that tends to pervade governance): it will always be limited and often subjective. But, it is to argue that ignoring or overlooking available information can result in a mix of lost opportunities to achieve wanted outcomes and misjudged risks of avoiding unwanted outcomes. In information theory terms, governments are wise to seek to avoid situations in which they are surprised by events simply because information that would have led them to estimate the relevant likelihood(s) differently was ignored and these likelihoods biased as a result. Complex circumstances can generate data that appear to be random (noise) but, as with the dripping tap, actually exhibit complex behaviours when the data are tested appropriately. Noise conceals a subtle signal.

This emphasis on the importance of making accurate diagnoses of the relative importance of information (the signal) and uncertainty (noise) is relevant to the way in which current *International Financial Reporting Standards* (IFRS) require that all widely known risks to the balance sheet value of a corporation are factored into the estimated net worth of the corporation. A failure to use widely available information to carry out this 'fair value' adjustment (including subtle patterns that may be assumed away as noise) opens a corporation to potential fines and even prison sentences for senior executives. This is because investors have effectively been misled by this missed opportunity to calculate fair value – which in the post–Enron and GFC world means corporate net worth may have been significantly over-stated.

Whilst governments have happily agreed to this policy stance towards large public companies in the business sector (these IFRS rules do not apply to smaller companies) – are they capable of applying the same criterion as regards their own performance in designing and delivering public policy? Indeed, using the concept of Public Value, the value to the electorate of what governments do (Moore, 1995), missed opportunities to learn in governance can be thought of as an IFRS-type distortion to Public Value: public policy stances that are not expressed on a 'fair value' basis in regards to *known* risks. The broader point here is that a stock-based rather than a flow-based perspective facilitates risk assessment. This issue is revisited in chapter three and revolves around the ways in which the current value of a stock of assets reflects the potential future stream of impacts of a range of opportunities and risks. By focusing attention on how the future may impact on the present value of assets, a link is made between future flows of activity and current stock values. Whilst the noise (random variability) experienced in these flows may make it hard to spot signals, that noise will have a calculable impact on the value of an asset stock linked to those future flows. For this reason approaches to national economic well-being based on national balance sheets rather than variable flows of national income provide a more robust basis for judging national economic performance. One role of governance is to try to minimise nasty surprises relating to the value of national balance sheets.

Framing the long-term challenge

The human mind is very good at identifying and testing generalised assertions from extremely sparse and uncertain sensory data (vision, hearing, touch).

50 *Limitations of risk-averse public policy*

The rapid learning that allows these generalised assertions to be developed by trial and error is possible because the mind is able to create and manipulate (i.e. select between, merge and re-merge) highly abstract conceptual representations of sensory data. This process links prior assumptions (based on a mix of experience and informed guess work) to the latest sensory data available.

For example the eye of a mammal can only work out what it believes to be the colour of an observed object via a complex process based on selecting the most plausible theory of the colours being observed. Perceiving the colour of any observed object involves dealing with the combined interactions of the spectrum of the surface of the object and the spectrum of the light from bouncing off that object. These spectra interact in complex ways. This means that there is no immediate 'right answer' as to what the colour of the observed object is. There are two unknown independent variables (the spectrum of the surface of the object and the spectrum of the light source bouncing off that object) that define the dependent variable (the light patterns arriving at the eye). The analytical task is to estimate the spectrum of the surface of the observed object with insufficient data to allow this equation to be solved. This means that without making prior assumptions that, in mathematical terms constrain the 'solution space' (the range of hypotheses relating to the colours being observed) at the start of an iterative process, it is impossible to work out which colour(s) are being observed. In other words, vision is a process of Bayesian inference (Brainard and Freeman, 1997).

When prior understanding (general assumptions about the state of the world) is applied to this problem then an iterative process of converging on the most plausible solution can commence via a process of hypothesis elimination – and usually be concluded with a maximum likelihood estimate (inconclusive solutions are rare but can arise when the spectrum of the observed object and the light source interact in certain ways). The process of determining the colour of an object is, consequently, not one of determining objective facts at the outset, but of the speed with which the most likely colour 'solution' is selected by a process of testing competing hypotheses using a combination of prior assumptions and current data.

This is an adaptive learning process. This sort of knowledge is not objective nor is it subjective in the sense of an opposition to the notion of an 'objective fact'. Rather, it is a learning process that quickly homes in on the most plausible solution to a problem by testing competing potential solutions against each other and on the basis of accumulated understanding from the past combined with the latest data available. The tendency to counter-pose concepts of objectivity and subjectivity independently of the processes that test competing hypotheses against sparse and uncertain data is, therefore, unhelpful. It is preferable to frame things in terms of the *speed* of the process that homes in on the most likely explanation or solution given sparse information. In other words, knowledge in a public policy context is a dynamic learning process subject to degrees of belief in facts rather than statements *of* facts.

Limitations of risk-averse public policy 51

This abstract conceptual dimension to cognition is of course the essence of creativity. It allows novel perspectives and hypotheses to be developed as potential solutions that may resolve what were previously puzzles, paradoxes or inconsistencies in our understanding. In this sense, creativity is a form of abductive reasoning (generating hypotheses from observations). Similarly, 'machine learning' of various types (cryptography, face recognition, automatic language translation, voice to text recognition, artificial intelligence, missile guidance systems, robotics, and information and communication systems generally) is also very successful in allowing rapid learning from available, often sparse and uncertain, data. In some cases machine learning relies simply on a Darwinian process of random mutation of hypotheses that are then selected between on the basis of relative performance (the use of 'genetic algorithms' for example). In other cases (and more recently) new hypotheses to be tested are generated in a more analytical manner, for example on the basis of pattern recognition.

For example in principle (the technical details tend to be classified secrets) a sophisticated automatic air-to-air missile guidance system may deliberately carry out a sequence of probing/test manoeuvres in its trajectory in order to monitor and learn from how the target responds. This process has the aim of attempting to define a 'guaranteed kill zone' – a time and airspace region in the future to which the missile will first attempt to provoke the target to move towards and then head to. Highly complex and rapid calculations are involved in this process. These calculations, crucially, can rely on deliberate 'experimental' changes in trajectory that attempt to discover both how quickly the target can adjust its own trajectory and to infer the most likely type of algorithms being used to change that trajectory in response to the attack. Without these experimental 'discovery' manoeuvres it is harder to reach the target because the potential for surprise (an unexpected manoeuvre by the target) is too high. In short, an air-to-air missile guidance system can actively invest in reducing the potential for surprise – it starts with very sparse and uncertain data but uses experimental ploys to try to reduce the sparcity and uncertainty in that data.

The vision example illustrates how past observational experience is used to try to develop a workable solution to a logically hard-to-solve interpretive problem, whilst the missile illustration deals with the challenge of coping with the need to anticipate and respond to possible future occurrences.

This unavoidable need for fast iterative convergence on a solution by combining prior understanding from experience (information) with the latest data available means that Bayesian inference has become an accepted means of characterising and modelling both cognitive processes and designing machine learning systems. Machine learning uses Bayesian inference, but also uses other methods – it is the combination of this range of adaptive learning methods that makes machine learning so effective (especially when a large number of machines are able to learn collectively from diverse experiences). This rapid convergence allows sparse and uncertain data to be used to arrive at conclusions and to make decisions on that basis. *Creativity reflected in hypothesis generation informed by what worked best in the past and attempting to anticipate*

52   *Limitations of risk-averse public policy*

what may occur in the future – a process able to compensate for sparse and uncertain data in the present.

In stark contrast, governments stress the utility of access to vast amounts of data (and spend a considerable amount of money on acquiring and storing that data) – *but* do not seem to learn very effectively at all. Costs are consistently under-estimated, policy interventions tend to be inflexible and do not adapt well to changing circumstances and unexpected developments.

The learning deficit in governance

In general terms, evaluations of government programmes are not closely coupled to adaptation and learning over the long run. Indeed, the public sector investments in developing structured procedures for designing, implementing and evaluating government interventions tend not to be associated with effective learning. For example in 2013 the UK National Audit Office (NAO) reported on a major assessment of the adequacy of evaluations of UK government programmes. The findings were striking in what they revealed about what is *not* being done to assist policy learning via robust evaluations. The NAO reviewed nearly 6,000 analytical and research documents published between 2006 and 2012 on seventeen main government department websites. It found that only 305 of these were impact evaluations; and that of these 305, only 70 made an assessment of cost-effectiveness (National Audit Office, 2013). Furthermore, the NAO found that '*only 14 evaluations were of a sufficient standard to give confidence in the effects attributed to policy because they had a robust counterfactual*' (National Audit Office, 2013, p. 7).

The author has completed a preliminary analysis of this dataset compiled by the NAO focusing on the potential for false positive test results for strong economic impacts (Matthews, 2016).[7] This study concluded that it is plausible that these methodological weaknesses are driving up the prevalence of false positives to levels so high that the ability to learn and adapt is severely compromised. Weak diagnostic capability is compromising adaptive governance.

This sort of finding reflects a generalised tendency for governments to focus attention on 'policy delivery' at the expense of policy learning. Given the strong compliance ethos at present towards both risk management and monitoring and evaluation processes, and the ways in which these functions are de-coupled rather than integrated, this neglect of learning is of little surprise – the tools available are not fit for purpose.

Consequently, because the potential to waste expenditure as a result of missed opportunities to learn is a major concern in governance, it is worth exploring the implications that stem from cognitive science and machine learning systems. Is this learning constraint in governance associated with the contrast between the ways in which there is a natural tendency for the mind to speculate at a highly conceptual level – whereas in public management and administration there is a self-conscious avoidance of speculative thinking – a stance that asserts the importance of 'evidence' as a basis for action? This is a plausible explanation because speculation on the basis of sparse data yields the hypotheses that, in turn, can be tested using available data and information. From this perspective it does seem strange that governments will fund the development and testing of very sophisticated decision-systems (e.g. the air-to-air missile guidance system described earlier) but not attempt to develop similar – adaptive learning system – capabilities to assist in formulating, delivering and learning from the process of governing.

Cognitive processes and machine learning both share a prioritised focus on generating speculative explanations of data that are tested as hypotheses *relative to each other* – often on a massive scale. The 'intelligence' in these processes stems from this speculative generation of hypotheses and their testing. This process can be modelled and understood using Bayesian inference methods that relate prior assumptions based on accumulated experience to date to the extent to which the most recent data supports these competing hypotheses.

In contrast, the norm in public policy is to avoid multiple competing hypotheses in preference to single preferred 'solutions' that demonstrate strong and decisive leadership and can be presented as such via the media. Cognitive processes and machine learning rely on *breadth* of analysis using competing hypotheses whereas public policy (currently) relies on *depth*: detailed justification of a single selected hypothesis framed against a notional null hypothesis of doing nothing. This depth priority is supported by tests of statistical significance based upon calculating the probability that the data observed could have been generated randomly (the lower that probability the greater the likelihood that a significant result has been obtained). In this way, conventional sampling theory–based tests of statistical significance tend to reinforce the depth approach because significance is assessed via comparison with a null hypothesis of no treatment effect rather than a comparative test of *competing* treatment effects. A missile guidance system operating on this basis is very unlikely to be effective – so why do governments persist with applying this test of significance when analysing the evidence deemed so crucial to effective policymaking?

Is it therefore the case that the solution to better governance lies in working out how to apply the rapid learning from sparse data and high uncertainty ethos that drives cognitive processes and machine learning? If so, then the critically important factor is the ability to speculate and generate a broad range of competing hypotheses – just as brains (that work with counts of relative frequencies of events) and, now, machines do.

If governance is to evolve in this direction then whilst Bayesian inference as currently configured is relevant at a conceptual level it is not relevant on a practical level. This is because it is overly complex and prone to 'gold-plating' in terms of the technical sophistication and mathematical 'flourish' applied, resulting in a situation in which Bayesian studies have been described as 'snowflakes' (each one is different) (Ferson, 2005). Just as cognitive scientists stress that the human mind (in most cases) cannot handle forms of Bayesian inference that require complex numerical calculations – so too in governance the trick is to develop a standardised framework that expresses the core Bayesian principle

54 *Limitations of risk-averse public policy*

of combining prior experience with the latest data to test competing hypotheses directly that avoids the need for complex customised numerical calculations. Just as the mind carries out a version of these Bayesian updates sub-consciously, so too the policy learning process should have access to a framework that achieves the same functional objectives.[8] It follows that the wide range of applications of the shared Bayesian principles of machine learning are well placed to provide this standardised framework for facilitating policy learning.

The critical enabler of such an approach would be to start to frame policy interventions as competing hypotheses and to monitor and evaluation progress in implementation as the comparative odds of each hypothesis being correct. In the simplest case of a single policy solution this would compare one hypothesis with the null hypothesis of no treatment effect. In more complex cases, the process would involve learning on the basis of the relative odds that competing hypotheses are true. This generic process applies to the diagnosis of policy problems, the generation of possible solutions (both as alternatives and as complements) and to the monitoring and evaluation of progress in implementation and lessons to emerge.

Is the major lesson simply that conceptions of 'good governance' are founded upon a mechanistic conceptualisation how governance should work (and be demonstrated to work) and that this paradigm persists because taxpayers (current and in future generations) have little choice over avoiding funding this waste? In other words, and despite political rhetoric, the public sector is not incentivised to get better at learning and adaptation. Rather, the problem is avoided by accumulating public debt (to be borne largely by future generations) and by transferring some public services to the private sector on the assumption that this privatisation will result in the necessary learning and adaptation (reflected in innovation and productivity growth) – something that experience has shown cannot be taken for granted (especially when natural monopolies are involved).

The public sector innovation agenda

In order to understand how innovation is currently approached in the public sector it is useful to briefly cover a little intellectual history concerning the study and understanding of science, technology and innovation in the private sector. This is important in order to explain the strengths and the weaknesses of the way in which the innovation agenda has recently been adopted in the public sector.

The interest in innovation in the private sector originated, in part, in a reaction against the difficulties faced by neo-classical economics in explaining technological advance. If one assumes a world of perfect information and a state of equilibrium in which markets are operating in a stable manner, then technological advances must be treated as externally originating deviations from these equilibrium conditions – processes of disruption to which the economic system must respond and adapt.

The finding from the early growth accounting studies that long-run productivity growth had a large 'residual' element that could not be explained by increases in the standard factors of production (capital and labour etc.) stimulated a large and productive line of investigation that eventually led to the 'innovation studies' work that is currently informing thinking on public sector innovation. As innovation studies has evolved it has moved away from economic theory and econometrics and towards more managerial approaches – with a particular (and useful) emphasis on documenting and understanding real practices in business.

Inevitably, this emphasis on how businesses *do* innovation in practice leads to a focus on how firms accumulate and exploit proprietary knowledge and capabilities: how they seek to exploit intangible assets that their competitors do not have. The emphasis is on *differences* between firms' capabilities – on how innovation drives markets in such a way that they are in continual evolution – rarely in states of equilibrium. It should be of little surprise that the management of uncertainty and risk feature strongly in this perspective on innovation.

Innovation is inherently risky and involves a strong element of 'learning-by-doing'. The greater the experience in innovating the lower the risk of failure faced when attempting to innovate. The value of this experience is recognised by venture capitalists, who prefer to invest in ventures in which the key proponents have prior experience of the incredible complexity and range of risks faced in the innovation process. This knowledge of how to navigate the 'white-water' risks faced when innovating is highly tacit and is therefore not easily taught outside of actual experience.

This learning-by-doing is not just personal, there is also a collective dimension. The groups of people who have innovated, or tried to innovate, gain valuable collective experience. This amounts to an intangible asset for a region or national economy. This is why US venture capitalists often invest strategically in industries rather than exclusively on the basis of case-by-case propositions. Investing in industries allows the intangible asset of collective experience and its associated flows of experienced people between different countries to be exploited. Economists call this type of intangible asset a 'positive externality'.

The movement from invention to innovation, that is to say the commercialisation of an invention, involves taking abnormally high investment risks in order to generate the (usually remote) possibility of making abnormally high returns. When this process is particularly successful the result is, in statistical terms, an 'outlier' – a rare event that deviates from the norm. Comparatively little attention is paid to these outliers in economics and econometrics because these events are viewed as transient phenomenon that reflect a temporary disturbance to normal competitive circumstances. Business schools also devote comparatively little attention to the leap from invention to innovation because these are, by definition, 'pre-competitive' activities. We therefore face not only a major gap in progressing from invention to innovation in terms of the capacity to manage the abnormal risks involved, we also face sparsely populated regions in the academic literature that analyse these processes (Hartmann and Myers, 2001).

56 Limitations of risk-averse public policy

Nonetheless, these 'outliers' often have a significant effect upon national and regional prosperity – and can sometimes create whole new industries or market segments. From a public policy perspective, although one cannot develop policies and commercialisation strategies based upon what are, in statistical terms, 'lightening strikes', one can seek to create more favourable conditions and incentives to encourage appropriately skilled people to take these abnormal risks. If these risks are not taken then the probability of creating these beneficial outliers in the distribution of returns against investments all but disappears. The objective is to create more favourable odds of generating abnormally high rates of company growth, but with no strong expectation that this can be forecasted or predicted on a case-by-case basis.

It is in this latter respect that encouraging research commercialisation by spin-offs, start-ups and licensing deals (all of which have merits) can clash with the 'risk-averse' approach to setting tightly specified performance targets in the public sector (i.e. clearly defined outputs and outcomes). The inherently risky nature of commercialisation, particularly as one seeks to move along the learning curve associated with improving the odds of success by trial and error, means that failures are to some extent inevitable – but that these failures are valuable. Unless we have a policy framework that explicitly recognises the value of learning-by-doing in investment risk management we may overlook the cumulative value of our history of successes and failures. Whilst we cannot base lessons for policymaking upon simply exploiting luck, we can examine the extent to which both the public and private sectors can develop strategies and tactics to buy better odds of success. Luck will still play a part, but we should aim to have more control over the odds that we face.

There has been a negative side effect for government from this pattern of evolution in thinking about innovation though. As work on 'innovation' has flourished and shifted from economics departments to business and management schools it has become a little too disconnected from our understanding of long-run productivity growth.

A lot of attention used to be paid to relating R&D expenditure to productivity growth. This was helped by the availability of pretty good data on R&D. We still have pretty good data, however many researchers who study innovation nowadays stress that R&D is essentially an accounting and tax break–based concept that does not reflect actual industrial realities in many sectors. We hear much less about R&D than we used to and more about innovation. One problem is that this shift in emphasis has weakened the link between measured productivity growth and innovation – the link it is asserted, the link makes intuitive sense, but we are actually rather poorly positioned nowadays to work out how future long-run productivity growth might behave – and to determine how it might react to efforts to simulate R&D and innovation investment.

Another problem is the tendency to ignore the 'inconvenient truth' – for the R&D and innovation advocates at least – that large chunks of publicly funded research expenditure have little or nothing to do (directly at least) with the generation of innovation outcomes. The so-called linear model that links R&D

to commercial innovation (scientists invent – industry applies) may be widely debunked amongst most of the cognoscenti – but persists in government policy frameworks and the media in a zombie-like manner – not properly alive but it won't die. Zombies are not good for public policy.

Arguably, we would benefit from efforts to re-connect our modern understanding of innovation with its genesis in growth accounting when thinking about public sector innovation. The use of a growth accounting framework in the Australian Treasury's approach to managing an ageing population, i.e. the three Ps of participation, population and productivity, is a clear signal of the importance of closing this loop (Australian Government, 2015). However, we must close this loop with a more realistic conception of what R&D and innovation are all about.

The private sector has well-established and understood mechanisms for managing the risks faced when investing in innovation. An 'appetite for risk' is a key component of corporate strategy and an influence on competitiveness. However, when it comes to fostering innovation in the public sector, it is unwise to attempt to simply transpose the private sector approach to innovation to the public sector.

As Mariana Mazzucato has powerfully argued, the state acts entrepreneurially: taking the calculated risks required to simulate and deliver innovations and seeking to shape markets in ways that help them to operate effectively (Mazzucato, 2011). Effective innovation is not the sole province of the private sector – innovation results from the effective coupling of functions that the private sector excels at and functions that the public sector excels at.

If the public sector innovation agenda really was pushing the boundaries of how governments act as the uncertainty and risk managers of last resort and contributing to demonstrated productivity growth, then there would be less grounds for being worried about the way in which the public sector innovation agenda is currently framed. The worrying thing is that there is little evidence of this connection between public sector innovation and governments' role as uncertainty and risk managers of last resort emerging.

The concept of public sector innovation tends to come across as a solution looking for problems, with innovation being banded about as an end in itself – with self-proclaimed experts on 'innovation' busily touting for business (and taxpayers' money). This new game is disturbingly disconnected from the reality of the nasty fast- and nasty slow-moving problems that governments must handle – *and that nobody else can handle.*

As with the new public management ethos in general, ideas and concepts have been adopted from the private sector in an attempt to frame an agenda able to address these challenges. Hence the emphasis placed on prototypes and experiments, incubators and the like. There is little evidence on relating public sector innovation to the distinctively more demanding challenges of learning and adapting as uncertainty and risk manager of last resort. Indeed, models of the public sector innovation process tend to focus on avoiding this learning cycle element. For example the influential paper by Albury and Mulgan advocates

58   *Limitations of risk-averse public policy*

models of the innovation process with little emphasis placed on learning and adaptation (Albury and Mulgan, 2003).

Arguably, the public sector innovation agenda started to wobble off its tracks precisely because it gained 'critical mass' and started to focus on innovation as a process. A process that needs surveying, a process that needs mapping etc. This process focus has been combined with the tendency to broaden the concept of what constitutes 'innovation' to such a scope that it means almost everything and hence loses its utility. From this perspective innovation in the public sector has become an over-spun and over-hyped slogan disconnected from the distinctive context in which governments operate. These issues can be examined using a formal model of the investment risk dimension to innovation – as follows.

A formal model of investment risk in the innovation process

It can be useful to use a risk-based formal model of the innovation process in order to highlight the ways in which risk-aversion in the public sector can be problematic. In generic terms, attempts at innovation can be treated as a process of driving up the probability of success (hence driving down the probability of failure) by spending what are usually increasingly large amounts of money. This process of risk reduction – but at a cost – can be represented in a fairly simple equation that balances the achieved probability of success combined with the Net Present Value (NPV) of that success with the probability of failure and the NPV of that failure (which will be the cost of failure offset by any recovered value from the innovation process). In economics and finance this is known as an Expected Value calculation. In economics and finance the impact of risk is sometimes assessed mathematically using calculations of 'Expected Value' that take the following basic form:

> Expected Value = $[P_s \times NPV_s] - [P_f \times NPV_f]$
> Where: P_s = Probability of Success
> P_f = Probability of Failure $(1 - P_s)$
> NPV_s = Net Present Value of Success
> NPV_f = Net Present Value of Failure (cost of failure less cost recovery)

From this Expected Value perspective, the standard research (and innovation) process follows the sort of pattern graphed in figure 2.2. This plots the characteristic pathways of the probability of success, the probability of failure and overall expected value (EV) in the innovation process.

Because we usually have to spend increasing amounts of money to drive up the probability of success (and drive down the probability of failure) it is usual for this risk-adjusted Net Present Value to become negative and get worse before finally improving and eventually entering positive territory. The key feature of this risk-taking process is that at the earlier stages in the innovation process it is common for the inter-play of the extent to which the probability of failure

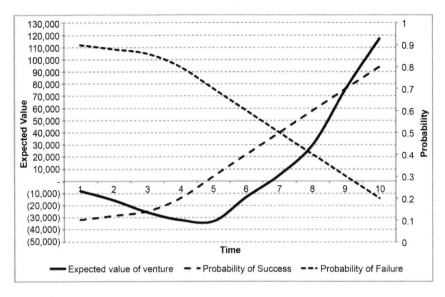

Figure 2.2 An expected value representation of the innovation process

is reduced to be set against the (high) cost of achieving this gain. This results in an expected value (i.e. risk-adjusted Net Present Value) that goes negative and gets worse before it gets better. It is government, via early-stage research funding, that supports the activities that translate substantive uncertainties into the sort of quantifiable pathways in this investment risk process. In this sense, these EV pathways are themselves an outcome from public spending.

There is, now, a large volume of accumulated case study research in the study of innovation in the private sector that highlights the importance of this 'valley of death', see Beard et al. (2009) for a recent discussion. It is the most perilous phase in the innovation process for the innovators and the investors in these innovators. In the business innovation process, venture capital and other investors characteristically invest at different points in this expected value trajectory. For instance, venture capitalists search for the critical junctures in the investment risk trajectory marked by minimised losses (points at which it may be possible to sell assets, notably intellectual property rights to offset investment losses). These junctures provide the exit options that play an important role in portfolio risk management strategies. In the process of allocating research funding (if this risk-based model is applied to academic research), then past track record is weighted heavily on the assumption that it is the most reliable way of reducing these 'investment risks'.

In the public sector this dip in the EV pathway can act as an impediment to achieving useful change. Whereas an 'appetite for risk' is an accepted feature of business strategy in the private sector, appetites for risk in the public sector tend

60 *Limitations of risk-averse public policy*

to sit less easily within the constraints of current transparency and accountability stances. The prospect of a failure in an attempt to achieve change (i.e. to innovate) can deter efforts. Formal investment appraisal methods in the public sector can constrain spending associated with this sort of investment risk trajectory. If the most plausible investment trajectory is described accurately when seeking funding (i.e. in this risk-taking manner) – a trajectory in which EV will often dip into negative territory for a sustained period – then the likelihood of securing public funds can decrease dramatically ('we don't gamble with taxpayers' funds'). This, in turn, can result in proposals downplaying the investment risks involved by putting a highly optimistic slant on things. In effect, proposals will plot an intended investment trajectory that is unrealistically optimistic in order to forecast a pathway that avoids the phase of negative value. Of course, these optimistically biased proposals increase the potential for nasty surprises to occur when it turns out that what actually takes place involves a sustained period in which EV is negative. In some circumstances projects can be cancelled when it becomes clear that the forecast was overly optimistic – thus wasting taxpayers' money.

This EV framework has been used to focus government–academic collaboration on those areas in which risk-averse procedures in government (which would otherwise block such activities) create opportunities for academics to take the necessary risks. This sort of partnership allows things to be achieved that would be less likely without such partnerships – but does require an appetite, on the academic side, for being blamed if things go wrong.[9]

In other cases, this EV pathway can result in risk-averse government innovation support stances that, in effect, only provide subsidies in the EV conditions under which the private sector would be willing to invest. This risk-aversion displaces private sector investment and undermines the effectiveness of the entrepreneurial state. The emphasis on quantification in the new public management ethos can act to undermine the entrepreneurial state.

The problem is of course that public sector investment appraisal methods can make it hard to articulate the sort of appetite for risk that is found in the private sector – where the risk–reward relationship plays a key role in competitive strategy. Whereas the risk–reward relationship balances the downside against the upside, the current public sector ethos makes it hard to create this sort of counter-balance, in part because methods for valuing options to act under uncertainty are not well developed (hence the relevance of framing policy options as competing hypotheses). Risk-aversion in the public sector can involve self-imposed limitations that increase the potential for nasty surprises to occur – and increase the potential for inflated levels of public debt as a result.

Chapters four and five consider ways of reducing the severity of this problem in the public sector. As they will stress, a stronger focus on treating public spending appraisals as tests of competing hypotheses (with the potential for diagnostic errors in the form of false positives and false negative test results) can help. However, the underlying challenge is to develop better ways of countering risk-aversion in such circumstances by being more realistic about the balance between substantive uncertainty and quantifiable risk. When substantive uncertainty is given no place in the risk assessment framework then it must be treated as if it is quantifiable risk – an assumption of convenience that can lead to a range of problems. A key challenge is to find better ways of treating substantive uncertainty in such situations – being able to articulate what we don't yet know and to highlight the benefits of reducing that uncertainty.

The growing chasm between robotic learning and learning in governance

It is fitting to end this chapter on the limitations of current uncertainty and risk-averse public policy stances by considering the growing chasm between the rapidity and ease with which robots are able to learn and adapt and the ability of governments to learn and adapt. At the time of writing this book considerable attention is being paid to the inter-connected issues of cars that can drive themselves and the government regulations that can encourage or restrict this capability. One emphasis in this machine learning process, found for example in the all-electric Tesla cars, is automated collective learning – a process already rolled out in the speech recognition algorithms used by smartphones and automated telephone systems used by some governments and corporations. These speech recognition systems use collective machine learning methods. What are effectively hypotheses framed mathematically are tested against data generated from real conditions in multiple circumstances and continuously updated in real time.

For example the precautionary braking of a car given the monitored changes in the estimated temperature of the road surface and given other environmental conditions such as the shape of the road, presence of pedestrians etc. If a range of sensors detect certain clusters of conditions the threshold at which braking is triggered may be reduced. When these vehicles do brake it is technically possible to measure the actual breaking time and distance against what had been assumed, given particular conditions, and adjust the decision-making algorithms accordingly (to maximise safety). These algorithm updates can be near instant and widely shared. Clearly, the greater the scope for this natural experimentation in real conditions the greater the ability of these machine learning systems to evolve the hypotheses they use in the light of real conditions and the experience in dealing with these conditions. This process of collective learning and adaptation is automated in machine learning. A range of competing hypotheses are tested in real conditions and these hypotheses are rapidly adjusted in order to increase the odds of them being true in the future given cumulative experiences to date. The greater the collective experience in this hypothesis-based machine learning system the greater the data available to evolve these hypotheses in order that they become *more true* over time via learning-by-doing. This is a Bayesian learning process. It applies to numerous technologies.

The collective dimension is particularly important. The ways in which real operational data (on a massively scaled level) can be instantly harvested, analysed and then sent out again as updated decision-algorithms (effectively sets

62 *Limitations of risk-averse public policy*

of hypotheses that detect and respond to rapidly changing conditions) enables very rapid learning and adaptation. These machines don't restrict themselves to classical tests of statistical significance based on calculating the probability that different hypotheses differ from a null hypothesis of no intervention effect given assumed but unobserved statistical distributions. It would be hard for cars to learn and adapt in this manner. Rather, these machine learning systems use all the available data from real conditions on a second-by-second basis to learn and adapt collectively. In a military sphere the potential of this machine learning is profound because manned and unmanned systems (drones etc.) are able to near instantly be aware of collective situational changes – when one drone obtains new data it is, in principle, possible for all drones to be given access to that data. Machine learning systems are able to process vast amounts of such data faster than human beings and to learn and adapt more effectively as a result. At present, we limit this automated learning and adaptation in some areas (especially in military domains) because the potential for automated decision-making over inflicting harm is of great concern. For example US tests of weaponised drones with autonomous attack decision abilities have had mixed results. However, in non-military areas (finance, road vehicles etc.) there is now considerable technological momentum to mass machine learning systems that learn and adapt without requiring human intervention. From a public policy perspective this growing gap between the rate at which some automated systems are able to learn and adapt and the constraints faced by governments in learning and adapting should be a matter of profound concern.

Conclusions

This chapter has considered a range of inter-connected problems in learning and adaptation in governance that stem from a self-imposed 'business-like' ethos (the 'new public management') in the public sector that limits governments' ability to act as the uncertainty and risk manager of last resort. These self-imposed constraints make a troubling situation worse than it might otherwise be. How can we effectively regulate private sector activities that use mass machine learning when we make so much effort, in effect, to limit both the understanding and ability to react in governments? To what extent might the careful and well-considered adoption of these (Bayesian) learning and adaptation methods in governance based on signal processing and machine learning methods inform how governments respond to such a challenge? Whilst the challenge is so severe that it may not be solvable, some ways of responding will be worse than others – and an examination of the potential to apply some of the very methods that underpin machine learning may at least make the situation less critical than it might otherwise be.

The chapter has highlighted the ways in which public policy approaches that attempt to avoid substantive uncertainty and quantifiable risk create self-imposed limitations to effective governance. Avoiding constructive engagement with uncertainty and risk rules out of bounds some useful ways of measuring outcomes from public sector activities (notably enhanced preparedness from public science) and limits the ability to frame public investment as a means of translating substantive uncertainty into quantifiable risk. The result is that there are persisting shortcomings in the ability to plan, learn and adapt that stem from these methodological weaknesses. When combined with the lack of a clear emphasis on governments' role as uncertainty and risk manager of 'last resort' and a pervasive use of performance measures and risk management standards and guidelines that reflect this uncertainty and risk reduction the result is a situation in which risks are amplified by increasing the likelihood for nasty surprises to occur. The growing emphasis in autonomous machine learning systems that can cope with ambiguity and subtle patterns now brings these problems to a head. This suggests that it is worthwhile for governments to examine the potential for using the very signal processing and machine learning methods that constitute a key challenge to governance as an area in which to search for ways of reforming governance that will be less ineffective than current bureaucratic alternatives.

Notes

1 It would be useful if future work in this area developed a transparent method for setting these discount rates on the basis of the measured and assumed rates of change in relevant conditions. Methodologically, this is similar to the ways in which economists calculate 'hedonic' price indexes (indices that estimate the affect of quality not just quantity changes over time).
2 As cited in O'Driscoll and Rizzo (1985), p. 1.
3 A very useful contemporary account of the long-term impact of Klein and Meckling's (1958) article and associated work can be found in Brady et al. (2012).
4 Indeed, maritime history has examples of these imagined charts being used to secure funding for exploratory voyages – such as attempts to discover a Northwest passage around the (then) ice-bound north pole of the planet.
5 Entropy can be a slippery concept to grasp. Apparently when Claude Shannon had developed his measure and consulted von Neumann on what to call it, von Neumann replied: '*Call it entropy. It is already in use under that name and besides, it will give you a great edge in debates because nobody knows what entropy is anyway*', quote taken from Georgii, 'Probabilistic Aspects of Entropy', 2003 as referred in Sargent (2012).
6 One of the key mathematical transformations used in wi-fi technology is the ability to filter noise in complex radio signals bouncing around moving objects in a room (resulting in the broadcast signal being received in several modified states with different and rapidly changing time lags).
7 This is published in an open source academic journal so freely available to the general public.
8 This point about the mind using 'a version of' Bayesian updating is, admittedly, referring to a fairly loose alignment given the substantial research in psychology and cognate areas (including behavioural economics) that tells us that we don't judge opportunities and risks in a precise Bayesian manner (Kahneman, 2011).
9 This was the 'risk-aware' approach adopted by the HC Coombs Policy Forum at the Australian National University – a collaboration between the Australian Government and that university.

64 *Limitations of risk-averse public policy*

References

Albury, D and Mulgan, G 2003, *Innovation in the Public Sector.* Strategy Unit Paper. Cabinet Office, London.

Ambravaneswaran, B, Phillips, S D and Basaran 2000, Theoretical analysis of a dripping faucet. *Physical Review Letters.* vol. 85, pp. 5332–5335.

Arena, M V, Younossi, O, Galway, L A, Fox, B, Graser, J C, Sollinger, J M, Wu, F and Wong, C 2006, *Impossible Certainty: Cost Risk Analysis for Air Force Systems.* Project Air Force. RAND MG415, Santa Monica.

Australian Government 2015, *2015 Intergenerational Report: Australia in 2055.* Australian Government, Canberra.

Beard, T R, Ford, G S, Koutsky, T M and Spiwak, L J 2009, A valley of death in the innovation sequence: An economic investigation. *Research Evaluation.* vol. 18, no. 5, pp. 343–356.

Brady, T, Davies, A and Nightingale, P 2012, Dealing with uncertainty in complex projects: Revisiting Klein and Meckling. *International Journal of Managing Projects in Business.* vol. 5, no. 4, pp. 718–736.

Brainard, D H and Freeman, W T 1997, Bayesian color constancy. *Journal of the Optical Society of America.* vol. 14, no. 7, pp. 1391–1411.

Crozier, M 1964, *The Bureaucratic Phenomenon.* University of Chicago Press, Chicago.

Ferson, S 2005, *Bayesian Methods in Risk Assessment.* Paper Prepared for Bureau de Recherches Géologiques et Minières (BRGM), France.

Hanger, I 2014, *Royal Commission into the Home Insulation Scheme.* Attorney-General's Department, Canberra.

Hartmann, G and Myers, M B 2001, Technical risk, product specifications, and market risk, in L Branscomb & P E Aursweld (eds.), *Taking Technical Risks: How Innovators, Executives, and Investors Manage High-Tech Risks,* The MIT Press, Cambridge, MA, pp. 30–43.

Hayward, D 2015, Performance budgeting: The power to persuade, control or deceive? in G Carey, K Landvogt & J Barraket (eds.), *Designing and Implementing Public Policy: Cross-Sectoral Debates,* Critical Studies in Public Management Series, Routledge, London, pp. 181–193.

Hood, C 1991, A public management for all seasons? *Public Administration.* vol. 69, pp. 3–19.

International Standards Organisation 2009 Risk management – principles and guidelines. International Standards Organisation, Geneva.

Kahneman, D 2011, *Thinking Fast and Slow.* Penguin, London.

Kay, J 2015, *Other People's Money: Masters of the Universe or Servants of the People?* Profile Books, London.

Klein, B and Meckling, W 1958, Application of operations research to development decisions. *Operations Research.* vol. 6, no. 3, pp. 352–363.

Matthews, M 2009, *Giving Preparedness a Central Role in Science and Innovation Policy.* Discussion Paper commissioned by the Federation of Australian Scientific and Technological Societies (FASTS), Canberra.

Matthews, M 2015, How better methods for coping with uncertainty and ambiguity can strengthen government – civil society collaboration, in G Carey, K Landvogt & J Barraket (eds.), *Designing and Implementing Public Policy: Cross-Sectoral Debates,* Routledge, London, pp. 159–180.

Matthews, M (Forthcoming) 2016, Using signal processing diagnostics to improve public sector evaluations. *Asia & Pacific Policy Studies.*

Mazzucato, M 2011, *The Entrepreneurial State.* Demos, London.

Moore, M 1995, *Creating Public Value.* Harvard University Press, Cambridge, MA.

Morris, P 1994, *The Management of Projects.* Thomas Telford, London.

National Audit Office 2013, *Evaluation in Government.* NAO, London.

O'Driscoll, G P and Rizzo, M J 1985, *The Economics of Time and Ignorance.* Basil Blackwell, Oxford.

Power, M 2004, *The Risk Management of Everything: Re-Thinking the Politics of Uncertainty.* Demos, London.

Sabel, C and Zeitlin, J 2012, Experimentalist governance, in D Levi-Faur (ed.), *The Oxford Handbook of Governance*, Oxford University Press, Oxford, pp. 169–183.

Sargent, T 2012, *Risk, Uncertainty, Value, and Public Policy. Presentation in Honor of Massimo Marinacci.* Presentation Slides.

Shannon, C E 1948, A mathematical theory of communication. *The Bell System Technical Journal.* vol. 27 (July), pp. 379–423.

Solesbury, W 2001, *Evidence Based Policy: Whence It Came and Where It's Going.* ESRC UK Centre for Evidence Based Policy and Practice: Working Paper 1, Queen Mary College, University of London, London.

Stevens, A 2011, Telling policy stories: An ethnographic study of the use of evidence in policy-making in the UK. *Journal of Social Policy.* vol. 40, no. 2 (April), pp. 237–255.

Stiglitz, J 2010, *Freefall: Free Markets and the Sinking of the Global Economy.* Penguin, London.

Wessel, N, Schumann, A, Schirdewan, A, Voss, A and Kurths, J 2000, *Entropy Measures in Heart Rate Variability Data.* Proceedings of the First International Symposium, ISMDA 2000 Frankfurt, Germany, September 29–30.

West, W 2011, *Program Budgeting and the Performance Movement: The Elusive Quest for Efficiency in Government.* Georgetown University Press, Washington, DC.

3 Government as uncertainty and risk manager of last resort

Chapters one and two considered various limitations of uncertainty and risk-averse approaches to governance, highlighting the ways in which the potential for nasty surprises (i.e. increased risks) can be amplified rather than reduced by risk-averse stances. The tendency for these nasty surprises to drive up the costs of governance and, in so doing, contribute to increased levels of public debt is a particularly worrying consequence of this aversion to uncertainty and risk.

The first part of this chapter expands this argument to consider the implications of adopting a more forthright stance towards uncertainty and risk that recognises governments' distinctive role regarding uncertainty and risk.

Governments must play the role of an 'immune system' and attempt to identify and pre-empt possible negative unintended consequences both of what they do, and what others do, to the nation's economy, society and environment and international relationships and obligations. Consequently, the risk-reward relationship for the public sector varies significantly from that of the private sector. It is important to recognise these differences in order to enhance the effectiveness of governance. Approaches to innovation in the private and in the public sector provide a useful illustration of this point.

A key difference between public sector innovation and private sector innovation is that market-based selection mechanisms play a different role in the innovation process. In the private sector, the litmus test for attempts at innovation is market success. Not all innovations prevail in the market, and indeed various other factors mean that the 'best' solutions may not become the dominant solutions. However, markets do enforce selection processes that tend to eliminate less competitive solutions. Competing firms therefore do their best to second-guess what will prevail in the market, often applying vigorous structured decision-making processes – such as Stage-Gate methods in innovation management (Cooper, 2001) – to weed out less promising concepts and solutions.

However, in the final analysis it is the market, and the social and cultural preferences that are reflected in markets, that will decide which innovations succeed and which do not. The academic and policy literature on how these processes work (and do not work) is well developed and full of useful insights. These insights work backwards from market processes into the R&D and demonstration stages that drive new product introduction. They also work forwards into how market processes drive the incremental innovations that continue once new products have been introduced into the market place.

In a public sector context, the relationship between innovation and markets (as selection mechanisms) is significantly different. Governments deal with the uncertainties and risks that markets cannot handle. This requires innovations in what governments seek to do. But, crucially, governments cannot rely on market processes to play the critical 'weed-out' stage in the innovation process by eliminating solutions that do not align well with the preferences expressed in markets and encouraging those that do. Rather, governments need to try to mimic this aspect of the functionality of market-based selection processes without the recourse of relying on markets to actually carry out this selection process. This requires that the public sector draw heavily upon external and internal expertise to weigh-up complex risks of generating negative externalities.

When there is no market-based 'shortcut' available the sheer weight of evidence that may need to be assessed poses major challenges, and raises important questions about whether 'hierarchies of evidence' are required to deal in a rational way with the sheer quantity and complexity of information available. The consequences of incorrectly judging what will and won't work when seeking to innovate are disproportionately greater for this type of public sector innovation than for private sector innovation.

Furthermore, when private sector innovation goes badly wrong (e.g. a new drug that has unforeseen and terrible side-effects) it is governments that bear the responsibility by virtue of their regulatory roles. This is why, in comparison to the private sector, public sector decision-making processes can appear cumbersome, risk-averse and time-consuming. The unintended consequences of getting it wrong are far too severe to rely on the market to correct problems – as in the private sector. The far greater complexity of what governments do generates ambiguity and confusion over *what* to do in response to challenges. The extraordinarily damaging potential associated with unintended consequences necessitates robust risk-averse decision-making.

On a practical level, this distinctive role for governments as the stewards for coping with a wide range of uncertainties and risks indicates that concepts and tools borrowed from the private sector are unlikely to be fit for purpose. This is why, in chapter four, attention is paid to the conceptual architecture of tools that would be more fit for purpose in a public sector context. The guiding principle in investigating options for developing such tools is that they should get to the heart of this distinctive role played by the public sector rather than fudge various aspects of this role: notably the distinction between substantive uncertainty and quantifiable risk and the related challenge of minimising the potential for nasty surprises to arise beyond levels that are effectively unavoidable.

It is worth stressing that, in some administrations, the very notion that there are problems is avoided in preference to 'challenges' when drafting statements and speeches. This choice of words reflects a sustained effort to downplay negative issues and to emphasise positive messages – a feature of the current paradigm

68   *Uncertainty, risk manager of last resort*

that militates against framing governance as, in part, a process of minimising the potential for nasty surprises as a key source of public value.

Science and innovation policy and the transformation of substantive uncertainty into quantifiable risk[1]

Science in its broadest sense, particularly basic research and public science, is our principal resource for helping us to grapple with the uncertainties and risks over what the future has in store for us. By attempting to understand how things work in an objective manner, as free as possible from ideology and bias (though these problems are always present and active), science alerts us to what *may* happen and what the consequences *might* be. Sometimes, science gives us early warnings well before future risks become empirically apparent – a major advantage of good theory.

The critically .important role played by science in helping us to deal with the uncertainties and risks we may face in the future is, however, complicated by a tendency to under-state the limits to our understanding of the future in public policy in general. The statement 'is the Treasury modeling right or wrong', as one politician put it in a debate over Australian Treasury projections, is revealing in what it tells us of the underlying assumptions about uncertainty and risk. When the scope of mathematical models extends into the future and complex systems such as economy are involved simple notions of veracity and falsification become problematic. What happens in the future is inherently hard to predict – so we do our best with the information and technical tools at our disposal – but our best is inevitably limited. In such circumstances, whether something is 'right' or 'wrong' can only be judged after the case, not before the case. Whilst forecasts (whether they be economic, social, environmental or in the national security domains) attempt to make the best of complex and difficult issues, they inevitably confront areas of fundamental uncertainty – which limits measurability.

Science also provides us with sophisticated tools for identifying, measuring and understanding complex phenomenon. Indeed, most areas of natural science involve a substantial investment in technical improvements to these tools. These tools are the technical means of translating uncertainty into risk. For example a new imaging technology developed via basic research will characteristically allow previously unseen features and processes to be viewed and analysed. Such imaging tools allow us to move from substantive uncertainty over what is happening to the risk that we have incorrectly hypothesised or interpreted what is happening. These principles apply to astronomy, physics and medicine, together with numerous other disciplines and subject areas. Technological innovation in imaging, analysis and modelling tools is the primary driver of progress in translating uncertainty into risk. We invest in the R&D to develop and improve these technologies because we have an aversion to ignorance and uncertainty and would in many cases prefer to know more about the risks that we face in order to be better prepared and to decide how to react.

Uncertainty, risk manager of last resort 69

This contribution of science is such a fundamental part of our lives that we tend to overlook the enormous value derived from reduced uncertainty over what the future may have in store for us. In our search for tangible 'outcomes' from science, the 'yield' on taxpayers' investments in innovation and the commercialisation of research, we often fail to give adequate weight to, and measure, the economic and social value of being forewarned and acting accordingly.

However, anyone familiar with public policy will be all too well aware of the ways in which policy definition and implementation tends to be an exploratory/experimental and therefore a *learning* process. Unintended consequences, positive and negative, are not unusual and are almost inevitable in such circumstances. These learning processes tend to operate in the grey area between substantive uncertainty and quantifiable risk.

Research and experimental development

In this context, it is useful to consider the links between the management of uncertainty and risk and research and experimental development (R&D). The so-called linear model of public R&D originated in the tri-partite distinction between basic research, applied research and experimental development proposed in 1945 by Vannavar Bush in his book *Science the Endless Frontier*. Bush had been asked by the US president to prepare a vision for US science policy in the post-war era. When his scientific colleagues suggested that this distinction was unrealistic as a representation of how research and its application actually takes place, Bush's response was that he was well aware of the mismatch between this model and reality, but that the point was that the model was easy to grasp, stressed the importance of 'basic' research, and would therefore help to secure funding from Congress.[2] This linear model concept and corresponding breakdown of R&D was subsequently adopted in the OECD's influential 'Frascati' manual and went on to define how OECD nations collect data on R&D expenditure.

The strength of this linear model is its simplicity – which has been beneficial in securing sustained support for long-term exploratory 'discovery' research by avoiding complexity and debate within the US. In contrast to many other OECD economies, business lobby groups in the US tend to be vocal in criticising federal funding for near-market applied research and experimental development as 'corporate welfare' – advocating a stronger emphasis on basic research as the key mission for federal funding. Again, this differs from business lobby positions outside of the US which have a greater tendency to criticise the relevance of curiosity-driven basic research to economic and competitive performance.

Indeed, even the hard-nosed White House *Office of Management and Budget* (OMB) seeks to stress the importance of basic research by reporting official budget estimates of the value of the net stock of federally funded R&D capital in which the value of basic research never depreciates (whereas the values of the stocks of applied research and of experimental development are depreciated at 10 per cent per annum).[3]

70 *Uncertainty, risk manager of last resort*

A great deal about what currently goes wrong in science and innovation policy can be understood once we recognise that the concept of R&D was developed in relation to public science and specifically in order to secure support for basic research via the deliberately crafted simple linear model assumption. The concept was then applied to what takes place in the business sector, but has never fitted comfortably either with how business innovation occurs or with how public science actually operates. In particular, the notion that basic research is divorced from practical applications has been promulgated via the Frascati definition of R&D produced by the OECD. The consequences for policy have been profound, and as is argued below, highly distorting.

The distortion stems from the failure to recognise that basic research, applied research and experimental development are closely coupled activities via which:

a   practical concerns influence 'open-ended' discovery objectives (e.g. we carry out undirected basic research on viruses because we want to understand how to handle these threats in the future);
b   practical applications reveal anomalies that cannot be explained by current vintages of theory – hence defining the objectives for future theoretical work, and;
c   technological advances in research instrumentation define the directions taken by, and the rate of progress of, discovery research – which consequently involves the 'experimental development' of new and improved research instruments as an integral part of the discovery process (in so doing generating important commercial spin-off activity).

Indeed, a substantial proportion of the 'experimental development' carried out in universities and public sector research organisations is not the experimental development of new products or processes in the linear model sense, it is the 'experimental development' of new and improved research instruments linked to basic and applied research. For example radio astronomy is a 'classic' blue-sky concern, yet the technologies, skills and expertise developed as the means to this end involved pushing the envelope in microprocessor design and signal processing. This, in turn, involved deliberate strategies for training graduate students in a range of trans-disciplinary areas of science and engineering. The highly skilled scientists and engineers developed via this strategy went on to found many companies and in so doing contributing to a substantial amount of wealth and employment creation, see Matthews and Frater (2003).

The distinctive feature of this sort of science- and engineering-enabled blue sky research is that it advances generic skills in identifying and reacting to patterns in highly complex situations. This requires skills in developing advanced technologies for communication and signal processing plus many other enabling areas, such as materials science and applied mathematics, which are used throughout modern economies. The critical factor in such work is that it involves advances in the fundamental theoretical understanding of complex processes and the skills required to do this.

Uncertainty, risk manager of last resort 71

The resistance of the research community to policymakers attempting to define precise utilitarian research objectives for 'blue sky' research is not based upon a reluctance to allow for practical objectives to be addressed via public science. Rather, it is based upon recognition that 'open-ended' inquiry may be required in order to explore and learn about complex phenomenon in this 'closely coupled' manner, and that peer-review mechanisms provide the best means of allocating resources to such exploratory activities because a tremendous amount of tacit knowledge is required to make robust judgements about scientific merit. Processes of discovery must be sufficiently open-ended if they are to be effective – the potential for useful surprises is a favourable not an unfavourable outcome.

The following illustration of the role of basic research in the private sector is taken from engineering design in technologically advanced industries like ICT and aerospace, however the principles are far more generic. High-tech businesses such as pharmaceutical and aerospace companies fund internal 'basic' research in the form of work on fundamental computationally based theoretical understanding (principally in the form of advanced applied mathematics describing natural behaviours). Some of this work is outsourced to universities and government research organisations, but the really critical work is kept in-house. They do this because better computationally based theory is a critical competitive asset. Possessing better theory than competitors allows new and improved products (such as an aero-engine or new chemical compound) to be developed faster and more cheaply than these competitors. This is largely because fewer design iterations are required to finalise a design, in turn because the better theory allows more accurate simulation models to be developed and used – thereby cutting down the number of 'real' prototypes that must be built and tested at great cost and over long periods of time.

In short, the better the theory (and the capability to apply that theory) the greater the confidence that the bulk of design targets can be met on the first attempt – and the lower the cost and shorter the lead time of subsequent attempts to meet these targets. The following diagram illustrates this principle (see figure 3.1).

This diagram represents different design capabilities in terms of confidence curves: the different probabilities of meeting or exceeding a given percentage of design targets on the first design iteration. These confidence curves apply to any science- and engineering-based design process. The better the design team the higher the percentage of the design targets that will be met or exceeded on the first iteration. 'Learning-by-doing' has the effect of shifting these confidence curves to the right. Pushing the 'design envelope' moves a team's confidence curve to the left because there is a reduced familiarity with the specific technical challenges and a decreased capacity to rely upon using existing solutions. The stronger the design capability the lower the requirements for learning and adaptation in meeting specified design objectives.

Drug design uses sophisticated databases and software models of molecular behaviour to push the confidence curve to the right. Similarly, Computer Aided

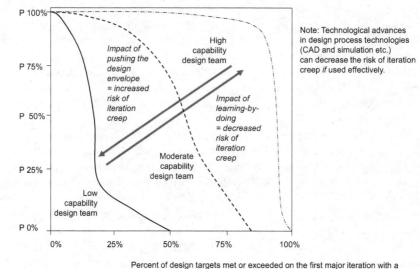

Figure 3.1 Design capabilities as confidence curves

Design (CAD) and other simulation technologies that assist designers also play a major role in allowing this curve to shift to the right – provided the skill exists to use these tools effectively. Given the severe cost and time-to-market penalties of substantial re-design work a strong confidence curve can be extraordinarily valuable (particularly if being first into the market brings with it a stream of substantial future commercial advantages).

This framework has been used to explain why some companies place a very high value on the teams of scientists and engineers who possess outlier skills in achieving ambitious design targets with very few (costly and time-to-market extending) design iterations.[4][5] The idea of applying 'confidence curves' to the innovation process drew upon the investment appraisal methods commonly used by oil companies to value oil deposits in the face of substantial uncertainties over how much oil is actually there and how economic it will be to extract it.[6]

The lesson is that advances in underpinning computationally based theory have powerful and pervasive economic and commercial impacts simply by virtue of how better computational capability allows for greater confidence that the right design targets have been set and that the scientists and engineers can meet these design targets with a low number of costly design iterations.

It is important to stress that the term 'theory' is used here in the specific sense of formal mathematical and computationally based methods that seek to describe and/or predict real phenomena. Consequently, this is a subset of the wider range of theoretical knowledge generated by science.

The same confidence curve principle applies to scientific human capital. The better the theory, the greater the confidence that the hypothesis to be tested is a useful one to test, and the faster and more effective the testing process. This points to the same underlying epistemological principle: *public science and industrial R&D involve logical reasoning in which the aim is to improve theory*. Outstanding problem definition skills in complex situations are a key enabler of this fast-tracking capability. As good Ph.D. supervisors (who want good completion rates) stress, the better the definition of the problem as a viable project the faster the work can be completed and the lower the risk of mistakes, blind alleys, re-work or non-completion. These efficiencies are particularly important with regards to how we think about human capital and in national preparedness for dealing with a range of risks and threats. As stressed earlier, these theory-based considerations are also central to strategies towards industrial R&D.

Consequently, scientifically trained human capital can be valuable intangible assets by virtue of the ability to define problems in a tractable (solvable) manner. A minimal number of experimental iterations are required to improve both fundamental theoretical understanding and achieve practical outcomes. Minimising the number of experiments holds down research costs and speeds the time to publication and to securing intellectual property rights – major benefits in global research competitiveness.

This perspective is useful for illuminating why peer review plays such an important role in public science. Peer review is not simply a mechanism for determining research excellence and professional reputation (promotion prospects etc.). The peer-review principle focuses on contested knowledge – mechanisms for validating theoretical claims on the basis of factual data and for encouraging explicit recognition of the cumulative nature of the knowledge thus generated via debates over veracity. As philosophers of science stress, a theory is never proven true it just remains, as yet, not disproved (a point often lost in the ways in which the media frames news relating to science).

The contested nature of claims of veracity is important from a highly practical standpoint. Good theory, derived from peer-review scrutiny of the match of theory with data, allows researchers to operate in the high confidence region of the above framework. Problems are defined in a tractable manner and, as a result, relatively few experimental iterations are then required to move forward in discrete steps in the discovery process. In effect, the stock of peer review–moderated cumulative knowledge reduces the risk of mis-specified research puzzles and experiments.

The drawback to peer review is, as many recognise, the problem that new perspectives and avenues of inquiry can be locked-out by conservative and/or risk-averse peer reviewers, in so doing holding back the advances in knowledge.[7] It is therefore essential that peer-review mechanisms allow for sufficient plurality and redundancy in investigations in order to avoid the weaknesses associated

74 *Uncertainty, risk manager of last resort*

with peer-review mechanisms blocking disruptive science whilst allowing for these benefits of strong theory to be exploited via the peer-review process.

In contrast, weak theoretical capability (either poor theory itself and/or inadequate application of that theory) tends to result in a larger number of experimental iterations and re-work loops as mis-specified problems and badly designed experiments waste time and cost. Once again, these are familiar issues in doctoral supervision. This is also a perspective that lends support for strengthening rather than watering down the emphasis placed upon advancing theory and research methodology in doctoral research.

The long shelf-life publications that are still being cited several decades after they were first published sometimes owe this to the way in which they defined a new, and more elegant and tractable analytical method that saves time and therefore cost in a research field. In effect, the long shelf-life stems from the way in which the research pushed the collective confidence curve to the right – allowing all researchers able to understand and apply the approach to be more efficient and effective in the discovery process – requiring fewer experimental iterations to make progress.

It follows from this argument that contested claims of theoretical veracity also serve as a means of generating valuable human capital skilled in defining and solving complex problems quickly and cost-effectively *throughout* the economy. This is why leading investment banks recruit physics, mathematics and engineering graduates – a rigorous scientific training generates valuable generic skills in problem definition and problem solution in complex situations in which timeliness is critical. Better theory and the skills in applying this theory allows given objectives to be achieved with a fewer number of problem-solving iterations, thereby generating competitive advantages in both cost-effectiveness and lead times.

From this perspective, the stock of scientifically trained human capital possesses the capability to progress knowledge via decision-making with minimal iterations resulting in lower cost and greater speed of progress. Re-work and scrap rates in the knowledge accumulation process are lower because the problem was well defined in the first place. It is not hard to see that this provides a basis for valuing scientific human capital in a manner that is relevant to all sectors of the economy in which scientific knowledge and data are pertinent to decision-making, i.e. from drug design in a company through to environmental policy advocacy in an NGO.

This approach would be based upon considering how much longer and more costly it would be to use less skilled and experienced human resources in the decision-making process. In short, the value of human capital can be derived from the cost savings associated with reduced re-work and scrap rates in the process of advancing knowledge and/or arriving at complex decisions. This concept is compatible with economists' approaches to human capital[8] and may be useful in allowing the value of scientific human capital to be estimated.

The implication is that public science and industrial R&D exploit the same epistemological capabilities. Science seeks to develop ever more parsimonious explanations of complex phenomena (critical to tractable problem definitions) via experimental testing aimed at selecting and evolving theory. If operating effectively (something that cannot be assumed) peer review plays a critical gate keeper role in reducing the incidence of incorrect theoretical propositions that risk wasted time and cost in future research if not spotted by the epistemological immune system. Similarly, industrial R&D uses experimental development to test theory and simulation models in order to avoid wasted time and cost in both future R&D and market introduction processes. Markets provide an alternative selection mechanism – but one that kicks in at a later stage in the process.

The differences between public science and industrial R&D are not epistemological (at the cutting-edge both share a concern with continuously advancing theoretical power), rather they lie in the subtleties over what the theory seeks to achieve. Thus, experimental development in industrial R&D seeks to use theories and formal models that can handle the added complexities of scale-up and related implementation issues of less relevance to public science.

Public science and the grey area between risk and uncertainty

Public R&D influences expectations about the future. The principle here is not dissimilar to the notion of rational expectations in economic theory – the proposition that all decision-makers will access and use the best available models and data.[9] For example as work on climate change modelling advances the potential exists for decision-makers throughout the global economy to access and use these forecasts to inform their own decision-making.

Whether or not the findings from this R&D are actually accessed is of course a critical policy issue, posing the question: are enough companies able to understand and use the methodologies and data? This is a matter of what economists term institutional failure (i.e. limits to management and human resource capability) rather than market failure per se. Institutional failure can be thought of as friction in the rational expectations model of how public R&D generates pervasive economic outcomes. In an uncertain world access to less imperfect information is valuable and R&D makes the information that we have less imperfect than would otherwise be the case.

This type of R&D impact may well be, by far, the most important means via which public R&D generates economic, social and environmental benefits. It is also a type of impact that the notion of prescience as an outcome class highlights.

If we think about both public policy and markets in this more open-ended way – as exploratory processes *and* selection mechanisms – then it is easier to understand their limitations and, hence, grasp why prescience and innovation are so important in helping us to manage uncertainty. Markets can, within boundaries, cope with risk (quantifiable likelihoods and estimateable consequences) but they cannot cope as easily with substantive ignorance and uncertainty.

76   *Uncertainty, risk manager of last resort*

In this context, economists often draw a useful pragmatic distinction between risk and 'Knightian' uncertainty: immeasurable risks and sheer ignorance about what may happen, see Knight (1921). Frank Knight's perspective on these matters was influenced by the 'Austrian' tradition of subjectivist economics. As stressed earlier in the book, this stream of thinking is distinguished from neo-classical economics in some fundamental ways, which are highly relevant to understanding both prescience and innovation. Rather than a world of quantitative uncertainty as defined within the empirical paradigm in risk and uncertainty analysis (quantifiable problems that yield a 'neutral' 50:50 balance of probabilities), the Austrian economic perspective describes a human condition in which creativity is a necessary response to qualitative uncertainty (effectively ignorance) over what the future has in store – both good and bad.[10] In some circumstances there are no probabilities to assign to future states of the world, but rather the necessity to act *creatively* in order to generate parameters that can be assigned probabilities (and hence managed 'rationally'). The resulting competition is *inherently* a process of discovery and innovation. From this standpoint, markets are inherently *exploratory* and *innovative* collective endeavours that operate via selection and in which pattern recognition plays an important role, see Kirzner (1973, 1979), and Hayek (1967).

The public sector faces the acute challenge of dealing with immeasurable risks, ignorance and uncertainties – managing the domains in which markets are ineffective as resource allocation mechanisms. Consequently, the government officials faced with these challenges stress the importance of the 'grey' area between measurable risks and ignorance/uncertainty. In practice, governments must deal with risks that are hard or impossible to quantify and quantified risks with large margins of error that attract little trust and credibility. Structured decision-making processes and discussions can help in addressing such challenges (hence the emphasis within the public sector on committee structures, inquiries, reviews and evaluations).

It is significant that the practitioners who engage in these structured processes sometimes express a wish that better formal methods were available and sometimes anticipate that the march of progress will eventually deliver technical solutions. This is a particular feature of funding programme reviews and evaluations. Again, this tends to reflect a lack of recognition of the problem of ignorance and substantive uncertainty. Many issues, including the rate of return on investment, are inherently unknowable for complex situations (other than over the very long term) *but* this does not mean that government interventions are neither useful in general nor critically important in some instances.

All public sector programmes focus on attempting to change the future in ways that are preferred over others, but this does not mean that a mechanistic validation of additionality is possible outside of some special cases: the systems are often far too complex and subject to second-guessing and complex feedback loops. Indeed, the more important the challenge, the more complex and intractable the problem, and the greater the likelihood of severe negative unintended consequences – the so-called wicked problems challenge (Churchman, 1967).

Looking for useful outcomes from public science (and innovation) in translating immeasurable uncertainty into measurable risk, and how these outcomes help us to cope with the grey area between uncertainty and risk, helps us to articulate a more realistic conception of the return on investment from public science. In so doing, this helps us to re-balance programme evaluation methods by avoiding reliance on the 'smoking gun' audit trail of tangible unitary outputs and outcomes (patents, spin-offs, license income etc.).

In contrast, over the last two decades or so a particularly strong emphasis has been placed upon this 'smoking gun' ethos: research commercialisation as *the* expected outcome from public R&D. The assumed simplicity – and measurability – of this type of outcome has undoubtedly contributed to the rise of this perspective. Patents, licenses, start-up companies and the like can all be measured as outputs. These tangible features tend to assist policymakers in budget negotiations and help to reassure the general community that value for money is being sought in a transparent manner. More recently, the policy narrative has started to focus on impediments to collaboration – framed as an end in itself rather than as a means to an end. Collaboration may be becoming the new commercialisation.

Arguably, there is a Panglossian tone to this perspective – rapid scientific and technological progress generates bountiful commercial opportunities – all we have to do is to reap these rewards if we are to live in the best of all possible worlds. We therefore search for the impediments to commercialisation and (more recently) collaboration on the assumption that there must be such impediments because both the level and timeliness of commercialisation and collaboration does not match our expectations given the levels of spending on R&D.

The result is that science policy has tended to be subsumed under innovation policy – leading to a defensive posture associated with attempts to frame many inherently worthwhile benefits from public science (notably prescience) as innovation-related outcomes (narrowly conceived in research commercialisation terms). It has proved difficult for the science community to articulate a compelling case for government support for science that moves beyond the research for its own sake ethos that has become increasingly unfavourably regarded in advanced OECD economies.

Theoretical power and investment risk: lessons from business and innovation

The manner in which a major new investment is to be financed can be critical to whether or not the potential investment is financially viable. For debt-financed investments the aim is to demonstrate, in as credible a manner as possible, that the investment risk is lower than a less well informed and in-depth analysis might conclude. For equity-financed investments the aim is to demonstrate that risk taking that exceeds market norms could, potentially, lead to returns-on-investment that exceed market norms.

78 Uncertainty, risk manager of last resort

In both cases the emphasis is upon striving for accurate estimates of the risk–reward relationship. This is one reason why major investment banks employ teams of experienced engineers and scientists. Scientific and engineering expertise is critical to judging investment risk. The same principle applies to areas of science in which there is significant commercialisation activity – such as in the bio-medical area.

It is for this reason that some industrialists are starting to stress a type of R&D outcome that is far less familiar to the majority of academic researchers (especially those without commercialisation experience) – namely lower investment risk relative to market norms – a factor known as *beta* in investment finance. On a number of occasions, discussions with industrialists over what they are looking for in research partnerships with universities and public sector organisations results in the phrase 'we are looking for a lower *beta*'.

This type of R&D outcome is explained in figure 3.2 in the form of the Capital Asset Pricing Model (CAPM). The CAPM[11] is widely used in large corporations, including banks as a convenient means of assessing the rate of

---

The Capital Asset Pricing Model (CAPM) is a frequently used, and relatively simply formal method for calculating the required rate of return on an investment on the basis of prevailing investment conditions. The standard equation used is as follows.

$$K_d = R_f + \beta[R_m - R_f]$$

Where:

K_d is the required rate of return from the investment (the cost of debt)
R_f is the risk free rate of return (usually taken as the 10 year govt bond rate)
β is the measure the specific project risks relative to general market risks
R_m is the expected rate of return in the market as a whole

The greater the estimated value of β the higher the required rate of return to compensate investors for the additional risk that they face and the lower the net present value (NPV) of an associated investment opportunity.

Estimates of β are widely used in the finance sector to inform decision-making. It is not hard to see that any R&D outcome that helps to demonstrate that β is lower than would otherwise be assumed to be the case can generate 'bankable feasibility' for an investment opportunity. Commercial-in-confidence studies do exist that examine how R&D generates bankable feasibility via *beta* – however none have been found in the public domain to date (precisely because they are so commercially important).

Figure 3.2 Reduced *beta* as the research outcome: understanding the value of research outcomes using the Capital Asset Pricing Model

return on a prospective investment that reflects the level of risk faced (to be specific the level of risk that cannot be offset by other mechanisms such as financial hedging).[12]

The principle of viewing research outcomes as reductions in *beta* is straightforward. Consider a new fossil fuel fired power station design that could greatly reduce greenhouse gas emissions. This design may involve bundling together different leading-edge technologies, many of which can be acquired from specialist providers. The result is that the design is a systems integration challenge – working out how best to get all these systems to work together. Until a real-world power station with the new bundle of technologies is built the risks must be estimated via simulation modelling but they cannot be demonstrated conclusively.[13] For a major debt-financed investment this risk dimension is a critical factor. Delays in the power station going online and/or cost overruns will also reduce the estimated net present value (NPV) of the investment proposition.

Irrespective of the precise method used by the investment banks or major corporations who will provide the finance, the general principle will follow the CAPM principle: the higher the estimate of *beta* the greater the required rate of return to offset the risk and/or the higher the discount rate applied in the NPV calculations. Whatever the approach, higher technical risk associated with pushing the envelope in innovation terms translates into a lower NPV via *beta*-related investment risk assessments.

This is why some industrialists are becoming very interested in using R&D outcomes to demonstrate what they term *bankable feasibility* by collating robust evidence that *beta* is in fact lower than their bankers and investors assume. This can involve a dialogue not dissimilar to that which takes place over the regulatory approval for a new drug, in which data that helps to set *beta* in scrutinised, challenged, and a particular *beta* value eventually agreed upon. On the basis of the available published evidence, drawing such a close connection between R&D and bankable feasibility via *beta* is currently an intention for many companies and a reality for a few rather than a well-developed and widely adopted methodology. Policymaking would benefit from paying attention to this dimension of the innovation process. Figure 3.3 illustrates the links via which collaboration between academia and business can generate bankable feasibility outcomes via reductions in *beta*.

This type of technological due diligence tends nowadays to revolve around correlations between the results of simulation modelling and data from large-scale experiments and prototypes, or even real systems being operated elsewhere. The better the correlation between theory and data the stronger the case for setting *beta* at a level that generates bankable feasibility.

Given the importance of *learning curves* (cumulative experience in building a particular design leads to lower unit costs, shorter lead times and reduced technical risk), simulation modelling that closely matches experimental data has the effect of allowing a number of 'virtual' systems to be built prior to the first real-world system. Considerable attention is paid to the First of a Kind (FOAK) design configuration in major engineering design projects as these provide a

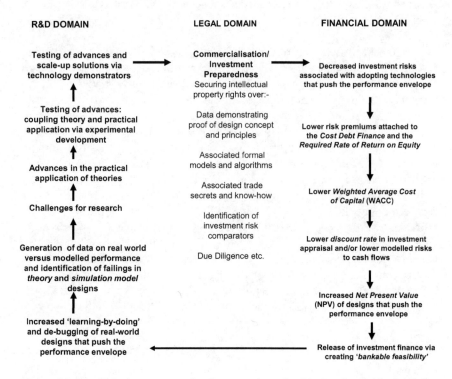

Figure 3.3 The links between academic research and achieving bankable feasibility for investments

starting point for both reaping learning-driven gains and demonstrating *beta* for subsequent projects. Significantly, scale-up issues are often central to the FOAK risk-assessment milestone. This is why so much attention is paid to developing simulation models that can accurately predict real, full-scale behaviours.[14] Figure 3.4 illustrates how an effective meshing of theory and simulation modelling can generate tangible productivity benefits by pushing the first real output further along the production learning curve (the unit cost differences between scenario A and B in this diagram).

The outcomes generated by partnerships via which universities link with companies to work on specific major design projects can be framed in terms of this virtual progress along learning curves. In effect, the all-important FOAK may be the third or the fourth unit built in learning curve terms because the R&D has allowed a significant amount of design de-bugging prior to the first build. For large, complex and expensive systems this is a major competitive advantage.

This perspective opens up a new regime for defining the outcomes from collaborative activities based on combining investment risk factors (*beta*) with

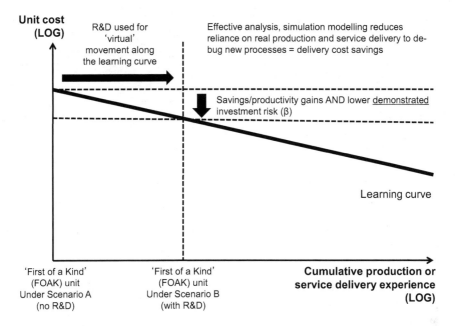

Figure 3.4 How simulation modelling pushes 'First of a Kind' along the learning curve

established learning curve methods. R&D partnerships can generate substantial benefits by securing *bankable feasibility* for designs that push the performance envelope – in so doing facilitating the diffusion of more advanced technologies that address global concerns such as climate change. Hence, the industrialists that look for the outcomes from R&D partnerships in terms of reductions in *beta* have identified a critical outcome from public sector R&D. This is not, unfortunately, an outcome that most governments accept as valid when carrying out project appraisals and selecting the projects to fund.

In my own experience, efforts by industry to get the *lower beta* approach accepted by governments have been rejected because this focus does not align well with the linear and sequential pathway to impact ethos encouraged by the new public management stance. In other words the identification of units of academic output (publications and patents) that are subsequently translated into units of commercial activity (firm start-ups, IP licensing deals etc.).

Consequently, whilst the potential exists to develop research impact metrics based on virtual progress along learning curves prior to the FOAK and the achievement of bankable feasibility via reduced *beta*, a shift in thinking away from a focus on 'units of output' within government is required in order to exploit this potential. Such approaches would be particularly useful in capturing the outcomes from engineering R&D – in which designs that are easier, hence less risky, to build can be important outputs in themselves.

82 *Uncertainty, risk manager of last resort*

An applicable theory can be thought of as a formal mathematical approach that can be related statistically to data from real-world experiences. As the correlation between the theory and real-world experience increases (by virtue of using data from experimental development to drive improvements in the underpinning theory) so the value of that theory increases. Being able to formally demonstrate a strong statistical correlation between theory and data can be critical to achieving bankable feasibility.

As noted earlier, the main difference between cutting-edge public science and cutting-edge industrial R&D does not appear to lie in how theory for competitive advantage is used so much as in the issues addressed by theory. In an industrial R&D context the challenge is to develop and use theoretical models to handle highly complex real-world issues such as scale-up – in which the number of variables required tends to increase dramatically in comparison to laboratory-scale models and analysis. This is why it is US government policy to encourage the weapons laboratories to commercialise older vintages of the highly sophisticated numerical methods used to simulate nuclear explosions as a substitute for real nuclear tests.[15] Disseminating advanced non-linear mathematical methods helps industry to reduce the time, cost and risk in scale-up efforts.

This is most clearly demonstrated in relation to the product families formed by successive design improvements. As any design is tweaked and improved there are likely to be major costs and long lead times associated with obtaining regulatory approval. The ability to frame the case for regulatory approval against statistically robust correlations between theory and practice is of great assistance in lowering the costs and lead times of the approval process. This is also an area where competitors can act to try to block fast tracking to regulatory approval.

For example several years ago one aero-engine manufacturer was seeking to obtain regulatory approval for an engine design derivative on the basis of mathematical modelling of that design, based in turn upon statistically robust data that demonstrated how effective the model was of actual engine behaviour for that design family. Because the design was a derivative of an already certified design, the US Federal Aviation Administration (FAA) was willing to certify the new design simply on the basis of the mathematical model of demonstrated explanatory power. Whilst for the industry as a whole this was the holy grail of applicable theory in R&D and market introduction processes, it became prudent for competitors to take legal action to block this precedent in order to seek to limit short-term competitive disadvantage. This regulatory compliance innovation and the litigation response highlighted the tremendous value of applicable theory backed by robust data.

Similar considerations apply with regards to the source code for advanced weapons systems. For example it has been rumoured that the lead-up to the French underground testing of nuclear weapons in the South Pacific in the mid-1990s involved attempts to obtain nuclear explosion simulation software for that class of warhead from the United States. When the US refused to provide the source code the French were forced to proceed with their own real test in order to assess the extent to which their own mathematically based

Uncertainty, risk manager of last resort   83

simulation models were accurate. This software *code validation* is an important issue for nuclear powers because they need to be able to assess the extent to which their stockpile of warheads is degrading over time. The nuclear 'pits', also known as the physics package, in nuclear weapons are long-lived and the manufacture of new pits is very rare. Rather, pits that may be decades old tend to be periodically re-packaged with updated guidance and delivery systems. Simulation models act as a substitute for test detonations of nuclear weapons (tests of both the old nuclear pits and the way in which they interact with the updated systems they are placed in).[16] Because these highly advanced simulation models cover nuclear stockpile shelf-life issues they are a vital aspect of US national security – these simulations reduce the potential for nasty surprises.

The US has a long-established tradition of not releasing source codes relating to a wide range of weapons systems – further emphasising the importance of applicable theory as a strategic asset – *advanced simulation software is applicable theory*.

It is also important to bear in mind the fact that there are major differences between research areas with regards to the scope for this type of theory-enhancing feedback within R&D. It is only possible for experimental development to drive theoretical advances in a major sense if the formal theory and the implementation of that theory in simulation models are able to begin to match the complexity of the real processes being studied. If this match is poor then nasty surprises can occur.

For example until the mathematics of computational fluid dynamics (CFD) was developed and implemented in software simulations, wind tunnels were the most effective means of optimising the aerodynamics of aircraft, motor vehicles and large structure designs (such as suspension bridges and skyscrapers). The data generated from these wind tunnel tests provided the raw material that defined the challenges for CFD theory and modelling. However, the ability to use the statistical correlations between formal theory and the experimental wind tunnel tests to identify anomalies between theoretical prediction and actual behaviour required that the theory was able to make predictions that were in the same ballpark as regards the nature and extent of the complex behaviour mapped by the experimental results.[17]

Similarly, the mathematical modelling and software simulations of complex bio-chemical processes is playing the same sort of role as CFD in reducing reliance on costly and time-consuming experimental development and compound screening in areas like drug design and genomics. The difference is that the greater levels of complexity and uncertainty over how biological systems behave may mean that formal theory faces more severe limits in efficacy than in the case of CFD. Consequently, the long-term scope for the fast-tracked progress associated with closely coupled advances in theory and experimentation differs markedly between research areas as a function of the sheer complexity of the processes involved.

The caveat to the importance of formal R&D is that in a number of high-technology industries, such as aerospace, R&D is viewed as an accounting and

84 *Uncertainty, risk manager of last resort*

tax treatment matter. In such industries, innovation strategies focus on broader concerns with capability acquisition and systems integration in extended technology supply chains. Formal R&D plays a role in facilitating capability acquisition and systems integration, but not the dominant role some commentators unfamiliar with actual corporate innovation strategies and practices assume. Consequently, emphasising the distinction between business innovation and technological innovation would help to clarify debate over the impact of business R&D spending on industrial competitiveness. However, scope would still remain for improving the accuracy of the assumptions about the role of formal R&D in those industries in which technological innovation is a key component of competitiveness.

Prescience as an outcome class

In reaction to the over-emphasis on traceable commercial outcomes from public science and an under-emphasis on the sort of uncertainty to risk pathway and its benefits discussed above, in 2006 the *Federation of Australian Scientific and Technological Societies* (FASTS) commissioned a paper that set out to increase the prominence of an important aspect of capacity-building in science and innovation – our 'preparedness' for anticipating and responding to undesirable and damaging future events (Matthews, 2006).

Previously, the term 'preparedness' was used mainly in relation to defence, counter-terrorism and natural hazards. The wider use of this term was deliberate, and attempted to focus policy thinking on the far more extensive aspects of how science helps us to deal with substantive uncertainty and quantifiable risk. Of course, science and innovation are also partly responsible for many of these unfavourable future scenarios (from endocrine disrupters in our water supply through to weapons of mass destruction). Indeed, the need for preparedness is generated in part by the unexpected consequences of science-based innovation – the unwelcome downside of modernity. Many areas of innovative activity address these unwelcome consequences of scientific and technological progress. We should not forget that the problem of climate disruption due to anthropogenic CO_2 emissions is largely a consequence of investments in industrial R&D of various types (e.g. in power station technologies, motor vehicles and aircraft) taking place since the Industrial Revolution. Whilst technological innovation is now a contributing solution to this major problem it is also a major, if unintended, cause of the problem.

In seeking to establish 'preparedness' as a more explicit outcome class in science and innovation policy, the 2006 paper highlighted the enormous economic, social, environmental and political benefits that are generated by 'prescience': being better informed (by public science) about what the future might have in store for us if we carry on acting as we are. The widespread dissemination of this information alters people's, and corporations', expectations about the future. This in turn, can lead to changes in current behaviour that change the likelihood of these undesirable future outcomes emerging. This line of argument was subsequently reinforced by the publication of the Stern Report in the UK, which empirically articulated this type of case in relation to the costs of delayed actions (and hence of *not* being forewarned and able to respond) (Stern, 2006).

The underlying principle in the case for treating preparedness as an outcome class is similar to the calculation of Net Present Value (NPV) in economics and finance. The understanding gleaned from public science alters the *current* value of economic assets because it alters the expectations about the future that determine what these current asset values are. This dimension provides a down-side mitigation argument that complements existing arguments over the social value of government support for science and innovation – a policy narrative that traditionally stresses the potential upside gains to be reaped from exploiting intellectual property rights, company start-ups and spin-offs etc. The term 'prescience' is used here to refer to this outcome class as it seems to be more appropriate. It also avoids the connotations of referring to 'preppers' (people who build bunkers and stockpile food and water in preparation for possible cataclysmic events and who often have strong anti-government views).

One very important aspect of the prescience outcome class is that it opens up an avenue for being clearer about the ways in which public science addresses inter-generational equity concerns (i.e. fairness to future generations). Greater awareness of future uncertainties and risks helps to counteract myopia in decision-making. By being better informed about what the future may have in store for us, and how we can therefore change the future by changing what we do today, public science helps to decrease what economists call the social rate of discount. This is the rate at which we collectively discount the value of things that may happen in the future. The lower the social rate of discount the higher the value we are willing to place on the future consequences of our current actions. If we have little information on how our current behaviours may affect future generations then it is understandable that we will tend to heavily discount the future. Public science helps us to value future states of the world more highly—with consequent impacts on current behaviour and investment decisions.

Indeed, the social rate of discount is a key factor in the financial discount rates used to calculate the Net Present Value of assets. The greater the discount rate the lower the Net Present Value of an asset. Of course, Net Present Value estimates will be over-stated if future uncertainties and risks are under-stated. This can lead to a situation in which there are nasty surprises – unfolding events lead to dramatic and unexpected drops in asset values. As the global financial crisis illustrates, these drops can be very de-stabilising – socially, economically and politically.

From this angle, the prescience outcome class helps to draw attention to the importance of seeking to avoid significant and unexpected drops in asset values by being better informed about future uncertainties and risks. Consequently, the prescience outcomes generated by public science generate the long-term benefit of enhanced fairness to future generations *and* the present term benefit of a reduced risk of unexpected and de-stabilising drops in the current value of economic assets.

86 *Uncertainty, risk manager of last resort*

Prescience and protecting the value of national balance sheets

The most recent United Nations guidelines for preparing National Accounts recommend that national balance sheets be compiled.[18] This is because these estimates of stocks of national net worth provide a measure of economic progress that compensates for weaknesses in the more widely used annual flows of gross domestic product and related measures. This limitation in flow-based measures is due to the potential for GDP growth to be based upon running down assets on the national balance sheet, see Thompson (2000). There is also now an additional set of joint UN, EU, OECD, IMF and World Bank national accounts guidelines designed to allow environmental impacts to be considered alongside economic performance – promulgating the concept of 'depletion adjusted net domestic product'.[19] This approach allows for the depletion and degradation of natural assets to be factored into estimates of net domestic product (gross domestic product net of capital consumption). In the new UN standard for integrated environmental and economic accounting the value of the depletion and degradation of natural capital associated with generating flows of economic activity is added to the value of economic capital consumption to produce an estimate of the overall value of capital consumption. See Australian Bureau of Statistics (2003).

These developments in national accounting are significant to understanding prescience outcomes. Public science examining long-term processes alerts decision-makers to the nature and extent of any risks to asset values (e.g. climate change impacts, environmental degradation, over-fishing etc.). Business decision-makers are then able to factor these future risks into the current market prices of assets such as agricultural and urban land (and in some countries water prices).

This process of adjusting asset values via market prices allows resource allocations made *now* that attempt to anticipate and mitigate future risks. In principle, this allows risk-mitigating investments to be made without overly penalising the current generation who must bear the costs generated by previous generations in order to limit the impact on future generations. This important issue in public policy is discussed in Arrow (1995).

Consequently, the preparedness value of the impact of public science lies in markets being 'forewarned' – avoiding the unexpected and more costly shocks caused by *not* being aware that there are risks to asset values. This opens up a means of valuing some types of prescience research on the basis of the extent to which costly impacts have been mitigated by being forewarned. Should a comprehensive analysis of this type of downside mitigation impact be carried out it may be comparable to, or even surpass, the economic impact of the narrow linear model research commercialisation pathway that is the dominant expected outcome in current science policy.

Policy implications

From a public policy perspective, these two benefits can reinforce each other in useful ways. Reducing the social rate of discount helps governments to address their key role in worrying about inter-generational equity issues (something markets cannot do as well). This longer-term perspective, in turn, reduces the risk that the current values of assets are over-stated in the face of risks and uncertainties – making markets more efficient as a means of allocating resources. In short, the enhanced levels of prescience arising from public science make markets more efficient in the present whilst also helping to counteract the short-termism that tends to be inherent in market behaviour.

Adopting prescience, and the key distinction between addressing substantive uncertainty versus risk management that this entails, could lead to more general transformations in how output-outcome budgeting is implemented at the programme level. In particular, it is necessary to adopt definitions of legitimate and desirable outcomes that emphasise reductions in uncertainty as being intrinsically valuable.

If we are to pursue a more balanced approach in science policy, in which commercialisation and prescience outcomes *both* receive the attention they deserve, then we need to articulate how prescience can be measured – and its value estimated. One advantage of prescience-based approaches is that they avoid the 'more jam tomorrow' problem: we obtain the benefits now because this is the point at which we judge the present value of future risks and associated costs – in exactly the same way that financial analysts calculate the present value of a future stream of investment yields. Prescience-based thinking opens up a rich new seam to mine as regards outcome measurement.

Five basic principles for moving forward in counter-balancing the research commercialisation approach to innovation with the prescience dimensions of public science suggest themselves.

First, policymakers need to work harder to create more receptive conditions for implementing prescience as an outcome by being more realistic (and honest) about the limitations to forecasts and other predictions. There is diminished scope for recognising the importance of prescience as an outcome class from public science if we pretend that governments, business and the general community do not face substantive uncertainty over what the future has in store for us. The more realistic and therefore honest we are about the limitations of our understanding of the future, the greater the value that we will place on investments that improve our understanding. In democracies, this means that widespread public debate over prescience-related issues is inherently useful because it requires us all to be more realistic about what governments can and cannot do in the face of substantive uncertainties that can affect us all. Greater honesty over the limitations to policy interventions encourages more effective debates over policy matters – debates in which substantive uncertainties are recognised and blame for failures, and credit for successes, makes more explicit recognition of contingent and unexpected events and processes.

Second, both policymakers and the general community need to make a far more explicit distinction between substantive uncertainty and quantifiable risk. The existence of immeasurable risks, and concerns, and in some cases sheer ignorance, over what may happen (a feature of pandemic preparedness), means that it is often inappropriate to allocate blame for policy and service delivery

88   Uncertainty, risk manager of last resort

failures. Whilst blame is worth allocating when relevant information was ignored, we all need to recognise that there are cases in which, without the benefit of hindsight, predicting what may happen was inherently *unknowable* at that time. The events concerned happen under conditions of substantive uncertainty rather than measurable risk. Whilst measurable risk, including financial risk, can be treated as a commodity – and offset, traded and allocated – uncertainty born of ignorance about what may happen is a shared problem that requires a collective response.

Third, given the importance of being more honest about the limits of our understanding of the future, and therefore of recognising the distinction between uncertainty and risk, those responsible for science policy should be far more active in stressing how science translates substantive uncertainty into quantifiable risk, and in so doing, elevating our levels of social, economic and environmental prescience. From this perspective, the objectives of innovation (as it is conventionally approached) are often set by the prescience outcomes created by public science. Prescience (the ends) and innovation (the means) have a complementary relationship to each other. Of course, as stressed recently by Helga Nowotny (2015), science and innovation also generate uncertainties – hence there is something of a 'tug of war' between these forces that reduce and increase uncertainty.

Fourth, it would be helpful to articulate new 'prescience friendly' guidelines for research funding allocations and performance evaluation. The adoption of more risk- and uncertainty-aware investment portfolio methods would assist in this regard. It would be preferable to bundle together discrete research projects addressing similar challenges into Prescience Research Portfolios. Prescience Research Portfolios could be funded and evaluated at a portfolio level – allowing for greater risk taking in the sense of exploratory and truly experimental work at the individual project level. The selection of these bundles of projects, which would require that appropriate levels of quality in research design and track record are achieved, would explicitly mix low- and higher-risk projects ('sure bets' with left field projects). Project selection would also pay attention to offsetting risks and uncertainties between projects in order to strengthen the portfolio as a whole. In evaluating Prescience Research Portfolios what matters is how the overall portfolio has performed. 'Failures' of some projects to achieve stated objectives can and should be tolerated as an inevitable consequence of this type of uncertainty and risk-aware approach to funding and evaluating research. The outcome of increasing levels of prescience (better awareness of, and options for dealing with, potential threats, hazards and other downside factors) would of course be an explicit attribute in selecting and evaluating this type of scientific research. This latter attribute would rectify a major shortcoming in current approaches – the penalisation of failures to 'follow through' on potentially useful advances in knowledge. Given the value that business places on the public science system developing prescience options for possible use should certain future circumstances emerge, the adoption of the Prescience Research Portfolios system is likely to receive widespread support from the business community. Firms require options in an uncertain world hence the provision of these options (in this case via collaboration with academia) is useful in itself and irrespective of whether or not those options are actually exercised – an aspect that the linear model aspects of the new public management ethos struggle with.

Finally, given the ways in which prescience outcomes are reflected in asset valuations (in the present) and inter-generational equity concerns (over the very long term) there is useful technical work still to be done on incorporating these outcomes into mainstream research evaluation methods. Capturing the value of prescience outcomes in this manner will hinge upon estimating how a better understanding of uncertainties and risks faced in the future affects asset values, and also on calculating the impact of any changes in the social rate of discount on these asset values. In each case, counter-factual assumptions based on the 'denial cost' of *not* possessing given prescience outcomes are required, and will be reflected in asset values that may be under-stated or over-stated depending upon complex circumstances. Success in these technical efforts can be defined as the availability of credible counter-factual estimates that capture the difference between asset valuations with and without the outcomes from given Prescience Research Portfolios. The larger the difference in asset valuations, and consequently the lower the severity of possible market corrections that might take place in the future, the greater the value of the prescience outcomes that have been achieved.

If we develop science and innovation policy in this manner then we will articulate a more balanced approach than exists at present. We don't need to rely on technochratic solutions in order to implement prescience as a policy framework – only greater *realism* and *honesty* over the challenges faced by public policy in general. We over-emphasise innovation outcomes and under-emphasise prescience outcomes (rather than the complementary relationship between the two) because we misrepresent the fundamental challenge faced in governance. This is that we inhabit a world beset by substantive uncertainty over what the future has in store for us – irrespective of how the new public management ethos attempts to conceal this reality.

Paradoxically, it may be the case that the major emphasis placed on innovation as an outcome from spending on science has contributed to the conditions for introducing prescience as a central feature in science policy. The adoption by governments of innovation-based narratives applied to what happens in the public sector brings with it the necessary recognition of the fundamental role of uncertainty management in governance. Hence, the increased emphasis on learning by exploration and experimentation within governance. Given this, we should do more to learn from post-Newtonian physics – whose intellectual authority stems from rejecting simple and unambiguous mechanical models and embracing and managing the existence of uncertainty, ambiguity, complexity, reflexivity between the observer and the observed – and to understand the consequent limits to prediction that stem from these conditions.

Prescience matters as an outcome class in science and innovation policy because it opens up a pathway to 'post-Newtonian' public administration in general – a

90 *Uncertainty, risk manager of last resort*

paradigm in which risk is not always something to be eliminated (like friction) and in which uncertainty may arise as an emergent property of the system itself (especially if it is complex).

Lessons from attempts to implement prescience as a research outcome

The Federation of Australian Scientific Societies (now known as Science and Technology Australia) used the 2006 paper articulating the case for preparedness (referred here as prescience) as an outcome class as the basis of its submission to the Australian Government Productivity Commission's *Review of Public Support for Science and Innovation* in 2006. The arguments gained traction with the Productivity Commission (PC) and, as a result, the PC's report stressed the importance of these types of benefit arising from scientific research, whilst also stressing how difficult such benefits are to measure. The arguments also gained traction with some senior government officials in Australia – for whom the argument made sense as a plausible approach and, as a result, was easily absorbed into mind-sets.

Following the Productivity Commission's support for this perspective (at a conceptual level), the notion that preparedness should be made explicit as an outcome class was supported by the standing committee of the *Prime Minister's Science, Engineering and Innovation Council* (PMSEIC) in Australia and also featured in new guidance on measuring research outcomes issued by the inter-departmental *Coordination Committee on Science and Technology* (CCST).

Following a change in government (from a liberal coalition to labour administration) a new *Review of the National Innovation System* was undertaken in 2008. That review chose not to endorse the emphasis placed on preparedness in the earlier Productivity Commission report. The reasons for this are unclear, but discussions held at the time indicated that this may have been because the case for preparedness was viewed by those advocating more support for innovation as a competing rather than as a complementary concept. The downplaying of this aspect of public science was also associated with moves by the incoming government to frame subsidies for a languishing automotive industry in Australia as support for innovation. The emphasis on innovation provided a useful and modern-looking means of representing such subsidies.

The lesson is that it is still important to explain and demonstrate how support for treating prescience as an outcome class in science policy reinforces support for innovation – and particularly industrial innovation. It was clear that, given the strong emphasis on quantification in the new public management ethos, efforts to introduce the new outcome class into the policy lexicon would only be successful if the concept (which made sense to many policymakers) could be translated into measurement tools compatible with the new public management stance. This challenge led to the exploration of signal processing methods as a public policy tool addressed in this book.

Conclusions

Just as the public sector tends to be the 'lender of last resort' so too it also acts as the uncertainty and risk manager of 'last resort'. The nasty surprises faced as uncertainty and risk manager of last resort can end up being reflected in levels of public debt – levels of debt that can be inflated if the ways in which we govern increases rather than decreases the potential for nasty surprises to occur. The greater the ability to minimise these nasty surprises above unavoidable levels, the greater the ability to keep public debt under control. Policy stances that seek legitimacy by adopting 'business-like' performance metrics can amplify the risks associated with these nasty surprises. The use of the concept of prescience as an outcome class for public science, especially when combined with an emphasis in impacts on stocks of assets rather than simply on flows of economic activity, focuses attention on these concerns and opens up new and important pathways of articulating the public value generated by public science.

Re-visiting the potential for surprise ratio introduced in chapter one, we can see that it is possible, in principle at least, to define prescience as an outcome using this ratio:

$$\text{Risk amplification} = \frac{\text{Achieved potential for surprise}}{\text{Unavoidable potential for surprise}}$$

In this context, prescience can be defined simply as a reduced achieved potential for surprise over and above the unavoidable potential for surprise, in turn reducing the risk amplification factor. The manner in which this is done, as suggested in this chapter, is by allowing research outcomes to be more explicitly framed as translating substantive uncertainty into quantifiable risk. In statistical terms, turning noise (random behaviour that maximises information entropy) into a signal. This process has the advantage of reducing the strength of both the nominator and the denominator because any translation of substantive uncertainty into quantifiable risk will also reduce the unavoidable potential for surprise as illustrated in the following version of the risk amplification ratio, which unpacks the balance between substantive uncertainty and quantifiable risk.

$$\text{Risk amplification} = \frac{\text{Achieved balance of substantive uncertainty to quantifiable risk}}{\text{Unavoidable balance of substantive uncertainty to quantifiable risk}}$$

Of course, as have practitioners stressed to me when this argument is run past them, the critically important issue is how to handle, in practice, the grey area between uncertainty and risk when it is couched in these terms – governments must deal with risks that are hard or impossible to quantify and quantified risks with large margins of error that attract little trust and credibility. As discussed in chapter four, information theory with its emphasis on concepts of entropy, noise and signals may provide a useful perspective on this challenge.

92 *Uncertainty, risk manager of last resort*

From this perspective the risk amplification ratio can be expressed in terms of governance entropy as:

$$\text{Risk amplification} = \frac{\text{Achieved governance entropy}}{\text{Unavoidable governance entropy}}$$

Chapter four takes a closer look at the potential for translating this signal processing perspective into a coherent analytical framework for use in public policy.

Notes

1 This section draws heavily on Matthews (2009).
2 See Stokes (1996).
3 See OMB *Analytical Perspectives* op. cit. The OMB R&D capital stock estimates do not align with those of the Bureau of Economic Analysis (BEA) – which does depreciate basic research on the assumption that the knowledge does become obsolete. Arguably, the most plausible approach would assume that it is only the value of fundamental theoretical breakthroughs that does not depreciate – as argued in this paper, this is a small subset of *all* R&D outcomes because advances in fundamental theory draw upon the testing carried out beyond basic research per se.
4 See Matthews and Frater (2003) op. cit.
5 Related arguments can be found in Dodgson et al. (2005).
6 Oil companies plot cumulative probability curves 'confidence curves' for the estimated NPV of oil deposits in an effort to quantify the uncertainty faced in deciding whether or not to proceed with major investments in oil extraction. These curves, derived from seismic analysis and geological patterns recognition, generate 'P90' and 'P50' and 'P10' NPV estimation points, i.e. a 90 per cent probability that the NPV is at least x, a 50 per cent probability that the NPV is at least y and a 10 per cent probability that the NPV is as high as z.
7 See Lakatos (1970).
8 There is a vast body of work in this area, most notably associated with Gary Becker's (1964) contribution entitled *Human Capital*. This tends to focus on the 'yield' from the stock of human capital with measures of educational attainment and professional experience used to estimate the quality of the stock (the greater the investment in acquiring knowledge, the greater the yield on that investment).
9 The original contribution that generated a large body of economic analyses of this issue was made by Muth (1961).
10 A useful discussion of different perspectives on ignorance and uncertainty can be found in Smithson (1998) and Smithson (2008).
11 Whilst strong criticisms have been levelled against the CAPM by academic financial economists, it is still used because it is tractable – 'generally true even if it is precisely wrong'.
12 Future and derivatives contracts are an important mechanism for hedging against uncertainty. For example electricity generators in de-regulated electricity markets used derivative contracts to hedge against unpredictability in weather that can drive spikes in the price of electricity and black-outs when demand exceeds supply.
13 Significantly, the brown coal–burning power station that has the highest thermal efficiency and the lowest carbon dioxide emissions in the world was built by a

publicly owned state utility in Germany. This was possible because it did not need to borrow the funding from the private sector and could therefore tolerate a greater level of technical and business risk (i.e. *beta*) than a privately financed solution. Once built, this 'first of a kind' (FOAK) power station has the effect of reducing *beta* for subsequent privately financed designs of this type – allowing these to achieve a level of 'bankable feasibility' that may not otherwise have existed.

14 Venture capitalists pay particular attention to scale-up risks because what works at the R&D scale can be a poor predictor of what works at a full operational scale.

15 Statements of intent and other information on this matter can be found on the official websites of the weapons laboratories, such as Los Alamos.

16 The US is currently undertaking a major upgrade of its nuclear arsenal, including re-using the physics package in the ageing B-61 nuclear weapon by placing it in a modern delivery system with highly adjustable nuclear detonation levels (not previously possible for that physics package) Lieber and Press (2011).

17 An excellent discussion of the epistemological dimension to engineering can be found in Vincenti (1990).

18 UN System of National Accounts 1993 (known as SNA93).

19 *Handbook of National Accounting: Integrated Environmental and Economic Accounting.* Joint draft guidelines issued by the United Nations, European Commission, International Monetary Fund, Organisation for Economic Co-operation and Development and the World Bank, 2003.

References

Arrow, K 1995, *Intergenerational Equity and the Rate of Discount in Long-Term Social Investment.* Paper Presented at the International Economic Association (IEA) World Congress, Tunis.

Australian Bureau of Statistics 2003, *Accounting for the Environment in the National Accounts in Environment by Numbers: Selected Articles on Australia's Environment.* Australian Bureau of Statistics, Canberra, Catalogue no. 4617.0 2003.

Becker, G 1964, *Human Capital: A Theoretical and Empirical Analysis, with Special Reference to Education.* University of Chicago Press, Chicago.

Bush, V 1945, *Science the Endless Frontier.* Report to the President by Vannevar Bush, Director of the Office of Scientific Research and Development, United States Government Printing Office, Washington, July.

Churchman, C W 1967, Wicked problems. *Management Science.* vol. 14, no. 4, pp. B141–B142.

Cooper, R G 2001, *Winning at New Products: Accelerating the Process from Idea to Launch,* 3rd edition. Perseus Books, Reading, MA.

Dodgson, M, Gann, D and Salter, A 2005, *Think, Play, Do: Innovation, Technology and Organisation.* Oxford University Press, Oxford.

Hayek, F A 1967, The theory of complex phenomena, in F A Hayek (ed.), *Studies in Philosophy, Politics and Economics,* Routledge & Kegan Paul, London, pp. 22–42.

Kirzner, I 1973, *Competition and Entrepreneurship.* University of Chicago Press, Chicago.

Kirzner, I 1979, *Perception, Opportunity and Profit.* University of Chicago Press, Chicago.

Knight, F 1921, *Risk, Uncertainty and Profit.* H Mifflin, Boston.

Lakatos, I 1970, Falsification and the methodology of scientific research programmes, in I Lakatos & A Musgrave (eds.), *Criticism and the Growth of Knowledge,* Cambridge University Press, Cambridge, pp. 91–196.

94 Uncertainty, risk manager of last resort

Lieber, K A and Press, D G 2011, Obama's nuclear upgrade: The case for modernizing America's nukes. *Foreign Affairs* (July), online postscript.

Matthews, M 2006, *Managing Uncertainty and Risk in Science, Innovation and Preparedness: Why Public Policy Should Pay More Attention to Geopolitical and Financial Considerations.* Federation of Australian Scientific and Technological Societies (FASTS) Policy Discussion Paper No. 1/2006, Canberra.

Matthews, M 2009, *Giving Preparedness a Central Role in Science and Innovation Policy.* Discussion Paper Commissioned by the Federation of Australian Scientific and Technological Societies (FASTS), Canberra.

Matthews, M and Frater, R 2003, *Creating and Exploiting Intangible Networks: How Radiata was Able to Improve Its Odds of Success in the Risky Process of Innovating.* Case Study Prepared for the Science and Innovation Mapping System Taskforce, Canberra.

Muth, J F 1961, Rational expectations and the theory of price movements. *Econometrica.* vol. 29, pp. 315–335.

Nowotny, H 2015, *The Cunning of Uncertainty.* Policy Press, Cambridge.

Office of Management and Budget (OMD) 2016, *Analytical Perspectives, Budget of the United States Government, Fiscal Year 2017.* Office of Management and Budget, White House, Washington, DC.

Smithson, M 1998, *Ignorance and Uncertainty: Emerging Paradigms.* Springer, New York, NY.

Smithson, M 2008, The many faces and masks of uncertainty, in G Bammer & M Smithson (eds.), *Uncertainty and Risk: Multidisciplinary Perspectives*, Earthscan Publications Ltd, London, pp. 13–25.

Stern, N 2006, *Stern Review on the Economics of Climate Change.* HM Treasury & Cabinet Office, London.

Stokes, D 1996, *Pasteur's Quadrant: Basic Science and Technological Innovation.* Brookings Institution, Washington, DC.

Thompson, S 2000, *Making Use of National and Sectoral Balance Sheets.* Paper Prepared for the 26th General Conference of the International Association for Research in Income and Wealth, Cracow, Poland, 27th August to 2nd September.

Vincenti, W 1990, *What Engineers Know and How They Know It.* Johns Hopkins Press, Baltimore.

4 Concepts for facilitating the transition

This chapter considers the concepts and tools that could provide a useful practical contribution to implementing adaptive governance by improving the ability to experiment, learn and adapt when formulating the delivering policy. The chapter focuses upon exploring the extent to which Bayesian inference might provide a practical basis for delivering the required decision-support information. The particular focus is on contemporary signal processing and machine learning that are based upon Bayesian principles that have been developed in a manner that makes them especially well suited to fast decision-making. In what follows, the term 'signal processing' is used to refer both to 'signal detection' and other technical methods associated with the mathematics of information that are concerned with error identification and error reduction in the transmission and receipt of signals. One striking feature of these technical methods is that they have been developed to cope with ambiguity, uncertainty and subtle patterns. They achieve this capability by focusing on the continuous improvement of methods for identifying signals hidden in noise and by a strong emphasis on measuring the prevalence of test errors (false positives and false negatives) in this process – with the aim of reducing these diagnostic error rates in the future. Whilst these attributes of signal processing are hidden to non-specialists they provide the foundations of the information age – the Internet, smart machines, wi-fi, telecommunications etc. This foundation rests upon error identification and error rectification. When information is communicated it can be corrupted. Signal processing methods, based in turn on the mathematics of information, allow this corruption to be identified and eliminated (if necessary by requiring repeated transmissions). Indeed, the technological foundation of the Internet lies in the ability to break up large amounts of information into small (duplicated) packets and send them via multiple pathways to be re-combined exactly as initially sent. The information age is founded upon learning and adaptation in error management.

These signal processing methods had their genesis in national security work (starting in the Second World War) and, in various guises, are still used within that community. In fact, for an area of work that has attracted such scorn from some statisticians, the volume of Bayesian work carried out in areas related to the military is astoundingly high. For instance, the Pentagon's Defense Technical Information Center provides online access to a wide range of declassified

96 *Concepts for facilitating the transition*

documents. In October 2015 a key word search revealed that 9,550 documents used the term Bayesian. This military Bayesian work has a long-standing focus on challenges such as working out the best ways of learning and adapting when firing artillery and missiles – a body of work that also had its origins in the Second World War.

One fairly well-known example of this sort of learning and adaptation analysis is Kolmogorov's Second World War work in the Soviet Union which pioneered the use of artificial dispersion artillery firing algorithms as a means of discovering and reacting to the combined impacts of various atmospheric conditions (wind, air temperature gradients etc.) that distort a unition's trajectory's. Rather than attempting to hit a target by repeatedly aiming directly at the target and attempting to adjust the trajectory in response to the observed pattern of misses (a suggestive metaphor for contemporary target-driven policy interventions), Kolmogorov's approach was based upon deliberately firing a pattern randomly around the target and responding to that richer set of observations on the outcomes. Using this spray of artificially dispersed shots generated more useful information for learning and adaptation than the narrower data generated by repeated attempts to hit the target.

There are other examples of this use of randomly generated 'tests' of a complex situation as a basis for developing learning and adaptation heuristics. They all share a Bayesian emphasis on the analytical value of using imprecise, arbitrary or random assumptions to kick off learning and adaptation processes that, over time, can converge on a workable solution to a highly complex problem without the need to tightly specify all relevant variables. In modern game theory terms this is referred to as a 'game against nature'. Indeed, some aspects of this mathematical work from the Second World War are still classified military secrets. The fact that much of the initial work on this highly practical use of Bayesian methods took place under a blanket of secrecy during the Cold War is pertinent to the way in which methodological arguments between the pro- and anti-Bayesian camps developed in the post-war period. Those arguments tended to focus on applications of statistical analysis that did not require urgency in decision-making or the necessity to make decisions when there is sparse, ambiguous and rapidly changing data. Indeed, there is a strong emphasis in classical tests of statistical significance on repeatability: experimental/sampling cycles that take place in a steady-state.

The parallels between this sort of use of Bayesian thinking by the military and public policy in general are striking. One way of summarising this parallel is that in an uncertain and risky world it is preferable to make decisions that are broadly correct but precisely wrong but to be very well positioned to learn and adapt in response to observed outcomes. This contrasts with the tendency in governance over the last few decades to define very tightly defined objectives and to develop programmes designed to deliver these objectives with minimal variance against targets and milestones allowed. The latter stance, in effect, places the burden of proof 'internally' onto the quality of the design of the programme rather than, as in Kolmogorov's approach, allowing the complex non-predictable and hard-to-analyse realities of the external situation to be treated as an experimental laboratory that yields useful information without requiring the intricacies of cause and effect to be pre-specified. If reality is complex and prone to evolution and unpredictability, yet decisions need to be made very quickly, then why not treat reality as a black box in analytical terms and simply test it with a range of inputs and track and react to the outputs observed?

One insight from the military work using Bayesian thinking is *elimination*. Hypotheses (e.g. the location of a missing submarine or an inert nuclear weapon dripped by mistake) are ruled out if they have little evidence to support them. This allows resources to be concentrated on more plausible hypotheses in an evolutionary manner. These approaches are still used on a regular basis – including in recent searches for a missing commercial airliner.

The remainder of this chapter takes a closer look at how these approaches to learning and adaptation might be configured so that they can be used as a more general approach to implementing adaptive governance – in so doing better equipping governments to cope with substantive uncertainties and quantifiable risks.

The intriguing history of Bayesian inference[1]

Bayesian inference, and the concept of probability used, differs in marked ways from the alternative (and more established) *sampling theory* approach (sometimes referred to as frequentalist, classical or orthodox probability). In the *sampling theory* definition, probability is treated as the long-run relative frequency of the *observed* occurrence of an event. The sample set can be either a sequence of events through time or a set of identically prepared systems (Loredo, 1990). In contrast, Bayesians treat probability (in effect) as the relative *plausibility* of propositions when knowledge is incomplete.

The term 'plausibility' is used here because Bayesian statisticians and classical sampling statisticians use the term 'probability' in different ways – generating semantic confusion. To a Bayesian, the concept of probability refers to the state of knowledge, expressed in terms of the degree to which different competing hypotheses may be correct given the available evidence. To a classical statistician, probability refers to the observed frequency of different events. In other words, one definition of probability refers to hypotheses given available data and the other, data independent of hypotheses. Given this semantic confusion it is preferable to avoid use of the term 'probability' in this context.

There has been a long and often vitriolic methodological argument between frequentists and Bayesians. In essence, frequentists assert that useful information can only be gleaned from situations in which there is a low probability of random processes generating the observed data. This threshold of statistical significance is usually (if arbitrarily) defined as a probability 0.05, with particle physics using a much higher probability threshold of five standard deviations, which (assuming normally distributed data) means a probability of around 0.0000005 that random processes generated the data captured to indicate a major discovery.

Leading frequentists, notably Ronald Fisher, never questioned the usefulness of Bayesian inference if any subjectivity in initially assumed likelihoods is removed

98   *Concepts for facilitating the transition*

from the picture. It is the subjective aspect of Bayesian inference that has been the cause of this controversy – for frequentists this subjectivity is unacceptable and not scientific. In a public policy context there are two issues at stake. First, that of whether introducing elements of subjectivity into an analysis contradicts scientific principles and, second (irrespective of scientific merit per se), whether subjectivity is a problem in public policy. The first issue was discussed at greater length in chapter three, which stressed that the all-important creative processes involved in hypothesis generation can be highly subjective in nature – what matters is the objectivity in their empirical testing. Thus, subjectivity does have a role in scientific endeavours – but as the seedbed for hypothesis generation rather than in regards to hypothesis testing. This requirement for creativity is acknowledged in the philosophy of science but does not receive much attention; far more attention is paid to the importance of testing these hypotheses (most notably in Karl Popper's work). As regards public policy, subjectivity is clearly important – political leaders must make decisions when there is no, or insufficient, evidence to articulate a 'scientific' basis for making those decisions. Consequently, the more we over-emphasise the 'objectivity' engendered by evidence-based public policy we put at risk our capacity of conjecture and speculate in ways that creatively generate new hypotheses. The utility of evidence stems from the creativity embodied in the hypotheses that are being tested to produce this evidence. Evidence is not simply an accumulation of data – as some in government seem to assume. Because these are the hypotheses that shape future interventions we compound the risks to effective governance by over-stating the utility of evidence in the face of substantive uncertainties about the future. If the world did not change very much from year to year then this would be less problematic. However, one aim of good public policy is to facilitate change (innovation, social progress, advances in health and medicine, improvements in national security etc.). Even if we disregard factors that drive change that cannot be controlled, there is an inconsistency in the way in which evidence-based policymaking is approached: namely that effective public policy will by definition seek to change circumstances – hence reducing the value for decision-making of relying on 'robust evidence' from the past. Effective public policy drives up the social rate of discount through multiple pathways (the social rate of discount is a concept used in economics to capture the lower value that people place in things that may happen in the future, the lower this value at a given time in the future the greater the social rate of discount).

The ways in which people and organisations themselves learn and adapt in response to their understanding of these policy interventions is of course an important aspect of this discount rate increase phenomenon. As familiarity with an intervention grows the intended subjects of that intervention are able to experiment, learn and adapt in order to get what they want from the intervention – which may not be what the intervention was intended to achieve. Whatever the evidence was that was used to design the intervention, then that evidence may become less relevant and useful as implementation takes place – 'learning-by-undoing'.

Terrorism provides an illustration of this issue. To a frequentist statistician if the data exhibits highly random behaviour then this is simply noise – there is

Concepts for facilitating the transition 99

no information present and no possibility of determining statistical significance. However, one terrorist strategy is to deliberately carry out random acts of terror on the assumption that this very randomness maximises the degree of terror engendered – and through that delivers the objectives sought. In this case, the randomness is clearly of policy significance because this (deliberate) randomness impacts directly on the degree of precision and anticipation possible in counter-terrorism strategy and tactics. To a policymaker, the statistician who dismisses data on a situation because it exhibits randomness is less helpful than a statistician who recognises that this very randomness constitutes the mode of attack, and who then proceeds to focus on possible weak signals of impending (random) attacks and/or the most useful responses to these random attacks. This aspect of frequentist thinking can be dangerous if threat management is based simply on sampling theory.

For example the random testing of shipping containers for various types of unwanted contents can be useful as a means of confirming that there are no significant levels of threat (i.e. attempted incursions) but, to use the terms articulated in this book, this testing does little to reduce the potential for nasty surprises to occur. Consequently, random testing (of the type we see at airports) is a reasonable way of confirming that things are okay, but it is not a good way of countering threats. When there are threats present the only way of addressing them is to quickly move from random sampling to more thorough checks (the safest being 100 per cent testing).

The more familiar one becomes with the ways in which Bayesian inference was used in the Second World War, usefully documented by McGrayne (2011), the clearer the impact of the fact that much of this work was classified state secrets seems to be. The range of examples of useful applications of Bayesian methods discussed by McGrayne gives us two main messages. First, the military in particular have been receptive to these methods because the Bayesian updating of estimates is so important as a part of rapid learning and adaptation. The ability to eliminate certain hypotheses as new evidence becomes available is a particularly important part of this updating process (e.g. search areas in a maritime context). Second, the potential benefits of using Bayesian methods more generally in governance face the major impediment that whilst the basic principle of 'updating' is easily grasped the reality of being exposed to the mathematics involved in the bulk of Bayesian analyses is a major impediment to uptake. As we will consider later on, this mathematical impediment stems from the way in which most applications of Bayesian methods use conditional probability. There are approaches that are easier to understand for non-specialists and hence it is these latter approaches that create the potential for a more practical version of Bayesian methods for use by non-specialists.

Figure 4.1 explains the basic (and very simple) principle behind Bayesian analysis, namely that we are able to update the assumed odds of something happening when new information is obtained. The new information may either confirm that the initially assumed odds should be retained, or may lead us to revise these odds. For the purposes of relating Bayesian inference to the policy cycle, the simple equation expressing new odds and a product of the old odds

Linear expression of Bayesian inference

New odds   =   Old odds   +   Analysis of new information

Circular/learning loop based expression of Bayesian inference

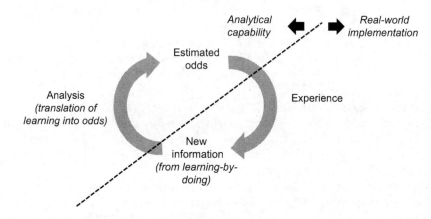

Figure 4.1 A Bayesian learning loop

plus the analysis of new information is re-framed as a circular learning process. Estimated odds, via experience, generate new information which when analysed allows estimated odds to be updated. This learning loop combines a real-world implementation phase (experiments in effect) with an analytical phase. Everything that government does is, in effect, in the implementation phase and consequently an experiment (either explicitly or implicitly). However, implementation/experimentation activities may not necessarily involve the new information being identified, collated and analysed. If the latter does not happen then the odds cannot be updated and, in effect, there has been a missed opportunity to learn (and manage risk in particular).

From this perspective, governments' monitoring, evaluation and learning (MEL) activities will have the greatest utility when the information obtained as a result of experience in implementing a policy intervention is related back to an initial (uncertainty and risk-based) assumption of the odds of success assumed for the intervention.[2] If MEL measures are not based on an explicit recognition of uncertainty and risk (i.e. the odds of success are not made explicit) then it is unlikely that useful learning will be captured *and used* even if useful learning takes place. This is because uncertainty and risk are marginalised rather than centralised in the analysis.

One major problem is that current approaches to MEL in the public sector favour firm targets that cannot be fudged ('Key Performance Indicators' or KPIs). These are often treated as counts of things happening – measures that can be verified as true or false. For example people who have managed overseas development projects report that government donors tend to prefer projects that meet their KPIs even though they generate little benefits compared to projects that do appear to generate benefits but do not meet their contractually specified KPIs – which characteristically become outdated as a result of accumulating experience. In contrast, a Bayesian implementation of the policy learning cycle would provide an alternative basis for MEL methods by more clearly specifying at the start the uncertainties and risks involved in delivering a policy intervention and (where relevant) targeted by that policy intervention. As a result, the actual outcomes from an intervention can be tracked as updated calculations of the odds that competing hypotheses are correct (calculated odds that incorporate uncertainties as reduced odds). Chapter five covers these issues in greater detail.

The next diagram (figure 4.2) provides an annotated version of the logical construction of Bayesian inference if conditional probabilities are used – and as conventionally presented. 'H' represents a hypothesis, 'P' the calculated probability that the hypothesis is correct and 'E' the evidence available to make that calculation. In essence, the calculations test hypotheses against new data on the basis of the previous estimated likelihood that a hypothesis is correct (given previously available data) combined with the theory-based likelihood that the new evidence would still be observed if that hypothesis were correct.[3]

That part of the calculation is then adjusted by the likelihood that the evidence being used was actually generated by the assumed model of the process

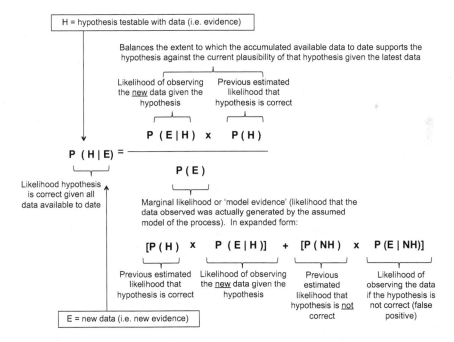

Figure 4.2 The conditional probability formula for Bayes rule

102   *Concepts for facilitating the transition*

to which the hypothese(s) relate. This includes a specific calculation relating to the impact of false positive results – an aspect that gives Bayesian methods a particular relevance to medicine. This latter element (the denominator in the equation) reflects a balance of likelihoods (including the likelihood of a false positive result) that in practice is usually complex to calculate. This aspect limited the application of Bayesian inference to simple problems until high-speed computing made it possible to calculate complex combinations of circumstances in the denominator, see Lilford and Braunholtz (1996). Indeed, if one reads Laplace's original work in astronomy, the first mathematical application of what we now call Bayesian inference (for a time known as 'inverse probability'), the sophistication of the calculations developed and then used with the very limited observational data then available is humbling. This mathematical sophistication acts as a substitute for the very sparse data (seeking to squeeze as much insight as possible from so little data) – a very different state of affairs than today. The complexity associated with calculating the denominator tends to be associated with extremely large technical variations in how Bayesian methods are implemented. As Scott Ferson comments, Bayesian approaches are rather like snowflakes in the sense that each one is unique (Ferson, 2005). This heterogeneity makes it hard for non-specialists to adopt these methods in a public policy context – and reinforces the importance of developing more standardised and simplified approaches for use in public policy.

Fortunately, as Gigerenzer (2002), drawing upon Kleiter (1994) and Aitchison and Dunsmore (1975), has stressed, Bayesian inference can be simplified if conditional probabilities are avoided and the raw 'natural frequencies' of data are used instead – an approach that is particularly useful for bringing clarity to the incidence of false positives and false negatives in diagnosis.[4] Rather than the complex formula commonly required when conditional probabilities are used, the natural frequencies version of the Bayesian equation for calculating the likelihood that a particular positive test result actually means the condition is present can be collapsed to a simpler ratio which expresses the observed True Positive Rate as a proportion of the sum of the True Positive Rate and the False Positive rate (we return to simplified versions of Bayes Rule shortly).[5] When this simple natural frequency expression of Bayes Rule is used, it is easy to grasp and intuitive. Indeed, experimental work in psychology supports the hypothesis that human cognition is 'hard wired' to deal with natural frequency data and, as a result, finds it harder to interpret probability-based expressions of the same phenomena (Gigerenzer and Hoffrage, 1995). Drawing upon Feynman (1967), Gigerenzer and Hoffrage (1995) also stress that the ways in which mathematically identical statements are communicated (such as conditional probability and natural frequency expressions of Bayes Rule) can affect interpretation – and as Feynman suggested the potential to develop creative responses. Feynman's famous use of diagrams to explain otherwise highly complex mathematical challenges is one example of putting this principle into practice. This latter aspect is of particular importance in a public policy environment: how we present evidence influences how creatively we are able to react to that evidence. In my own engagement with government

Concepts for facilitating the transition 103

I have found that using the metaphor of the seen and unseen valley to express the distinction between the evidence that we currently have and the conjectures that we must make over the evidence that we don't yet have gains more traction than attempting to get the same message across in more technical terms.

Perhaps the most famous demonstration of the power of Bayesian inference is found early on in the mathematical development of the techniques used in astronomy – via the seminal work of Laplace in the eighteenth century. Laplace sought to estimate the most plausible estimate of the mass of the planet Saturn based on the (limited) astronomical data available at the time (the observed perturbations of the orbits of Jupiter and Saturn) combined with other commonsense assumptions that imposed limits on what the mass could be (large enough not to lose its rings but not large enough to de-stabilise the solar system as a whole). He estimated that the most plausible mass of Saturn would be 1/3512 of the solar mass and specified a probability of 0.99991 that the actual mass would be within a margin of error of 1 per cent of that estimated value. The addition of another 150 years of astronomical data (and considerable additional expense and effort) improved this margin of error estimate from 1 to 0.63 per cent (Loredo, 1990). This is a powerful illustration of the power (and very high cost-effectiveness) of the use of Bayesian inference to interpret available but incomplete information in order to produce the most plausible estimate possible at that point in time.

Decision-making in public policy shares the key characteristics exhibited by this aspect of Laplace's work: it is necessary to work with incomplete data, combined with a range of assumptions in order to assess a situation in a manner that can inform timely decision-making. The Bayesian emphasis on estimating the relative plausibility of different hypotheses is well suited to this environment. Arguably, orthodox sample theory–based definitions of probability and tests of statistical significance are better suited to an academic research context because they encourage continued investigation and debate over technical subtleties (especially as regards the wide choices to make over methods to test hypotheses) without the 'pinch point' associated with the need to make a decision *now* on the basis of everything that we believe we know and understand. The Bayesian approach also recognises that a simpler model should be preferred to a more complex model (this Occam's Razor aspect is built into the calculations via the denominator, which effectively treats greater complexity as an increased likelihood of a false positive test result).

The distinction between sampling theory and Bayesian approaches has resulted in a long debate between the two camps characterised by misunderstood concepts and underpinning philosophical assumptions (see Jaynes, 1957, 1984). The orthodox stance tests hypotheses in a discrete manner (not relative to each other) and on the basis of the likelihood that a particular null hypothesis of no treatment effect can be safely rejected as being very unlikely to have been produced randomly. The standard threshold for stating statistical significance in the social sciences is that there is a less than 5 per cent probability that random events could have produced the phenomena captured in the data.[6]

104 Concepts for facilitating the transition

Forward-looking forecasts and predictions may then (if required) be derived from model(s) that pass these significance thresholds.[7]

In contrast, Bayesian analysis works with the data that we actually have without requiring it to be treated as a random sample of a larger unobserved yet theoretically possible dataset in order to determine the degree of support for a hypothesis. The use of Bayesian methods in fields such as astrophysics (where there may be a very limited number of observations of some very hard-to-detect sub-atomic particles such as neutrinos) has helped to counter-balance the view that Bayesian approaches are reliant on subjective assumptions (Loredo, 1990). Significantly, in 2006 the US Food and Drug Administration (FDA) published guidelines (published in draft form in 2010) for the use of Bayesian inference in testing medical devices. The FDA guidance stressed the importance of using Bayesian prior distributions (i.e. initially assumed odds in the learning cycle) that are based only upon previous Randomised Control Trial (RCT) studies rather than less robust sources (Food and Drug Administration, 2010). This approach removes the subjectivity objection of the anti-Bayesian camp who, from an academic perspective, have understandable reservations about the robustness of results that are based in part upon prior assumptions.

The final key point about Bayesian inference is that it provides a direct measure of the relative plausibility of different competing hypotheses – simply by comparing the different values of the Bayesian calculation with the latest information available. A similar measure of the *Weight of Evidence* (known as a Ban and its log derivative the Deciban) was used to particular effect by Alan Turing and colleagues in efforts to break the German Enigma code in the Second World War, see Good (1979). Turing did not explicitly base his code breaking work on Bayesian inference – when asked by a colleague whether he was using Bayesian inference he reportedly responded 'I suppose so' (Gillies, 1990). Although, as Gillies argues, technical details of the approach adopted by Turing (which was a classified government secret for many years) suggest that it is closer to Popper's concept of the *Severity of a Test* (Popper, 1934). The concept of the *Severity of a Test* asserts that the preferred test of hypotheses should be the severity of the hypothesis tests applied and not simply the number of corroborating instances that have been counted.

Turing's metric proved itself to be very useful as a numerical guide to which decryption solution(s) had the greatest promise given available (highly ambiguous and uncertain) data. Such a metric is especially useful as a research resource allocation tool because it provides a clear indicator of the relative plausibility of different explanations that can be updated as new data becomes available (in Turing's case on a daily basis). As such, this kind of summary metric provides a particularly useful approach to the policy learning process. Turing made a conscious decision to use the odds in favour of competing hypotheses because this provided an easier conceptual link to the available evidence – literally as the relative 'weight' of this evidence in favour and against specific hypotheses. In effect, Turing developed a system for placing bets on the relative appeal of different solutions given the sparse information available. These bets were used to allocate staff time on the following day – resulting in an adaptive learning process with a high clock speed. We return to consider the best way of implementing this type of hypothesis test in a governance context in chapter six.

The evolution of signal processing and machine learning methods from their Bayesian roots

Writing shortly after the end of the Second World War, Claude Shannon distinguished between information and uncertainty (defined as entropy) and expressed the value of new information that might be received in terms of the assumed likelihood of an event happening *and* being observed. In that framework, which has been incredibly useful in information technology, the less likely an event is assumed to be – the greater the information gain *if* it is observed (Shannon, 1948).[8] When plotted as the relationship between the probability and entropy coefficient, Shannon entropy describes a curve that reaches its maximum value when there are even odds (a probability of 0.5) of observing a specific symbol. Entropy declines as this probability increases and decreases and is zero when the probability is zero or is 1.0. This relationship between probability of occurrence and entropy is graphed in figure 4.3.

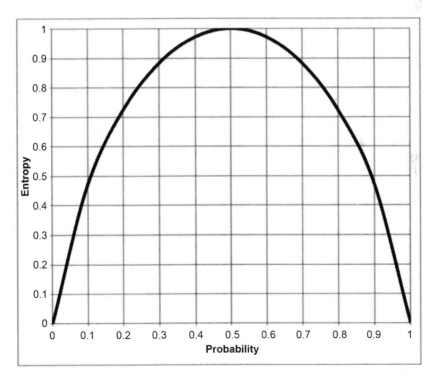

Figure 4.3 Shannon entropy

106 Concepts for facilitating the transition

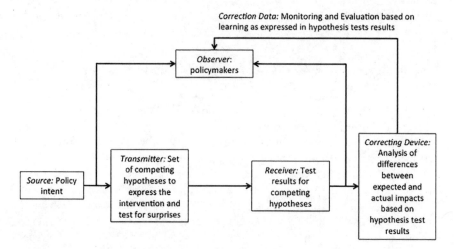

Figure 4.4 Shannon error correction model framed in a public policy context

Turing and Shannon were given opportunities to share ideas (rather than collaborate on a more formal basis) when Turing was sent across the Atlantic to be co-located with Shannon for a while (McGrayne, 2011). The Shannon model is conceptually appealing in a public policy context (particularly in a risk management sense) because it highlights the importance of noise and error identification and correction. If noise and error correction functions are not effective, then the signal received may not be the same as the signal sent and decisions may consequently be based on incorrect information.

Of course, a real policy context can be far more complex than a communications or encryption system in the sense that there are many more dimensions, each of which is subject to uncertainty. But it is in regards to the methods for handling this complexity that information theory can be useful in a policy context. This is because the mathematical solutions make use of complex multidimensionality but seek to reduce that complexity to the levels that calculations can be made.

Information theory, in its practical application, tells us that an especially effective way of handling the noise and error correction (adaptation) loop is to introduce a specially designed error detection signal. By monitoring distortions to that error detection signal (specifically designed to reveal potential errors), it is possible to correct the signal carrying the information – thus minimising transmission errors.

The use of a deliberately introduced error correction signal played a key role in the development of modern wi-fi communication. The potential for the wi-fi signal to be disrupted by both static and dynamic factors in a room (chairs, tables and people moving around) is great. An error correction signal provides the basis for making very fast mathematical adjustments to the main signal in such a way that these errors are reduced. Whilst each packet of substantive information is checked for integrity this slows down the communication rate, hence sophisticated methods able to pre-empt and/or indicate the best way of rectifying this signal corruption are important (Matthews and Frater, 2003). Figure 4.4 contains a version of Shannon's error correction model adjusted to align with a public policy context.

In a public policy context, this corresponds to a failure to understand why what actually happened when a policy was implemented differed from what was intended to happen – and to adapt future policies on the basis of that analysis. In Shannon's terms, this represents operating with a higher level of entropy in the policy process than would otherwise be the case (i.e. if learning opportunities had not been overlooked).

Shannon's use of the concept of entropy in the Second World War had a very specific national security objective: the need to be able to calculate the minimum volume of information required to encrypt a message given the statistical frequencies with which different letters are expected to appear for linguistic reasons. Shannon entropy is therefore an expression of statistical uncertainty based only on available information (or noise) rather than being treated as a sample of additional but unknown data (as in frequentalist/sampling theory–based statistics).

Figure 4.5 contains the basic analytical taxonomy used in signal processing and machine learning. This is sometimes (usefully) referred to as a 'confusion matrix' in artificial intelligence because it draws out the ways in which binary test results can be wrong and, in combination, contradictory and, hence, cause confusion. In a machine learning context, based on the use of algorithms, this confusion paralyses learning and adaptation. In a policy context, the impact on human judgement can be equally paralysing, or can lead to decisions being made that

Test result	Condition assessment	
	Yes	No
Positive	(a) True positive rate Referred to in statistics as test **'Sensitivity'**	(b) False positive rate
Negative	(c) False negative rate	(d) True negative rate Referred to in statistics as test **'Specificity'**

Figure 4.5 The Confusion Matrix

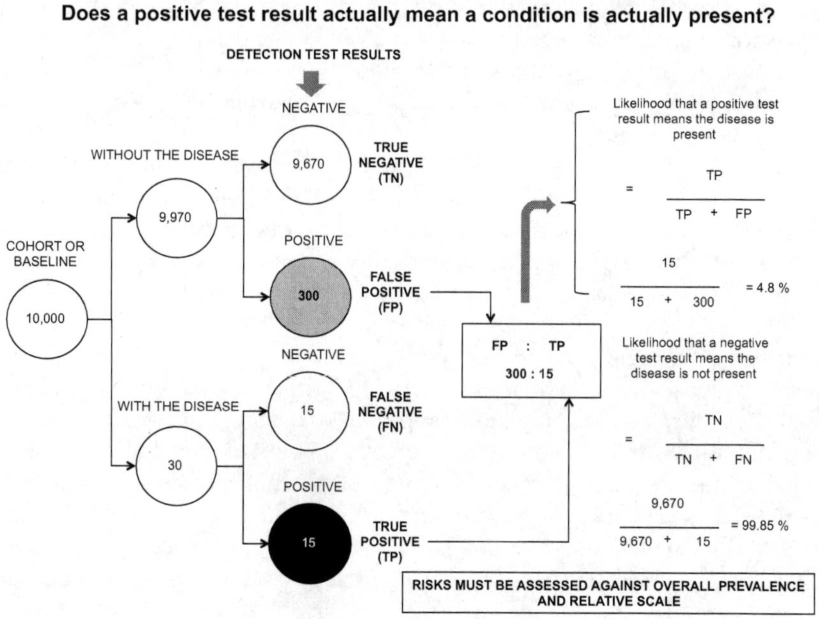

108 *Concepts for facilitating the transition*

Does a positive test result actually mean a condition is actually present?

Figure 4.6 A Natural Frequency expression of Bayes Rule

arbitrarily ignore this confusion. This can lock interventions into problematic developmental pathways if not corrected at later stages.

As the confusion matrix highlights, we should prefer policy and regulatory stances (if expressed as competing hypotheses with binary answers) that maximise the true positive rate and the true negative rate and that also minimise the false positive and the false negative rates. Whenever there are false positive and false negative test results the response of the policy framework is *itself* a risk to effective policy delivery (actions may be taken that are unnecessary or actions that should be taken are not taken).

Figure 4.6 contains an illustration of the significance of test result errors in a clinical context (using data from Gigerenzer, 2002). For many people this 'natural frequency' based expression of the situation, which clearly communicates relative scale, is far easier to grasp than the standard Bayesian equation using conditional probabilities (as laid out in figure 4.2).

In presenting the data in this manner it is clear that a positive test result (in this case for colorectal cancer) means that there is only a 4.8 per cent likelihood that a particular patient actually has the condition. This is simply because the 3 per cent false positive rate (300 false positives in every 10,000 cases) results in 300 cases of false positives relative to only 15 true positives. Hence, for an individual patient one must consider the implications of this ratio of 300 false positives

Concepts for facilitating the transition 109

against 15 true positives (the odds from which favour a particular test result being a false positive). This highlights the way in which the overall prevalence of a disease in the population, combined with the rates of true and false positives (and true and false negatives) in test results, generates this gap between a naïve interpretation of a particular test result and a more thoughtful evidence-based interpretation.

Figure 4.7 contains the more conventional Bayesian expression of this same situation. Unless one is highly familiar with conditional probability (which many people working in government and in stakeholder organisations are not), then this way of calculating test sensitivity is hard to grasp. This unnecessary complexity is created by avoiding the use of natural frequencies in preference for reliance on the mathematics of conditional probability. As figure 4.8 demonstrates, the use

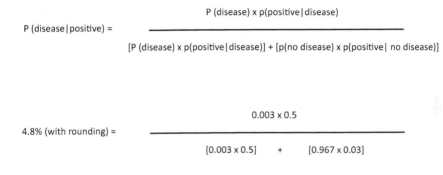

Expressing Bayes Rule using conditional probabilities makes it overly complex and hard to grasp.

Figure 4.7 Conditional probability expression of Bayes Rule

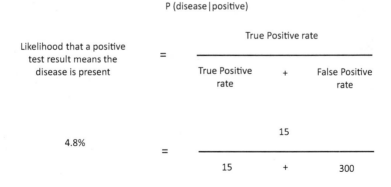

Figure 4.8 The simplified Bayes Rule

of natural frequencies makes Bayes Rule far easier to understand – it is simply the sensitivity of the test to the rate of false positives given the prevalence of a condition.

It is easy to see how this use of Bayesian signal processing and machine learning concepts (especially when expressed in natural frequency terms) provides a robust and intuitively straight-forward basis for assessing aspects of the efficiency and the effectiveness of policy interventions. The approach makes clear where problems caused by test inaccuracies lie, highlights the implications for response decisions and provides a basis for measuring historical changes in diagnostic capability. Crucially, this approach places risk-related concerns centrally in the policy process.

This issue of diagnostic capability is formally expressed in signal processing and machine learning in the following manner (see figure 4.9).

For historical reasons this is referred to as the *Receiver Operating Characteristic* curve (an ROC Curve in short). An ROC curve plots the false positive rate against the true positive rate and was originally developed to assess the abilities of radar operators in the Second World War. As a diagnostic tool, it provides a useful means of measuring the accuracy of test results in a robust and coherent manner. The version used here adds the true negative and false negative rates

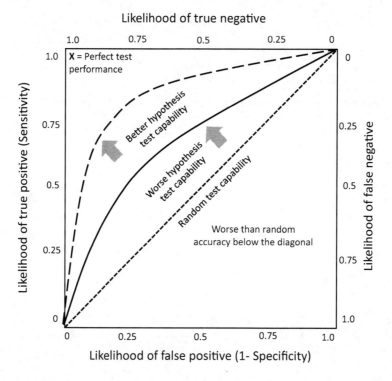

Figure 4.9 The Receiver Operating Characteristic

Concepts for facilitating the transition 111

for consistency. As such, ROC curves reflect the principles behind the use of Randomised Control Trials (RCTs) in public policy – but in a more generally applicable framework (indeed ROC curves are used in medicine to assess the adequacy of RCT results). For a useful overview of the use of ROC curves in a range of contexts see Swets et al. (2000).

The best possible performing hypothesis test lies in the top left-hand corner (a test that is 100 per cent sensitive and has a zero false positive rate). Random test results lie on the diagonal (e.g. someone guessing the toss result of a coin would expect to eventually end up at the 0.5, 0.5 point in the middle of the diagonal). Test results that are worse than random lie below that diagonal (thus providing a particularly useful diagnostic). In a public policy context, the potential to waste public funds increases the further that capabilities lie from the ideal diagnostic point in the top left-hand corner of the ROC space. Particular test capabilities can be represented as curves in this space: the further above the diagonal and the greater this curvature the more reliable the hypothesis test is. Shifts in capability over time can be reflected as shifts in these curves. The Appendix contains some more details on the ROC framework and how it can be used in a public policy context.

Figure 4.10 reinforces the potential utility of this diagnostic framework in a governance context by indicating some of the possible positions of organisational capability (strong, weak and harmful). In the latter case, test accuracy is worse than

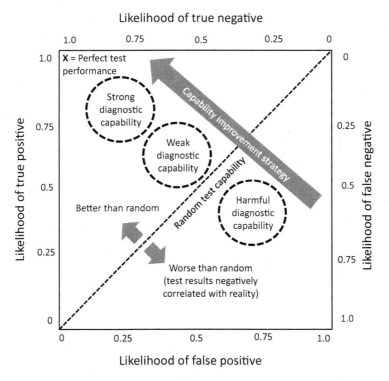

Figure 4.10 Measuring diagnostic capability in organisations

112　*Concepts for facilitating the transition*

random in the sense that test results are negatively correlated with reality. This is not as rare an occurrence in risk management (and indeed public policy in general) as many would assume. This can be caused by cherry picking 'evidence' to support political aims, weak analytical capacity that introduces errors, inappropriate uses of performance targets and other shortcomings that can distort decision-making. Consequently, the notion of worse than random diagnostic capability that emerges from this application of signal processing methods to public policy is a potentially useful tool for examining impediments and distortions to learning and adaptation. Aside from some interesting work using signal detection methods in subjectivist economics, e.g. Heiner (1986), the ROC framework is an under-exploited tool in public policy.

Applying signal processing methods to governance

As noted in chapter one, a core proposition to be explored in this book is an attempt to frame governance objectives in terms of reducing the potential for surprise – in practical terms this means minimising the extent to which an unavoidable potential for surprise is made worse by the ways in which practices, procedures and beliefs are used. The signal processing concepts and methods outlined above reflect this interest in framing capabilities in governance in relation to the extent to which they reduce or increase this potential for surprise. The greater the incidence of false positive and false negative diagnostic test results, i.e. the further away from the top left-hand corner of the ROC plot that organisations' capability lies – the greater the potential for nasty surprises. Worse than random diagnostic performance can have a particularly damaging effect on the risk amplification ratio.

Drawing upon this key insight from information theory, this perspective on organisational capability can be expressed in the following ratio:

$$\text{Risk amplification} = \frac{\text{Achieved potential for surprise}}{\text{Unavoidable potential for surprise}}$$

This simple ratio tells us that governments face a range of complex and unavoidable factors that can surprise them.

Usefully, risk is defined in a manner aligned with the most recent incarnation of the international risk management standard ISO31000: 2009 as 'uncertainty over objectives'.

This simple equation also provides another potentially useful concept and measure:

$$\text{Governance Entropy} = \text{Achieved potential for surprise} \\ - \text{Unavoidable potential for surprise}$$

This expression of the relationship highlights the ways in which the amplification of risk stemming from the mind-sets, practices and procedures of governance can be viewed as a decrease in the capacity to anticipate events, resulting in an increased

Concepts for facilitating the transition 113

potential for surprise. In this sense, governance entropy is an expression of the well-understood tendency for bureaucracies to self-organise around internal interests and incentives rather than generate public value outside of governance. In this case, the result is an increased potential for nasty surprises. Of course, worse than random diagnostic capability, such as politically motivated misrepresentations of understanding such as the deliberate fabrication of security intelligence information, can seriously increase the potential for surprise above the unavoidable level.

Consequently, this risk amplification ratio provides a clear high-level measure of both current capability challenges in governance and a basis for planning future improvements in capability and assessing the progress made. The simplicity of a bird's-eye-view metric of this type is important because one can easily get lost in the complexity and detail of real governance processes and procedures – approaches that seem to amplify rather than simplify complexity. These very detailed methods can, in effect, come across as noise that conceals the signal.

The risk amplification ratio is proposed as a *heuristic* (i.e. means of facilitating learning) rather than as a definitively testable proposition. As a heuristic, it helps to focus attention on the ways in which emerging events can create nasty surprises for decision-makers – nasty surprises that are made worse by the choices over risk management methodologies; assumed statistical distributions are other factors that can compromise an organisations' ability to handle uncertainties and risks (assumptions that can impact on diagnostic test accuracy). In line with Austrian/subjectivist economic thinking summarised in chapter two, the heuristic does not pretend that the unavoidable potential for surprise can be measured in any definitive sense. It simply recognises the reality that whatever the future throws up as regards nasty surprises there will be better and worse ways of being prepared for these surprises or reacting to them.

Given this subjective aspect, one useful feature of the heuristic is that it can allow for situations in which an organisation adopts a specific risk management approach, puts effort into ensuring compliance with that approach and, as a result of the assumptions made, ends up having to deal with a nasty surprise when things happen that were not considered in that risk management framework. Compliance with standards and guidelines alone is not a sufficient criterion for reducing the potential for nasty surprises. Restricting risk management to compliance can mean that weak signals of looming problems may be missed and that the range of assumptions made in any specific risk management approach can result in aspects of risk being overlooked. This is an aspect in which the deliberate generation of 'what if' hypotheses can play a useful role in reducing the potential for nasty surprises. However, if this is to happen then it not only needs to be allowed to happen it needs to be encouraged to happen. This sort of 'red team' activity does happen in the national security community, mainly because the consequences of failing to do this can be so terrible that it is worth bearing the additional cost of such activities.

The challenge outside of the national security domain, and especially in times of austerity in the public sector, is that red team and related activities need methodologies that make them cost-effective – and to be demonstrated as such. This is why this form of heuristic based on the concept of the amplification of

114 *Concepts for facilitating the transition*

risk can be useful. It focuses attention on the importance of both generating 'what if' hypotheses and on developing faster and more cost-effective means of formulating and testing these hypotheses.

To provide a realistic example, a government or airline might decide to implement a specific security standard to attempt to protect against a terrorist threat. Expert advice, with an eye on cost burdens, may use statistical data to justify various 'cut off' criteria designed to minimise security compliance costs. These will characteristically relate to what are deemed to be relatively unlikely events because they are rare or non-existent in experience to date and are judged to continue to be unlikely in the future. Risk matrices are commonly used to summarise this sort of information and assumptions (we return to a discussion of the problems with using risk matrices as a 'where the buck stops' methodology shortly). Clearly, the first principle is to avoid being transparent about what these assumptions are as this makes it easy for adversaries to target their threats. This can be very difficult when security risks are approached as a collective compliance exercise because the standards and guidelines become well known. A second principle, which in part can help to reduce the risks of these standards and guidelines becoming known to adversaries and being used to target threats is to try to avoid fixing the rules over what is not scrutinised. Some deliberately introduced random variation in where these exclusion boundaries are drawn on a day-to-day basis can be useful here. A third principle is of course to try to break whatever the system is to identify weak spots.

However, despite the commonsense nature of these ploys, something of a paradox is encountered in studying actual practice: the risk management as compliance norm can dominate behaviour and as a result amplify risks by engendering a false sense of security that avoids putting adequate effort into the three approaches noted above. One highly plausible explanation for this norm is simply that the prevailing public sector management ethos used outside of the national security community is not well suited to facilitating the development and testing of any types of hypothesis as an explicit part of the policy cycle. The intelligence cycle, in which senior policymakers can issue requests for intelligence gathering and analysis in response to their concerns, is well suited to public policy in general (provided that it is done honestly). However, the required ethos and methodologies for testing hypotheses (which does happen in security intelligence) simply do not exist on a sufficient scale in the general public policy domain. This methodological deficit problem can spillover into the national security community due to the pervasive nature of this norm.

This is why a risk amplification ratio, framed as a heuristic can be a useful counter-balance to such a norm and the complacency that it can engender. The risk amplification heuristic encourages a more explicit and forthright effort to develop approaches to risk in the public sector that can mitigate the harmful aspects of compliance culture–based risk management stances. Those who take the initiative and demonstrate the creativity required to probe and test for weaknesses in mind-sets and various technical assumptions are more likely to

Concepts for facilitating the transition 115

be valued and rewarded when there is an over-arching heuristic designed to draw attention to the consequences of complacency. Just as with Kolmorgov's tactic of the artificial (random) dispersion in artillery fire that is able to reveal how unobserved complex interactions distort an intended trajectory, in so doing increasing the ability to learn and adapt in hitting a precise target, so too the encouragement of 'dispersed thinking' in approaching uncertainties and risks can increase the likelihood of achieving useful outcomes in public policy more generally – but only if this exploration is tracked and rewarded.

From this perspective, the use of risk matrices (which relate the likelihood of occurrence to the consequences of occurrence), while useful in some settings, can also increase the potential for nasty surprises, and hence amplify risk.[9] There are five reasons for this concern. First, the matrices specifically downplay low probability and high consequence outcomes. The 'red zones', or the areas that score highest, are in the high probability and consequence categories. While this is fine in itself, it generally shifts attention from the outcomes that are worthy of considerable attention. Second, the matrices always result in 'range compression' (Cox, 2008). In one category or box, for example the designated range in probability measure may range from, say, 0 to 20 per cent. The problem here is that for many especially high consequence outcomes, a change in probability from 10 to 15 per cent of a given outcome can be crucial. But this distinction is simply buried in the given range or box being considered. Third, the ranges themselves do not always map out in symmetric boxes (e.g. 20 per cent blocks), and this can cause confusion over range intervals and what is being measured. Fourth, a lack of a 'common language' often causes misunderstanding. Categories in the matrix designated as 'catastrophic' or 'almost certain' can mean very different things to those who do risk assessments.

Finally, risk matrices totally obscure problems with 'false negatives' and 'false positives' in security and risk measures, as discussed earlier, and can never account for 'jumps' in probability assessments or states of nature that are common with nasty surprises. This latter point is essential. Probability measures of potentially severe outcomes cannot only change or 'drift' from one box in the matrix to another over time, but can take discrete jumps. Accounting for these jumps and militating against is especially important for high-consequence events.

The result of this range of problems is that risk management frameworks can, paradoxically, act as risk amplifiers by increasing the achieved potential for surprise above the unavoidable level.

Four examples of risk management failures can be used to illustrate how risk can be amplified by choices made over how to handle uncertainties and risks. First, as Australia's recent Royal Commission into the implementation of the flawed home insulation scheme (that resulted in four deaths) highlighted the way in which a top-level political priority on policy 'delivery'–dominated thinking with risk management tended to be viewed as a 'speed bump' to delivery made it hard for officials to adopt a more prudent approach to risks (Hanger, 2014). This was exacerbated by the prevalent tendency in government to treat risk management as a compliance ritual to be got out of the way as easily as

116 *Concepts for facilitating the transition*

possible and, where possible, even outsourced to consultants for convenience. This 'sidelined' stance meant that prior information on relevant risks from states within Australia and from New Zealand was ignored. The Royal Commission's investigation revealed both specific departmental capability shortcomings but also pointed to more general systemic limitations in risk management in the loosely federal Australian system of government: (a) risk as an inconvenience in delivering policy, (b) a 'tick box' (do and forget) mentality rather than the basis for learning and adaptation, and (c) poor flows of relevant information across administrative boundaries. In short, this tendency to treat risk management as a compliance ritual is *itself* an amplifier of risk.

Second, NASA's *Challenger* space shuttle disaster in 1986 demonstrates how technical choices made over risk management methodologies can amplify risks. In the lead-up to the disaster there were two alternative risk assessments for the space shuttle system (McGrayne, 2011).[10] A 1 in 100,000 risk of catastrophic system failure calculated by NASA and the findings from a 1983 US Air Force–funded review by Teledyne Energy Systems that used Bayesian methods that put the risk of catastrophic system failure much higher (and dangerously so) at 1 in 35. Teledyne had examined failure rates in similar solid fuel rocket systems (as used in Poseidon submarine missiles, Minuteman ICBMs) and used these estimates as prior risk factors in a Bayesian analysis (with a prior of 32 confirmed failures out of 1,902 rocket launches) augmented by subjective probabilities and based on lessons from real operating experience. Perhaps due to the Bayesian impact on cryptography in the Second World War, the Pentagon has always been more receptive to Bayesian concepts than NASA. Worryingly, NASA instructed the company it had hired to study shuttle risks to ignore such 'prior' data – even though the rockets were essentially identical. This was partly because NASA's risk management methodology worked on system-specific technical engineering safety margins that sought to eliminate risk via system redundancy rather than use probabilistic risk assessments that have stronger implications for the operational decision-making able to respond to unusual events (such as cold weather) – a narrow 'hard' data-driven approach that, in fact, amplified risk.

Third, there is the case of the Hoover Dam. This was designed on the basis of what later turned out to be statistical data on rainfall and consequent river levels from an unusually dry period. This leaves it at risk of collapse unless water is released to pre-empt a rapid rise in the dam level caused by the spring snow melt, in turn the combined consequence of rainfall and snow depositions earlier in the year and the rate at which the snow mass melts due to rising temperatures. As a result, the dam came close to failure in 1983 partly because this pre-emption was not carried out – a decision influenced by assumptions over expected deluge likelihoods (the likelihoods of actual water inflows threatening the dam are greater than the *assumed* likelihoods). These likelihoods are best updated and used to drive operational decision-making rather than sticking to the rule book (based on non-updated likelihoods). The Hoover Dam illustrates the way in which assumed statistical distributions used in design specifications,

Concepts for facilitating the transition 117

coupled with risk management solely as compliance (especially when used to define regulatory frameworks), can also amplify risk.

Fourth, the way in which government regulation of the banking and finance sector has involved assuming a normal distribution to threats to asset values that paid little attention to so-called fat tails (greater likelihoods of very dramatic risks than a normal distribution assumes). The multivariate version of the normal distribution (known as a Gaussian copula) played an important role in creating the conditions that led to the global financial crisis. These highly complex models, so complex as regards the fully specified models that overnight and weekend computational runs were required to solve the risk exposure calculations (even with very high levels of networked computing power), engendered a false sense of security in risk management in investment banking, see MacKenzie and Spears (2014a, 2014b) for a sociology of science perspective on this issue. Assumed statistical distributions that are not themselves adapted by being tested against reality on a regular basis can drive the amplification of risk.

Thus, even though a bank may have been fully compliant with regulations relating to risk, that compliance (and the assumptions upon which the regulatory framework had been designed) meant that this compliance had in reality amplified rather than mitigated risks. In other words, it is not hard to find examples of risk amplification that lend support to the utility of using the potential for surprise ratio as a diagnostic tool in policy analysis and risk assessment.

Another pertinent example to consider is that of the risk of the unintended detonation of a nuclear weapon. This was the subject of a classic Bayesian study performed for the US Air Force by the RAND Corporation completed in 1958 (Ikle et al., 1958). The policy challenge at the time (and that, thankfully, remains today) is that there is no data on *actual* unintended nuclear weapons detonations. There had been a series of accidents of various types in which things went wrong with a nuclear weapon – in some cases the conventional explosives detonated and in others they did not. In all of these accidents the safety features designed to prevent a nuclear detonation worked effectively – but mainly (at that time) because the 'physics package' comprising the nuclear materials had been removed. It is worth bearing in mind that the report was sanitised for public release hence it is not possible to get a complete picture of the failure modes at that time.

In such circumstances, with no statistical data on unintended nuclear detonations to work with, it simply was not possible to apply a frequentist analysis. Nevertheless, the US Air Force required a formal estimate of the likelihood of an unintended nuclear weapon detonation in order to inform risk management approaches.

The RAND study therefore opted to examine the failure modes found in the evidence available at that date. It did this from the perspective of the prevalence of the *opportunities* that were evident in which this worst-case accident could potentially have happened. This was a useful approach to take because as the Cold War evolved the increasing levels of activities involving the storage, transport and operational deployment of nuclear weapons would create an increased

118   *Concepts for facilitating the transition*

number of these opportunities for accidents to happen. The key to the analysis was therefore to estimate the probability that an accidental nuclear detonation could take place given this prevalence of opportunities with the parameters defined by the range of things that could go wrong and the effectiveness of the safeguards in place if they did go wrong. This is a classic expression of the Bayesian principle that the parameters under study are subject to random effects but the data is known (the only data we know is the data we currently have, this data is not a random sample of assumed parameters as in the classical/ frequentist approach). Interestingly, the analysis of failure modes highlighted the risks associated with human factors (including mental instability) and the (now declassified) RAND report has an extensive appendix on what was understood about these human factor–driven risks.

The study concluded that if there were 3,000 flights with nuclear weapons per year (key opportunities for accidents to happen) then the US Air Force could be 99.1 per cent sure that the probability of their being at least one accident in the following decade would be no greater than 0.05. Of course, if there are more flights per year then this estimate would increase.

From the point of view of practitioners in the US Air Force this type of analysis is useful to decision-making precisely because it sought to diagnose failure modes whilst also giving an indication of the severity of the risks faced (in this case a risk to be very concerned about). Note the way in which the risk estimate reverses the classical/frequentist approach by providing an estimate of the confidence range for a specific risk magnitude (in a similar manner to Laplace's estimate that the mass of Saturn would be within specified boundaries). To return to the risk amplification ratio, this example shows how a Bayesian analysis can be used to reduce the achieved potential for surprise by providing useful decision-support information. The RAND risk assessment is useful precisely because it works only with the available data whilst treating the complex parameters responsible for generating that data (in this case the failure modes) as being subject to random factors. From this perspective Bayesian approaches have a greater utility in relation to reducing the potential for nasty surprises than do classical statistical approaches.

One key lesson from these examples of risk amplification is that the incidence of false positives and false negatives in diagnostic tests used in risk management can be an important source of the amplification of risk. In each of the examples summarised above that preceded the discussion of the RAND study there was a false negative conclusion to the test for system failure risk. In the case of the space shuttle the false negative was caused by methodological restrictions imposed by NASA on itself that constrained risk assessment as regards prior data on failures in similar systems and avoided a probabilistic approach to risk management in preference for engineered safety margins (a methodological choice that impacted upon decision-making over risks). In the case of the Hoover Dam, design tolerances and operational guidelines that impact on risk were based on biased statistical data on rainfall patterns. In the case of the Australian home insulation scheme false negatives arose because risk management was treated as

Concepts for facilitating the transition   119

a compliance ritual and an impediment to rapid programme delivery (rather than being placed at the centre of the design and delivery of the intervention). In financial regulation the *assumed* statistical distributions that characterise frequentist regulatory stances, and that are not therefore subject to learning and adaptation as a matter of course, can be the source of nasty surprises.

These false negatives amplified the potential for nasty surprises above unavoidable levels. In other words, risk was amplified because organisations made choices over risk management that increased the likelihood of false negatives for tests of potential system failure but did not calibrate these methodological choices against an over-arching framework. The lesson is that risk management is most effective when diverse methods are calibrated against each other rather than one method being complied with. In addition, as the discussion of the limitations to some forms of risk matrix has illustrated, this approach can also amplify risks by increasing the potential for nasty surprises.

Given the importance of this 'amplification' aspect of risk management, an analytical means of dealing with the challenge of reducing false negatives (and false positives) in tests relating to risk is provided in the following section. The key enabler of this approach is to frame risk management as binary (true or false) hypothesis tests and to break down complex sets of inter-relationships into these binary links.

In practice, it can be difficult to calculate the unavoidable potential for surprise but it is possible to estimate the consequences of the ways in which risk is handled (defined broadly to encompass programme management, monitoring and evaluation processes and other aspects of the day-to-day business of spending government money and accounting for that spending). This means that the potential for surprises ratio can be modified to treat the unavoidable potential for surprise as an estimated factor as follows:

$$\text{Unavoidable potential for surprise} = \frac{\text{Achieved potential for surprise}}{\text{Risk amplification (\textit{estimated using process characterisations})}}$$

Indeed, for many practical purposes those working in government (and collaborating with government) will be more interested in the actually achieved potential for surprise and the associated risk amplification factor. This means that the unavoidable potential for surprise can be set in a fairly arbitrary manner for some purposes (such as formulating risk management strategies). What matters most is the ability to mimimise risk amplification.

It is important to stress that this approach is only analytically tractable if it is subjectively based in the sense that it only tries to work with what is understood at present as sparse and ambiguous information, rather than frame understanding against an ideal type of objective information. The advantage of adopting a subjective approach to risk expressed as the potential for surprise is that we can carry out calculations without having to be overly concerned about the enormity of what we don't know or understand. All we need to concern

120   *Concepts for facilitating the transition*

ourselves with is what we do believe we know and understand. As alluded to earlier, it is this ability to learn using sparse, ambiguous and changing information that allows human cognition and machine learning to out-perform analyses of decision-relevant information based on classical frequentist approaches to statistical analysis. The confidence we are able to place in analytical results stems from tests of the relative odds that competing hypotheses are true. This means that even if all these odds are weak we choose (as Turing did) the hypothesis with the best odds and focus our investment in learning in that area. If the odds of other explanations being true improve then we change the learning strategy accordingly.

This contrasts with the absolute levels of statistical significance used in sampling theory–based analysis – where statistical significance is defined as the (low) probability of random factors generating the observed data and each hypothesis is tested independently against a null hypothesis of no treatment effect. As Ziliak and McCloskey stress, the 'objectivity' of sampling theory–based definitions of statistical significance does not encourage scrutiny and use (in decision-making) of the strength of relative treatment effects of different treatment solutions. This can result in beneficial treatments (interventions that improve conditions) not being adopted due to a failure to achieve statistical significance on the basis of the sample size–related characteristics that dominate analytical methods, see Ziliak and McCloskey (2014).

In contrast, subjectivist approaches do not need to assume an unknown statistical distribution from which the observed data are sampled in order to determine whether or not a finding is 'significant'.

The strongest support for using the risk amplification ratio as a policy tool is that governments naturally seek to minimise this potential for surprise. From this perspective, large chunks of government budgets seek to reduce this potential for surprise: swathes of intelligence spending (e.g. in the USA, National Security Agency, National Reconnaissance Office, parts of the Central Intelligence Agency budget and a myriad of other high-cost entities and programmes). The costs of regulating the financial sector – and businesses generally. A large proportion of research and experimental development (R&D) budgets also effectively aim to reduce the potential for surprise. In aggregate the spending on these entities and programmes acts to reduce the amplification of risk by decreasing the actually achieved potential for surprise over the unavoidable potential for surprise (whilst also improving understanding of the unavoidable potential for surprise that sets the threshold level of risk).

Mapping substantive uncertainty, stochastic risk and controllable risk

One way of conceptualising the differences between, and the implications of, substantive uncertainty and risk is to approach the challenge by visually mapping the knowledge pathways via which we learn. A visual mapping addresses Feynman's emphasis on alternative expressions of the same phenomenon in order

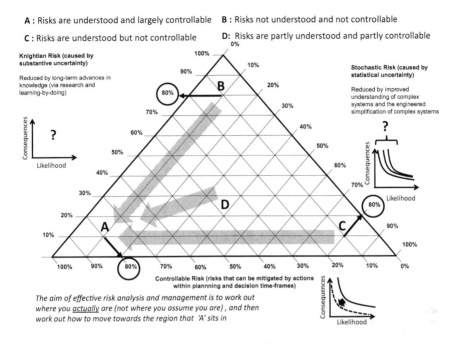

Figure 4.11 A Ternary representation of knowledge acquisition phases

to stimulate creativity and innovation. In doing this it is useful to distinguish between stochastic risk and what might be termed controllable risk – the distinction being that the former exhibits random behaviours over which we have little or no control whereas the latter involve risks that we do have some control over. From this perspective an ideal type knowledge gain involves a transition from an initial state of substantive uncertainty into a phase of stochastic uncertainty and then (if we are fortunate) into a controllable risk phase. These phase transitions are visualised in the 'ternary' graph in figure 4.11 (note, figures 4.11, 4.12 and 4.13 were created using a spreadsheet provided in Graham and Midgley (2000)). Ternary graphs of this type are used in the natural sciences to map systems in which the state of physical systems reflects three interacting factors and results in specific circumstances that reflect distinct combinations of these conditions. As such they are particularly useful for marking out phase states and transitions between these states (such as between gases and liquids under different pressures). In this context, a ternary graph is a useful means of emphasising that any particular policy situation will involve a distinctive mix of substantive uncertainty, stochastic risk and controllable risk.

The distinguishing characteristics of the three phases are that when substantive uncertainty exists we are unable to assign a probability to a potential occurrence. In other words, we avoid using Laplace's 0.5 probability assumption to express uncertainty in favour of directly stating our ignorance over something.

122 Concepts for facilitating the transition

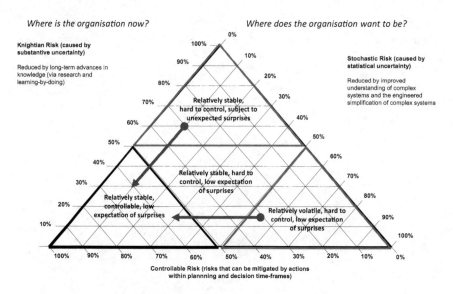

Figure 4.12 A Ternary representation of knowledge domains

For stochastic risk the driving factors result in random behaviours over which we have insufficient control to give us what might be termed actionable information on risk factors. Finally, there may be a phase in which we are in a position to influence these risks – they become controllable (in principle at least). Figure 4.12 identifies four regions in this ternary framework with regards to the mix of stability (or volatility), potential for control and, as a result, the potential for nasty surprises to occur.

In practice of course there will be a range of pathways exhibited in this ternary space, often expressing 'stunted' development in knowledge of risks because it has not proved to be possible to move from one phase to the next (e.g. from stochastic risks to controllable risks). For decision-makers, there is a set of challenges stemming from the potential for *assumptions* about where an organisation (or project) sits and where it actually sits if these factors are assessed more accurately. This dislocation of assumptions from reality is expressed in figure 4.13. This is one way of visualising the risk amplification ratio because the assumption that we are able to control risks that are in reality too stochastic to control to a sufficient degree increases the achieved potential for surprise over the unavoidable potential for surprise.

From this ternary perspective, the types of impediments to effective governance and public policy covered in this book can be treated as situations in which the rules, guidelines and procedures that dictate how government departments operate distort reality. They do this by not allowing for high levels of substantive uncertainty and/or high levels of stochastic risk and by assuming (i.e. forcing behaviour) into the controllable risks dominated region when these risks are

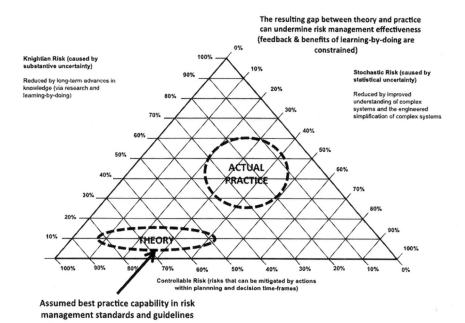

Figure 4.13 A Ternary representation of the disjuncture between theory and practice in risk management

not in fact as controllable as is assumed. As discussed earlier, public sector budgeting procedures encourage this dislocation between theory and reality as regards substantive uncertainty by forcing spurious precision on cost estimates that are subject to high levels of substantive uncertainty and attempts to hit performance milestones that are effectively long-odds bets – with the result that nasty surprises are almost inevitable.

In this context, one pertinent insight from research on cognition (in both humans and other animals) is that what this work refers to as 'subjective contours' plays an important role in influencing decision-making. These subjective contours are used in the mind to find patterns in visual data based on what is *not* seen rather than what *is* seen (e.g. to infer patterns in white spaces suggested by the implied spaces defined by black shapes). The inter-play between the distinctive features of the left- and right-hand sides of brains has an influence on how effectively these subjective contours are perceived. In general terms, as Vallortigara et al. summarise 'the left hemisphere sets up rules based on experience, and the right hemisphere avoids rules in order to detect details and unique features that allow it to decide what is familiar and what is novel' (Vallortigara et al., 2008, p. 213). These subjective contours emerge from this complex inter-play between building and using rules that allow details in data to be ignored – enabling fast decisions in identifying and responding to existential threats – and then suspending these rapid recognition rules in order to examine details and to decide whether these rules need to be modified. When this creative

124 *Concepts for facilitating the transition*

tension does not work effectively then various cognitive consequences arise (such as an enhanced ability to perceive details in data but a reduced ability to generate and use pattern recognition rules, including rules associated with subjective contours). These subjective contours are in effect conjectures that create illusory patterns – but these illusory patterns can be very useful in making sense of what is being observed.

In the Bayesian terms being explored here, these subjective contours can be thought of as new hypotheses about patterns that have been induced from missing data (in philosophical terms abductive reasoning on the basis of missing information). The odds in favour of such hypotheses are based on what is not observed (at present) but that appears as gaps in data. This characteristic stands to play an important role in a public policy context because it points to uses of structured hypotheses testing able to cope with risks generated by substantive uncertainty – threats defined by missing evidence rather than proof based on available evidence (we currently obsesses about the latter and miss opportunities to factor missing evidence into our risk-related decisions).

Conclusions

This chapter has considered the advantages of approaching governance and public policy as a Bayesian process of learning and adaptation. It has highlighted the ways in which using the analytical methods used in signal processing and machine learning provide a more easily grasped version of Bayesian methods. These methods emphasise diagnostic accuracy (as reflected in false positive and false negative test results), as such they provide a basis for measuring diagnostic performance in governance. The concept of a risk amplification ratio based on the ratio of the achieved potential for surprise over the unavoidable potential for surprise provides a useful heuristic for guiding the formulation of policy and the monitoring, evaluation and learning that guides implementation. Finally, a ternary framework for emphasising what can go wrong when actual configurations of substantive uncertainty, stochastic risk and controllable risk are distorted by norms, standards, rules and guidelines has been proposed.

The following chapter considers how this conceptual approach can be translated into practical tools for use in government.

Notes

1 This section draws upon arguments in Matthews (2015).
2 See Matthews and White (2013) for a discussion of an experimental project that used structured hypothesis testing as an MEL methodology.
3 This method is derived from the principles of conditional probability in mathematics.
4 Natural frequencies are simply the counts of the occurrences of possible permutations expressed in raw terms (and ideally using a graphical mapping of the structure of these permutations). This is both simpler and (for many people) a more intuitive way of dealing with risks and uncertainties, see Gigerenzer (2002) for an explanation using a range of examples.

Concepts for facilitating the transition   125

5 Details of how this natural frequency–based approach can be used to test hypotheses in a public policy setting using worked examples and systematic reviews of evaluations of public sector programmes and projects (and including further elaboration on a Bayesian expression of the policy cycle) can be found online at: http://marklmatthews.com/transformational-public-policy/ ⌐
6 In some branches of physics where large amounts of data are available a deviation of three standard deviations from the mean is used as the criteria for attributing the status of 'evidence' and five standard deviations from the mean for attributing a 'discovery'.
7 See Ziliak and McCloskey (2014) for a discussion of the shortcomings in classical statistical significance testing.
8 See Pierce (1961) for a non-technical explanation of Shannon's work.
9 This summary of the problems associated with a compliance-dominated use of risk matrices is based on my co-author Tom Kompas's contribution to Matthews and Kompas (2015).
10 This summary also draws on a range of internal NASA documents bearing upon risk management shortcomings.

References

Aitchison, J and Dunsmore, I R 1975, *Statistical Prediction Analysis*. Cambridge University Press, Cambridge.

Cox, L L 2008, What's wrong with risk matrices. *Risk Analysis*. vol. 28, no. 2, pp. 497–512.

Ferson, S 2005, *Bayesian Methods in Risk Assessment*. Paper Prepared for Bureau de Recherches Géologiques et Minières (BRGM), France.

Feynman, R 1967, *The Character of a Physical Law*. MIT Press, Cambridge, MA.

Food and Drug Administration 2010, *Guidance for the Use of Bayesian Statistics in Medical Device Clinical Trials*. Food and Drug Administration, Center for Devices and Radiological Health, Silver Spring, MD.

Gigerenzer, G 2002, *Reckoning with Risk: Learning to Live with Uncertainty*. Penguin, London.

Gigerenzer, G and Hoffrage, U 1995, How to improve Bayesian reasoning without instruction: Frequency formats. *Psychological Review*. vol. 102, no. 4, pp. 684–704.

Gillies, D 1990, The Turing-Good weight of evidence function and Popper's measure of the severity of a test. *British Journal of the Philosophy of Science*. vol. 41, pp. 143–146.

Good, I J 1979, Turing's statistical work in World War II. *Biometrika*. vol. 66, no. 2, pp. 393–396.

Graham, D and Midgley, N 2000, Graphical representation of particle shape using triangular diagrams: An Excel spreadsheet method. Technical Communication. *Earth Surface Processes and Landforms*. vol. 25, pp. 1473–1477.

Hanger, I 2014, *Royal Commission into the Home Insulation Scheme*. Attorney-General's Department, Canberra.

Heiner, R A 1986, Uncertainty, signal-detection experiments, and modeling behavior, in R N Langlois (ed) *Economics as a Process: Essays in the New Institutional Economics*. Cambridge University Press, Cambridge.

Ikle, F C, Aronson, G J and Madansky, A 1958, *On the Risk of an Accidental or Unauthorised Nuclear Detonation*. RM-2251. US Air Force Project RAND, Santa Monica.

Jaynes, E T 1957, Information theory and statistical mechanics. *Physical Review*, Series II. vol. 106, no. 4, pp. 620–630.

126 Concepts for facilitating the transition

Jaynes, E T 1984, *Bayesian Methods: General Background: An Introductory Tutorial*. Paper Presented at the Fourth Annual Workshop on Bayesian/Maximum Entropy Methods, August 1984, Calgary.

Kleiter, G D 1994, Natural sampling: Rationality without base rates, in G H Fisher & D Laming (eds.), *Contributions to Mathematical Psychology, Psychometrics, and Methodology*, Springer, New York, pp. 357–388.

Lilford, R J and Braunholtz, D 1996, The statistical basis of public policy: A paradigm shift is overdue. *British Medical Journal*. vol. 313, pp. 603–607.

Loredo, T J 1990, From Laplace to supernova SN 1987: A Bayesian inference in astrophysics, in P F Fougere (ed.), *Maximum Entropy and Bayesian Methods*, Kluwer Academic Publishers, The Netherlands.

MacKenzie, D and Spears, T 2014a, The formula that killed Wall Street: The Gaussian copula and modelling practices in investment banking. *Social Studies of Science*. vol. 44, no. 3, pp. 393–417.

MacKenzie, D and Spears, T 2014b, A device for being able to book P&L: The organizational embedding of the Gaussian copula. *Social Studies of Science*. vol. 44, no. 3, pp. 418–440.

Matthews, M 2015, How better methods for coping with uncertainty and ambiguity can strengthen government – civil society collaboration, in G Carey, K Landvogt & J Barraket (eds.), *Designing and Implementing Public Policy: Cross-Sectoral Debates*, Studies in Governance and Public Policy Series, Routledge, London, pp. 159–180.

Matthews, M and Frater, R 2003, *Creating and Exploiting Intangible Networks: How Radiata was Able to Improve Its Odds of Success in the Risky Process of Innovating*. Detailed Analytical Case Study Prepared for the Science and Innovation Mapping System Taskforce, Australian Government Department of Education, Science and Training, Canberra.

Matthews, M and Kompas, T 2015, Coping with nasty surprises: Improving risk management in the public sector using simplified Bayesian methods. *Asia & the Pacific Policy Studies*. vol 2, no. 3, pp. 452–466.

Matthews, M and White, G 2013, Faster, smarter and cheaper: Hypothesis-testing in policy and program evaluation. *Evaluation Connections. Newsletter of the European Evaluation Society* (December), Prague, pp. 13–14.

McGrayne, S B 2011, *The Theory That Would Not Die*. Yale University Press, New Haven.

Pierce, J R 1961, *Symbols, Signals and Noise: The Nature and Process of Communication*. Harper & Brothers, New York.

Popper, K R 1934, *The Logic of Scientific Discovery*, 6th Impression. Hutchinson, London, 1972.

Shannon, C E 1948, A mathematical theory of communication. *The Bell System Technical Journal*. vol. XXVII (July), pp. 379–423.

Swets, J A, Dawes, R M and Monahan, J 2000, Psychological science can improve diagnostic decisions. *Psychological Science in the Public Interest*. vol. 1, pp. 1–26.

Vallortigara, G, Snyder, A, Kaplan, G, Bateson, P, Clayton, N S and Rogers, L J 2008, Are animals autistic savants? *PLOS Biology*. vol. 6, no. 2, pp. 208–14.

Ziliak, S T and McCloskey, D N 2014, *The Cult of Statistical Significance: How the Standard Error Costs Us Jobs, Justice and Lives*. The University of Michigan Press, Ann Arbor.

5 Implementing the transition

This chapter draws upon the preceding arguments to develop a methodological 'manifesto' for delivering the transition to ways of doing public policy that are better equipped to cope with uncertainties and risks. It discusses how signal processing methods could be adapted to facilitate learning and adaptation in public policy using structured hypotheses testing techniques and stresses a range of advantages to be exploited if such a transition were to be made.

The limitations currently faced

In OECD countries, the formal monitoring and evaluation frameworks that are, in theory, a key driver of policy learning can be excessively 'administrative' and focused on compliance with funding contracts and/or standards and guidelines rather than on maximising opportunities to learn-by-doing in policy implementation.[1] Indeed, there is currently a notable disconnect between the factors that drive policy forward and the administrative practices and procedures that are used to manage *and learn* how to deliver policy more effectively.

This disconnect means that the ways in which OECD governments handle evaluation (and use evidence more generally) in the context of their broader public sector reform agendas is not necessarily a capability that nations actively building up their policy capacity are wise to emulate. It would be wiser to explore capacity-building approaches with the potential to jump beyond current 'best practices'. A focus on using Bayesian inference, framed in signal processing terms to facilitate learning and adaptation, is one potential approach to articulating this sort of capability 'leap-frog' strategy.

Arguably, one reason for the disconnect between the factors that drive policy forward and the administrative practices and procedures that are used to manage the delivery of policy is that policymakers do not currently have access to a generic and comprehensive analytical model of the policy learning and adaptation process specifically designed to facilitate capacity-building via a focus on identifying inaccurate test results. Whilst there are idealised models of the policy formulation and delivery cycle, most practitioners recognise that these are very much 'ideal types' that guide and inform real practices – but may not directly assist with those real practices.[2]

128 *Implementing the transition*

The reasons for this are a combination of political expediency, urgency in responding to unexpected surprises and other factors. The result is that these models of the policy process, like the monitoring and evaluation function that appears in different guises as a stage in this cycle, tend to play a ritualistic and referential role at some distance from actual practice.

Arguably, however, the complexity and requirements for detail that practitioners tend to encounter when attempting to use M&E frameworks are an impediment to effective policy learning. M&E is a specialist activity with its own distinctive jargon and methods (Log Frames, Theories of Change etc.). This complexity can be even harder to cope with in situations in which technically sophisticated statistical analyses are used (including econometric studies). The methodologies applied can themselves be a source of ambiguity and confusion to officials without specific technical expertise and experience.

Current approaches tend to result in long and complex lists of evaluation parameters that make it hard to take a top-down view that gets to the heart of what has really happened. It is not unusual for key conclusions from evaluations to be watered down for political expediency simply by editing reports and via subtle changes in wording. This aspect can increase cynicism amongst generalists in government and, as result, get in the way of identifying key lessons for moving forward. This is especially the case when an M&E framework is excessively focused on complying with a range of specific contractual performance indicators – leading to the familiar problem of 'managing to contract' vis-à-vis 'managing for results'.

These characteristics tend to result in a de-coupling of the pragmatic (and often chaotic) process of doing real public policy and the frameworks that are taught to new government officials but only used ideally and/or when people have the chance. This de-coupling is not helpful for M&E activities because it limits the feedback from non-specialist policy officers – a feedback loop that, if configured appropriately, has the potential to force a simplification and standardisation of methodologies via learning-by-doing.

As argued in chapter four, methodological insights from signal processing and machine learning based on adopting a binary (true or false) characterisation of hypothesis-based evaluation findings should be explored. This binary framework (widely used in clinical diagnosis) is framed in terms of the estimated likelihoods of obtaining false positive and false negative test results in evaluation studies – based on the combination of specific evaluation test results *and* what is known about the more general prevalence of test inaccuracies. The suggestion is that this is an approach that could also, potentially, simplify and improve the utility of monitoring and evaluation (M&E) frameworks by integrating that specific activity more fully into the broader collective policy learning process – including linking more effectively with the challenge of how uncertainty and risk are managed. Uncertainties and risks can stem from the use of inaccurate test results, thereby increasing the potential for nasty surprises.

In an uncertain and risky world, governments should seek to maximise the availability of decision-support information they have access to. If they do not, then there is a risk that a better decision could have been made – *given what is currently understood and assumed to be the case*. Whilst information will always be imperfect there are, of course, degrees of imperfection that can have a major impact on policy decisions.

As stressed earlier, information theory can be applied to missed opportunities to learn in public policy. From this perspective, governments should aim to minimise the extent to which the assumptions they hold over the range of wanted and unwanted events (i.e. risks *and* opportunities) are distorted by failures to use all available information to calculate the odds they are working with. This is not to argue that this available information will always be adequate from the perspective of idealised models and frameworks (not least the neo-classical economic thinking that tends to pervade governance): it will always be limited and often subjective. But, it is to argue that ignoring or overlooking available information can result in a mix of lost opportunities to achieve wanted outcomes and misjudged risks of avoiding unwanted outcomes – the calculated odds diverge from the data upon which these odds should be based. In information theory terms, governments are wise to seek to avoid situations in which they are surprised by events simply because information that would have led them to calculate relevant odds differently was ignored.

We use the United Kingdom's experience as an illustration of these generic challenges because there is an established (and influential) history of promoting evidence-based policymaking matched with significant attention paid to the methodological challenges involved in actually delivering this approach in practice.

The British Government currently uses the ROAMEF definition of the policy learning cycle, illustrated in figure 5.1. This comprises the following distinct

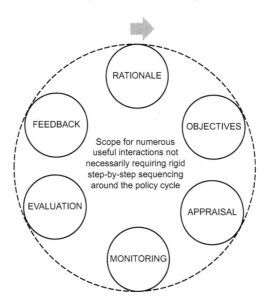

Figure 5.1 Diagrammatic representation of the UK ROAMEF policy learning framework

130 *Implementing the transition*

functions: Rationale, Objectives, Appraisal, Monitoring, Evaluation and Feedback (HM Treasury, 2011).

That is the theory. Actual practice is rather different. In 2013 the UK National Audit Office (NAO) reported on a major assessment of the adequacy of evaluations of UK government programmes. The findings were striking in what they revealed about what is *not* being done to assist policy learning via robust evaluations. Whilst the UK NAO findings had a noticeable impact on public sector evaluation practices in the UK (leading to greater attention being paid to using more robust methodologies), these findings, and their implications, are of more general relevance outside of the UK as regards highlighting problems and framing where to search for solutions.

As noted in chapter four, the NAO reviewed nearly 6,000 analytical and research documents published between 2006 and 2012 on seventeen main government department websites. It found that only 305 of these were impact evaluations; and that of these 305, only 70 made an assessment of cost-effectiveness. The NAO was able to identify £12.3 billion of overall programme expenditure (in cash terms) evaluated by 41 of those evaluations (National Audit Office, 2013).

The main message to emerge from the NAO's assessment was that the evaluation function is not delivering what it should deliver – robust conclusions on what is working well and what is working less well, or even badly – and why this is the case.

One noteworthy aspect of UK experience is the strong emphasis now placed on approaches to evidence-based policymaking (like the concept itself) that originated in health and medicine. This is resulting in the growing use of Randomised Control Trials (RCTs) and the promotion of a hierarchy of evidence. This hierarchical approach is explicitly reflected in the use of the Maryland Scientific Methods Scale by the NAO. This framework is expressed graphically (by the author) in figure 5.2 below and is based upon identifying five categories of scientific evidence – the most powerful of which are RCT studies.

The Maryland Scale has been used in the UK to assess the quality of evidence used in public policy. Of 33 published evaluations in four policy areas examined by the NAO (spatial policy, labour markets, business support and education), 3 (8.8 per cent) conformed to Level 5 quality evidence, 8 (23.5 per cent) conformed to Level 4, and 3 (8.8 per cent) to Level 3. Finally, 13 conformed to Level 2 (38.2 per cent) and 6 to Level 1 (5.8 per cent).

In other words, 44 per cent fell within the 'weaker/riskier research designs' category. In the NAO's view, this skewed diversity in evaluation quality is a matter of concern because it indicates that UK government departments should make a greater effort to conduct evaluations using high-confidence methods (it noted that weaker methods tended to be associated with more positive conclusions).

Two observations can be made about this NAO assessment. First, the growing emphasis on drawing attention to the robustness of evaluation methods is a significant development – especially as regards capacity-building. If policy is to be informed by robust evidence then it will take a significant effort (and possibly greater cost) to achieve high evidence quality thresholds. Second, the type of

Implementing the transition 131

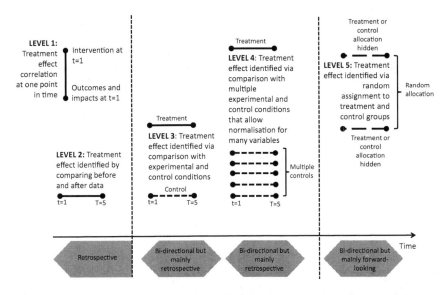

Figure 5.2 Diagrammatic illustration of the Maryland Scientific Methods Scale

approach being put in place in the UK may be effective in retrospective assessments and in driving robust (RCT-style) assessments for future use – *but* is poorly positioned to assist policymakers forced to make decisions (as is often the case) when available information is sparse, and/or ambiguous and therefore confusing. We cannot, and should not, assume that solutions lie only in more better data on experience to date when the major challenges for decision-making stem from coping with future conditions that may only relate weakly to such data.

Re-formulating risk management

The first step to building stronger capacity to learn and adapt in governance is to re-think approaches to risk management. This is because a failure to do this will most likely result in the rules, guidelines and procedures that currently characterise risk management acting as an impediment to transformation. This re-positioning of risk management can be thought of as a process of broadening the boundaries of risk management by introducing elements not usually covered – notably ways of thinking and innovating. This philosophy is summarised in the following diagram (figure 5.3).

In this approach, organisation-specific rules, guidelines and standards play an important role in risk management – but risk management is not exclusively a matter of compliance with those factors. Similarly, data and simulation modelling also play an important role – but as a means of interfacing with both rules, guidelines and standards and, the most important consideration for effective risk management: ways of thinking and innovating. The Venn diagram in figure 5.3 emphasises the balancing acts required. First, there is the need to balance the

Implementing the transition

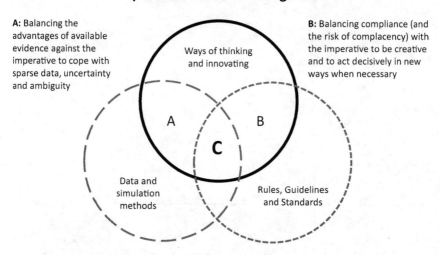

Figure 5.3 Different perspectives on risk management

advantages of having data (and other formal contributions such as results from simulation models) against the need to be able to make decisions when there is only sparse, uncertain and ambiguous information to rely on (domain A). Second, the need to balance compliance with rules, guidelines and standards against the need to act creatively and decisively when necessary – even though this may go against current rules etc. (domain B). Finally, the need to find an effective balance between all of these considerations by recognising that it will rarely be the case that there is a 'right' solution – only more or less worse solutions (domain C).

The notion of a risk amplification factor based upon the ratio of the achieved potential for surprise over the unavoidable potential for surprise provides a useful means of obtaining perspective on these challenges – as illustrated in figure 5.4. This is because it provides a top-level concept for considering the strengths and weaknesses of different ways of balancing these trade-offs in coping with uncertainty and risk. As the examples given in chapter four highlighted, an excessive emphasis on any particular aspect of this set of considerations (e.g. on specific statistical distributions and/or slavish compliance to standards and guidelines) can result in amplified risk.

Finally as regards risk management approaches, and as stressed throughout the book, it is essential to link this adaptive and creative approach to risk management to a more seamless approach to the appraisal, implementation and the monitoring and evaluation of interventions. This is illustrated in figure 5.5 below. This sets up a set of connections to pay attention to in day-to-day activities.

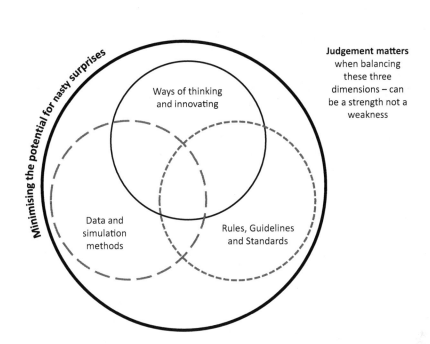

Figure 5.4 The scope for integrating different perspectives on risk management

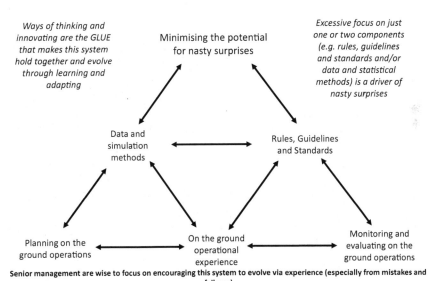

Figure 5.5 Exploiting synergies in risk management

134 *Implementing the transition*

Achieving transformational public policy: 'brownfield' versus 'greenfield' sites

Given the emphasis placed on better diagnostic capability as an enabler of learning and adaptation the first step to achieving the transformation outlined in this book is improved awareness of current diagnostic strengths and limitations. This can be achieved by gradually introducing signal processing diagnostics into the policy formulation and delivery process.

Where there are well-established mechanisms in place, characteristically in central government, this can involve 'piggybacking' signal processing diagnostics onto existing policy formulation work and also into monitoring, evaluation and learning (MEL) studies. One current challenge in such situations is that public sector austerity measures lead to reductions in spending on monitoring, evaluation and learning. Evaluations will be carried out if they are required in the specification of the intervention (and unavoidable activities), but if these are not specified in this tight manner it is likely that evaluation won't happen. As stressed at various points in this book, this marginalisation of evaluation tells us a lot about the utility of that function as a means of policy learning given current methods. This marginalisation further reinforces the importance of transitioning to more effective methods that create a seamless link between appraisal and evaluation (and as such drive learning and adaptation). If this re-invention of methods does not happen then the risk is that the current austerity measures will simply lock governance into slower, costly and less useful appraisal and evaluation methods than would otherwise be the case.

However, in situations in which that sort of existing policy capacity is not well developed, which is characteristic of devolved policy strategies, this sort of 'piggybacking' is not necessary – the opportunity exists to move straight to implementing newer and more innovative approaches. In some respects these 'greenfield' sites (as opposed to the 'brownfield' sites associated with central government) provide the most compelling environment for trying out these new methods. Unlike central government, which has a legacy and corporate memory of better days with more money to spend, these greenfield sites do not have established ways of doing things. The situation is similar to that of industrial productivity – a process in which new ways of making productivity gains can be developed during difficult competitive and general economic circumstances (because there is no alternative) with the move to more comfortable trading conditions allowing these productivity gains to be exploited as activities scale-up. The situation is also similar to the way in which radical, potentially disruptive, innovations are best achieved outside of existing corporate structures. This is why established corporations prefer to 'spin-off' some types of innovation into start-up companies in which they take an equity stake (which gives them to option to acquire the start-up if the innovation looks promising commercially or in other ways of use to the 'parent' company). The innovating teams are encouraged to leave and set up the new company – and may of course re-join the parent if things don't work out.

Interventions as hypothesis tests

For policy formulation, the first step is to frame the proposed intervention as a set of competing hypotheses relating to cause and effect. Aspects of this approach are already found in many intervention rationales, all that is required is to frame these rationales more explicitly as a set of succinct hypotheses. These will usually be bundled together as complements in the sense that they all reflect particular aspects of the intervention rationale. However, they are also competing hypotheses in the sense that there is uncertainty over which aspects of the intervention will work best (and worse) – with the subsequent tests of these competing hypotheses being used to discover what works best and what works less well. These questions should revolve around assessing the potential for the evidence and beliefs that drive a proposed policy intervention to create true positive, false positive, false negative and true negative hypothesis test results.

Where funding contracts are used, this hypothesis-based approach has some major advantages. Current contractual arrangements are highly risk-averse and attempt to stipulate as many grounds for default and blame as possible. Performance metrics are detailed (as grounds for default), rigid delivery milestones are often set. In contrast, in a hypothesis testing based framework funding contracts can be far simpler (and therefore cheaper to complete) and also more permissive and recognise explicitly that uncertainties and risks are unavoidable – indeed the very existence of these uncertainties and risks often constitutes the reason for the government intervention (a point often lost on the lawyers who handle government contracts). As stressed in chapter three, the public sector invests in a range of activities that, in effect, seek to translate substantive uncertainty into quantifiable risk (academic research in particular). When these uncertainty and risk-averse contractual arrangements are applied to such investments, the very behaviours that the funding seeks to encourage (discovery) can be distorted by contractual compliance.

One way around this problem in academia is for researchers to effectively do the discovery work prior to seeking funding to perform that discovery work. This allows them to take risks – to explore – without facing the risks associated with attempting that exploration under a specified contract. This system actually works rather effectively and should, therefore, not be viewed as problematic behaviour. It is particularly appropriate when scientific instruments or relevant data are available that are able to perform key aspects of a highly exploratory work without the need for a new contract.

What can be problematic, however, are situations in which research funding is secured but the experimental work does not proceed as anticipated and should ideally be abandoned or re-focused. In science, this will characteristically be a situation in which access to specialised research instruments is required and which requires dedicated funding for that access. In these situations, rigid 'delivery' focused funding agreements can be highly problematic. Some researchers have expressed a preference for more flexible research funding agreements to be available that would allow research to be curtailed in such situations with the unspent funds returned to donors.[3]

136 *Implementing the transition*

In such situations, funding agreements based explicitly on tests of competing hypotheses and with 'fail early' provisions based explicitly on these hypothesis tests could be especially useful. Competing hypotheses are relevant because they can be structured in such a way that they cover the 'fail early' option. Of course, academic research is a useful example of the utility of formal hypothesis tests precisely because research proposals tend to be couched in these terms anyway. The main difference would be a clearer use of this approach to address abandonment options – or greater leeway provided for major re-directions of the research.

There is also the issue of excessive red tape in academic funding agreements. Rather than rely on hypothesis test based progress reporting, contracts for academic research tend to apply 'business-like' key performance measures and progress milestones more suited to a building construction project being overseen by an architect – in which the objective is to deliver the stipulated building design against a stipulated timetable. This aspect could be reduced via a stronger emphasis on the core of the work being funded, i.e. the advances in knowledge obtained (or not).

More generally, however, hypothesis test based funding agreements are rare. This contractual form is being used by one government department that funds academic research (as a result of a pilot project involving the author). The reported advantages of using this approach are cost-effectiveness and shorter contract preparation lead times via the reduced administrative requirements associated with greater simplicity. These funding agreements simply list the set of mutually agreed hypotheses that define the intervention rationale and state that it is up to the funding recipient to decide on the range of evidence that will be provided to test these hypotheses as the research proceeds.

In a hypothesis testing approach, the only role for key performance indicators and progress milestones of a traditional type is when there are activities such as building construction (where it is useful to know whether or not the foundations have been completed on schedule and if not why not). This tight performance metric-based ethos need not be carried forward into the research carried out when the building is completed. Progress in the research is judged by the progress made in testing the hypotheses that defined the intervention. This is a process that can allow for the evolution of these hypotheses if necessary (these tend to take the form of subsidiary hypotheses that can be nested within the main tests being carried out). In other words, KPIs are only used in a fit for purpose manner and are not used in an unfit for purpose manner.

For MEL work, this approach greatly reduces the burden of red tape on funding recipients for three main reasons. First, the decision over how to demonstrate progress using evidence is left to them, it is not specified *a priori* in the funding contract. Second, as experience evolves in unexpected directions, it is not necessary to attempt to shape what was actually done to fit original (outdated) expectations – something that can be very time-consuming in contractual reporting. New hypotheses can be introduced with an explanation of why they arose that highlights the advances in understanding thus achieved. Third, in cases in which an intervention was a high-level political imperative, and therefore may not have had a tightly defined rationale, there is no need to attempt to retrospectively create that intervention rationale in great detail in order to then proceed with drawing up the *ex ante* 'theory of change' and other conventional public sector evaluation requirements on an invented *ex post* timeline. It is much easier, and cheaper, to re-frame the original political imperative as a set of hypotheses without the necessity of re-creating robust rationales and theories of change.

In my own experience in conducting public sector evaluations this attempt to retrospectively create a detailed intervention logic when none originally existed simply because a senior politician had taken the initiative (sometimes very creatively) to act and to act quickly can be a major advantage. It is far easier to simply translate that top-level political statement of what the intervention seeks to achieve into a set of high-level hypotheses and then leave it to the funding recipients to decide how to present their case as to how well they spent the funds they were given. Indeed, these projects launched by senior politicians tend, by definition, to be at the larger end of the size range. Hence, adopting the recommended approach helps to deal with a major challenge in evaluation work (relatively large amounts of public money being spent on interventions that do not have rationales that comply closely to the detailed specifications that central economic ministries tend to stipulate).

This retrospective use of hypotheses cuts out what can be a difficult adversarial process via which funding donors and recipients clash over how to create a detailed intervention rationale when none originally existed. At present, funding recipients seek to shape the retrospectively created detailed intervention logic to fit their current situation, which reflects a complex mix of things they have not done but should have done and things they have done that were not anticipated when the funding agreement was initiated. The funding donors seek to shape the retrospectively created detailed intervention logic to cover their own backs politically – demonstrating transparency and accountability in the prudent use of public funds. This negotiation can result in an impasse and, even if it does not, can be very expensive in the use of staff time on both sides. Indeed, the hypothesis-testing framework was used with great success in such a situation – and allowed both parties to move forward and agree on a mutually acceptable compromise far faster and more cheaply than would otherwise have been the case. The following box contains a short article from an evaluation practitioners newsletter summarising this experience.

Whilst this does, on face value, appear to be a logical and practical approach, in practice it can be hard to learn how to frame an intervention as a set of competing hypotheses (whether retrospectively or forward-looking). This is mainly an issue of learning-by-doing – generating the necessary tacit knowledge by going through the hypotheses-framing process for real cases. In scientific research, this is a critically important aspect of research training – how to identify problems/puzzles that can *in principle* be solved, and to translate those problems into testable hypotheses. Indeed, this is an area in which this established scientific expertise could, in a 'research outcomes and impact' context, play a useful role in helping government. A transition towards framing policy interventions as hypotheses would greatly enhance pathways to impact for academic research.

138   *Implementing the transition*

Faster, smarter and cheaper: hypothesis-testing in policy and program evaluation

We were commissioned by a State government in Australia to review its approach to the evaluation of a major investment in science and innovation that it made over a decade ago. It quickly became clear to us that the traditional auditing process adopted by our client which relied on reconstruction of the original objectives and targets of the investment was inappropriate. It boosted costs, slowed down the evaluation and sapped the goodwill of stakeholders – without contributing much by way of evidence on the impact and value for money of the investment.

Apart from the obvious finding that an evaluation framework should have been specified at the outset of the intervention, we concluded that the audit approach was cumbersome and expensive. It required reconsideration. Accordingly, we suggested an alternative designed to increase the speed, effectiveness and efficiency of the evaluation. Our advice might have wider applicability not only in the science and innovation policy field but more generally for the assessment of major investments implemented in uncertain contexts.

The specific solution we proposed drew on the *structured hypothesis testing* techniques used by the US security intelligence community. It involves assessing the investment by formulating and testing succinct propositions against summaries of available evidence in a structured and sequential manner. It reverses the time-line of the audit approach (tracking the intervention as it unfolds over time) by identifying the contribution of the intervention from a formative perspective – how we might move forward taking account of current budgetary and policy priorities.

The approach aims to maximize the signal to noise ratio by quickly testing hypotheses against the balance of probabilities and by reporting the results in a concise fashion according to a format suitable for use at later dates. A critical aspect of the approach is that it allows for, and encourages, an iterative process by which hypotheses are readily reformulated and evaluation results revised as fresh evidence becomes available – without recourse to major and costly re-writing of unwieldy reports.

The hypothesis testing approach we piloted proved to be effective in getting the State government evaluation back on track and engaging stakeholders in a positive dialogue about preparing for the future (rather than just reflecting on the past). It also demonstrated potentially significant cost savings compared with the audit-based approach. Consequently, the State government is now adopting the approach more widely and further developing its key components, namely:

*   Engagement of stakeholders in jointly specifying and agreeing the key hypotheses underpinning the intervention program to be tested and adjusted as development proceeds.

- Agreement amongst stakeholders at the outset of the program on the design of the monitoring and evaluation questions, framework, methods and reporting arrangements and their respective roles in providing the necessary data.
- Mixed evaluation methods and a process of triangulation to assess convergence of the emerging evidence – to reduce complexity as the intervention unfolds
- Tracking mechanisms to ensure that the evaluation can help reduce uncertainty and inform decisions in a clear and simple way especially at anticipated 'forks' in the road of program development
- Methods by which evaluation design and reporting can be standardized and the integrity of the evaluation process protected – including protocols that guarantee evaluators' independence regardless of whether they are internally or externally commissioned.

The approach we piloted is promising for more widespread use given its following compelling attributes:

Firstly, by reducing the complexity and workload of evaluations it lowers their cost and duration. If applied in a continuous developmental manner, such evaluations could spot early program failures and contribute to better use of resources.

Secondly, it offers a clear and standardized discipline for the design and conduct of program evaluations. It enables public authorities to become smarter commissioners of evaluations, recipients of government funding to be clearer about evaluation information needs, and evaluators to be more consistent in the conduct and reporting of evaluations.

Finally, the approach can be set up at the start of a program and at low cost. Hence, program managers will know at the outset what the key evaluation issues are and how they will be assessed. The resulting discipline of continuously monitoring and evaluating how public value is being generated (or not) by testing hypotheses against available evidence increases the likelihood of generating benefits for taxpayers by fostering continuous improvement.

On the basis of experience to date, the hypothesis testing method could help to bridge theory of change approaches and real time developmental evaluation in a pragmatic and rigorous way. It could contribute to the integration of policy and program design with the evaluation methods to be used before, during and after the intervention.

This potential exists because policy and program design in complex and uncertain contexts is itself often based on hypotheses about the underlying theory of change and the appropriate form for program architectures and delivery mechanisms. Consequently, the approach can also be used to collate and analyse the evidence that drives policy and program design by

140   *Implementing the transition*

integrating, assessing and reporting research findings from different interventions in a single comprehensive framework.

Reproduced from the *European Evaluation Society Newsletter*, December 2013, pages 13–14.

Value-for-money measures

'Value for money' estimates are clearly important in demonstrating transparency
and legitimacy. It is therefore essential that a seamless integration of appraisal
with MEL and risk management includes a means of measuring the value for
money of policy initiatives.

These measures can based on the cost of achieving advances in understanding
as reflected in updated odds of competing hypotheses being correct. This is a
process that is able to capture the impact of decreases in substantive uncertainty
as it shifts to quantifiable risk because this will be reflected in the changing odds.
This process is similar to the way in which Alan Turing developed a means of
calculating the odds that different competing decryption solutions were correct at
the end of each daily code breaking cycle – based on the (often limited) information available on that day. As noted in chapter four, this allowed Turing, in effect, to
place an 'evidence-based bet' on how best to allocate code breaking resources on
the following day. Thus, this odds-based approach would have the advantage of
reflecting decreases in uncertainty as improved odds of certain hypotheses being
true – in so doing allowing a return-on-investment calculation ('truth comes at a
price': public investment is a means of buying more favourable odds in the future).

This sort of approach would be particularly useful in providing a basis for
expressing the return on investment in academic research rather than relying
too narrowly on research commercialisation concepts – hence providing a basis
for implementing the concept of prescience outcomes discussed in chapter three.

A practical method for assigning odds in hypothesis tests

The aim here is to formulate an accessible means of implementing aspects of a
Bayesian approach to structured hypothesis testing in a public policy environment. In what follows, only one subset of Bayesian methods is used: binary
tests of hypotheses. There is a far wider set of Bayesian methods such as Bayesian
belief networks, and non-binary hypothesis tests that require complex simulation
modelling, see Fenton and Neil (2013) for a comprehensive coverage of these
methods. Given the emphasis on searching for simplified ways of implementing
Bayesian hypothesis tests in a public policy environment, these complex
approaches are not covered here. O'Hagan and West (2010) provide a broad
ranging collection of examples of these technically complex Bayesian analyses.

Figure 5.6 captures the essence of the proposed approach to integrating
appraisal with evaluation using structured hypothesis testing. The appraisal

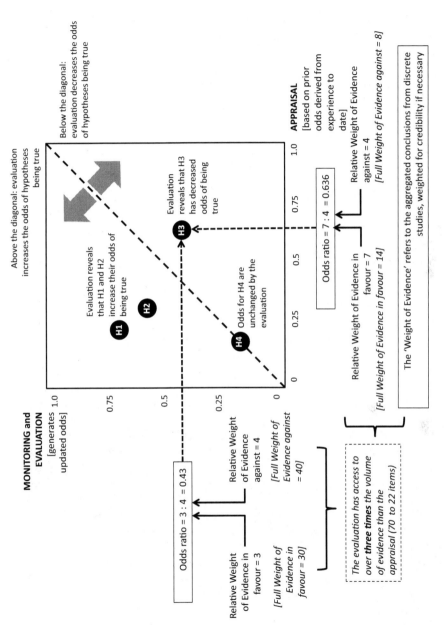

Figure 5.6 Odds-based hypothesis tests in appraisal and evaluation

142 *Implementing the transition*

function is mapped on the horizontal axis and the subsequent monitoring and evaluation function on the vertical axis. Four hypotheses are mapped (H1, H2, H3, H4), which collectively define the intervention in the sense that they reflect the theory of change being used. These hypotheses are framed in such a way that they are tests of specific aspects of the theory of change not tests of the theory of change as a whole. This decomposition allows for learning and adaptation by adjusting the theory of change in the light of accumulating experience. Put another way, whether or not the theory of change turns out to be true or false rests on the performance of its composite elements.

Figure 5.7, which is taken from a discussion of this approach in White and Matthews (2016), shows how this approach can be used to track updated odds over time, and from the very start of a policy intervention.

In order to produce this plot the odds for and against each hypothesis being true are expressed as probabilities by calculating the ratio of odds in favour to the total of odds in favour and odds against (i.e. the nominator divided by the sum of the nominator and the denominator). These odds can be calculated by systematic reviews of the available evidence using appropriate aggregation methods (discussed in greater detail below).

The key issue is how the credibility of different types of evidence should be assessed in the systematic reviews used to generate odds-based hypothesis tests. As noted in chapter one, the concept of a hierarchy of evidence is primarily an effort to minimise the incidence of diagnostic errors. Hence, a robust RCT is viewed as a particularly reliable means of minimising diagnostic errors (i.e. the rates of false positives and false negatives). From this signal processing angle, the rankings in any hierarchy of evidence should be determined simply on the basis of the accumulated evidence of the prevalence of diagnostic errors. This solution reduces the risks of distorted evidence-weightings associated with prior assumptions over the graduations in credibility between different types of evidence.

These diagnostic errors are easily measured using the simplified natural frequency version of Bayes Rule discussed in chapter four, which is simply the ratio of true positive test results to the sum of true positive and false positive test results. Such a ranking, and most important the relative scores using Bayes Rule in this ranking, will tell us how to weight the relative credibility of the evidence used to calculate the odds in favour and against each hypothesis. Aside from accuracy, one advantage of using this signal processing approach is that it allows the full range of signal processing analytics to be used (if this is necessary), including the diagnostic capability plots discussed in chapter four. Indeed, it would be particularly useful to use diagnostic capability plots to map the relative performance of different types of evidence. This is especially useful given that RCTs can yield diagnostic errors as a result of the use of classical significance tests in which large expenditure allowing large sample sizes can under some conditions result in spurious statistical significance test results, see Meehl (1978).

What this means in practice is that types of evidence based on credibility weightings are best developed as an analytical *output* rather than via assumed *input* parameters. These outputs can only be produced via systematic reviews

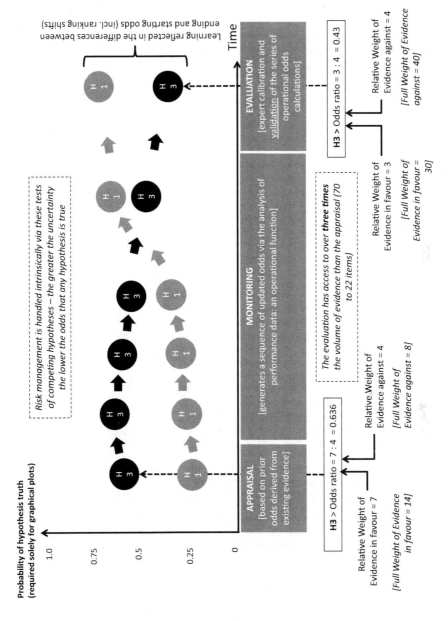

Figure 5.7 Using updated odds to integrate appraisal and evaluation

144 *Implementing the transition*

of the diagnostic errors associated with the use of different types of evidence in different policy domains. In such situations, diagnostic errors can only be measured with hindsight – they are identified when more recent tests reveal that older test results were wrong. Usefully, however, this hypothesis-based approach allows regular monitoring functions to serve as Bayesian updating processes. As information on progress (or the lack of it) becomes available the weights of evidence for and against each hypothesis can be calculated, in so doing providing a timely series of updates to hypothesis test odds. This, in turn, allows trajectories of these changing odds to be tracked (details of this dynamic approach are discussed below). These trajectories will give an indication of likelihood of any reversals in test results, i.e. cases in which the odds for and against specific hypotheses look like they may be about to 'flip' between a balance in favour to a balance against (or vice versa). This ability to track evolving trends in the odds-based tests provides a basis for 'weak signals' analysis.

The resulting data can then be used *ex ante* in subsequent intervention appraisals to give a sense of the potential for a specific test to generate a false positive or a false negative – adding a cautionary dimension based on collective experience. This cautionary dimension allows decision-makers to consider not just the findings from a specific appraisal but to also consider what these more general statistics on diagnostic errors suggest for how accurate that particular appraisal may eventually turn out to be. This rapid update capability (via regular monitoring) introduces a useful cost-reduction tactic. Evaluation studies conducted at particular stages become less important for learning and adaptation and become more of a calibration exercise that checks the accuracy of the monitoring-based hypothesis tests. This important role for systematic reviews using signal processing diagnostics creates an opportunity for academic research to contribute to public policy by fulfilling an important role (an issue we return to later).

Whatever the system of evidence credibility weightings used, it will need to be expressed in integer form in order to maintain integer-based Weight of Evidence measures. This is not hard to do technically. Most important, there are major technical advantages in using Boolean (i.e. true of false) evidence-assessment methods as this allows for a direct interface with binary signal processing methods. The latter allows for the extent of randomness in data to be measured using entropy measures whilst also being 'interoperable' with established Boolean analysis methods, notably Qualitative Causal Analysis (QCA) of the type pioneered by Charles Ragin, see Ragin (1987).

One advantage of using the visual approach in figure 5.7 is that sensitivity analyses (for example in the application of credibility weightings) can be grasped visually as relative effects. Sensitivity analyses will produce scattered positions for each hypothesis, this makes it very easy to see whether the scatters overlap or not and to compare the relative size of the regions of these scatters.

The relevant evidence available at the appraisal stage is used to calculate the odds for and against each of these hypotheses being true ex ante. As implementation unfolds these hypotheses are then used to make sense of the additional information obtained. This results in a greater volume of evidence being available

Implementing the transition 145

(in this case over three times more) and updated odds that each of these hypotheses is true. In the situation portrayed in figure 5.6, H4 remains unaffected by the new evidence, H1 and H2 exhibit increased odds of being true whilst H3's odds of being true decrease. This tells us that we have learned from this particular intervention that H1 and H2 are stronger performing aspects of the theory of change than H4 and H3. It also tells us that H3 may be a candidate for removal when the theory of change is adjusted – but ideally only when tested via a few interventions in differing conditions.

For economic impacts, the appraisal can develop a set of competing hypotheses for the range of potential rates of return on the investment, with the currently available evidence used to estimate the odds in favour of each of these potential rates of return being achieved. The evaluation then updates these odds allowing the rates of return with the strongest odds of being true to be treated as the result. This approach is particularly useful when, as discussed below, political imperatives have set a minimum threshold rate of return on the public investment because that becomes the most important hypothesis to test.

Figure 5.8 illustrates how odds-based tests of a set of competing hypotheses over rates of return on investment can be expressed visually. As the available evidence increases, which in turn allows tests of competing hypotheses to be refined, then the plateau of uncertainty at the start of the process gradually transforms into a ridge of more likely conclusions, in this illustration the starting probabilities for each hypothesis reflecting uncertainty are all set at 1.0 and become more accurate, and lower, over time. The outcomes in this graph are expressed in monetary terms but they can easily be expressed as ROI ratios

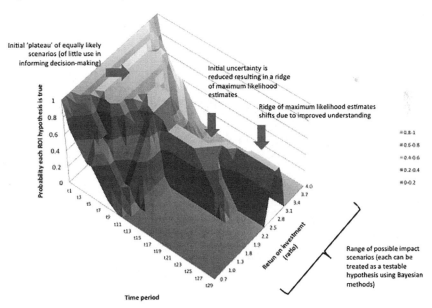

Figure 5.8 Visualising uncertainty and risk in return-on-investment calculations

146 *Implementing the transition*

(an ROI of 1.3 etc.). This is an approach that also applies to risk-aware budgeting. In that context, uncertainty over possible cost outturns is similarly reflected as a plateau with accumulating experience resulting in this plateau also (hopefully) transforming into a ridge. Referring back to the discussion of the differences between target-driven and discovery modes of intervention, budget overruns due to uncertainty over cost factors tend to occur when the target-driven ethos is applied to situations in which the discovery mode is more appropriate (given the high levels of substantive uncertainty faced). This sort of graphical expression of the situation together with the ternary characterisation of substantive uncertainty vis-à-vis stochastic risk and controllable risks could help decision-makers to question such assumptions and guide appropriate responses.

One advantage of this unified approach to appraisal, monitoring and evaluation is that it allows for an odds-based measurement of *information gains* to be calculated. This is simply because we can measure the changes in the odds that the hypothesis describing the theory of change are true. This provides a basis for calculating a summary measure of the information gain (the flip side of the reduction in uncertainty) in the simplest form simply as an average of the calculated odds. These measures of information gain, in turn, provide a basis for calculating the return on investment in information terms (the cost of obtaining these updated odds) – returns over and above the substantive benefits estimated for the intervention. This aspect opens up a potentially very useful opportunity for contributing to performance measurement in the public sector, particularly in regards to assessing prescience outcomes. Similarly, the ability to express reductions in uncertainty as improved odds via these hypothesis tests is also useful as a performance measure.

As explained in chapter three, prescience as an outcome class involves being better informed about the uncertainties and risks that we face in the future (a core benefit of public science in particular) and, as a result, being better positioned to invest in innovation and the other activities that help us to address these uncertainties and risks. When the updated odds of hypotheses being true increase this can be used as a contributing measure of prescience (we are less unsure than we used to be).

A major advantage of this simplified approach is that it allows pairs of hypotheses to be compared via the ratio of their odds of being true. In Bayesian inference these ratios reflect the relative weight of evidence and are referred to as the Bayes factor – a useful method of selecting between competing hypotheses. This aspect can be particularly useful when opposed teams are used to contest the interpretation of evidence (red teams etc.) because it provides a useful summary measure of this contested process, a measure that can in turn stimulate useful competition between these teams. This can be useful when pilots and experiments of alternative approaches are used. It is more useful to be able to directly compare competing pilots (i.e. sets of hypotheses) using odds measures than to use classical statistical significance tests based on comparing each competing pilot against a null hypothesis.

Perhaps most usefully, new understanding can be expressed in new hypotheses introduced into the set being tested as the intervention proceeds – creating an

Implementing the transition 147

adaptive process. Indeed, this ability to innovate in hypothesis creation in direct response to the evident limitations in explaining available data is a particularly useful aspect of using Bayesian methods. The ability to directly compare different hypotheses provides a useful (and quick) basis for both judging relative odds of being true and for identifying the 'reverse salients' in a set of explanatory hypotheses (inward bulges in the frontline of understanding that hold back advances – in this context reflected in lower odds of being true than found for the bulk of the hypotheses being used). Scrutiny of the reasons why existing hypotheses fail to gain support provides a stimulus for developing new and updated hypotheses – with the advantage of quantified odds to draw attention to these 'reverse salients'. This is an important aspect of machine learning that opens up important opportunities in public policy.

These new hypotheses will often undergo a distinctive life cycle. As new hypotheses they may well have minimal evidence to test them. Consequently, their odds of being true will be low due to the high uncertainty involved. As the existence of the new hypotheses stimulates research, resulting in more evidence available to test them, the odds will evolve. Some hypotheses will be ruled out whilst others will exhibit increased odds of being true.

Finally as regards useful attributes, the ability to relate the overall volume of evidence to the weights of evidence for and against specific hypotheses provides a basis for assessing the extent to which cumulative experience (which generates more information) is impacting upon advances in understanding as reflected in the updated odds of the hypothesis tests. It is useful to track this aspect because in some situations the accumulation of more evidence may not result in corresponding changes in hypothesis test odds. This flattening out of the gains in understanding is a consideration when deciding upon future priorities for monitoring and evaluation budgets. It is preferable to spend more on evaluations more likely to yield strong information gains (i.e., surprise us) – especially when systems exist for collating and using the results obtained from multiple evaluations in the same policy area.

To conclude this part of the argument, a number of useful practical advantages are created as soon as appraisal and evaluation are linked (seamlessly) by framing interventions as explicit tests of hypotheses and by capitalising on this advantage by using signal processing methods and odds-based tests of binary (i.e., true or false) likelihoods to implement a simple Bayesian method for testing these hypotheses.

Calculating odds-based hypotheses test results

Odds-based hypothesis tests (the odds for and against competing hypotheses being true) can be calculated using approaches used in security intelligence analysis. These analytical methods are based on scientific methods (the empirical refutation of competing hypotheses) but prioritise practical expediency. This expediency requires: rapid decisions given incomplete information; the ability to quickly update conclusions when new or re-calibrated evidence becomes

148   *Implementing the transition*

available; and providing busy and stressed senior decision-makers with an easily grasped summary of the (contestable) link between evidence and conclusions that does not require them to go through the subtle details of different technical studies.

This focus on practitioners' needs means that the choices made over analytical methods prioritise the (minimal) time to the conclusion and (usually unavoidable) decision stage. This contrasts with academic research and, to a great extent with current evidence-based evaluation methods, in which more time is available to improve the quality of the analysis (in signal processing terms to reduce the risk of false positive and false negative test results). This trade-off between time and quality usually means that security intelligence analysis is costly compared to academic research and to evaluation studies – but these costs tend to be associated with intelligence collection, a process in which calibration using diverse sources requires duplication (e.g. signals intelligence and human intelligence sources). Given the often dramatically damaging consequences of the decisions that need to be made, the risk of a misdiagnosis is addressed by this diversity in intelligence sources. In contrast, in the academic research and the evaluation domains the risk of misdiagnosis tends to be addressed via analytical methodologies. To some extent, the growing emphasis on systematic reviews in evaluation work reflects the power of the breadth of data sources in reducing the risk of misdiagnosis. From a security intelligence perspective, diversity in information sources is an important consideration – greater *scope* across different types of evidence can be more useful than greater *scale* in more restricted sources of evidence. Consequently, intelligence assessment methods place a strong emphasis on the ability to assess different types of evidence quickly – hence the use of 'correlated intelligence'. Diversity across sources reduces the risk that adversaries are deliberately feeding misleading intelligence into the assessment process.

Both academic research and evaluation work tend to be characterised by a clear interest in, and commitment to (indeed in some cases loyalty to), particular analytical methods. Even 'mixed methods' in the social sciences risks itself becoming just such an analytical specialism. As a result, debates on methodology quickly become immersed in levels of technical detail that defeat practitioners who, unless they happen to be familiar with the technical intricacies of those particular methods, can dis-engage. This tendency to generate 'baroque' methodological debates in academia and evaluation is itself an impediment to effective government–academic engagement.

As noted in chapter one, government officials who attend university seminars on policy-relevant issues tend to come away dissatisfied because so much of the discussion has focused on debates over the adequacy of data sources and the analytical methods used. On the other hand, academics who have participated in meetings and workshops within government tend to come away concerned by the lack of attention paid to potential biases in data sources and the analytical methods used (usually viewed as over-simplistic). Finding a way forward requires appropriate trade-offs to be made that balance precision against utility for decision-making.

One clue as to how to approach this challenge can be found in the Second World War code breaking discussed at various points in this book. That work developed an explicit utilitarian definition of precision – defined as the smallest difference in the odds in favour (or against) a hypothesis that is intelligible to a human being. In effect, this approach provided a framework for benefit–cost approaches because it set a precision threshold above which it is pointless to invest in further improvements.

In this approach, a change of odds from even (1:1) to 5:4, in probability terms the shift from 0.5 to 0.56 (rounded), i.e. a proportional increase in probability of + 12 per cent, is viewed as the degree of precision in any result that decision-makers will be able to make sense of, and react to (Good, 1979). This means that it is not worth the effort of striving to obtain precision of greater than this increment, i.e. a difference in the likelihood that a hypothesis is correct *within* the interval 0.5 to 0.56. This is an important principle because it focuses attention on analyses that are fit for purpose from this end-user perspective. This highly pragmatic, decision-focused, aspect of Turing's odds-based approach is clearly relevant to public policy.

The following diagram (figure 5.9) reinforces this line of argument by overlaying the approach adopted by Turing and Good with the UK defence intelligence categories that are used to indicate how reliable intelligence is. Superimposing the Turing–Good curve allows, in particular, two key points to be highlighted: situations in which something becomes a 'realistic' probability, marked by Log_{10} likelihood coefficients between –0.3 and –0.6 (i.e. probabilities less than 0.5 and greater than 0.25). In this diagram the lowest practical interval used by Turing and Good (e.g. that between 50 and 56 per cent) would encompass just a little more than the gap between a 'realistic probability' and 'probable or likely'). Similarly, this sort of minimum interval would account for around one third of the range covered by 'probable or likely'.

This continuous representation of confidence in evidence, which can be implemented using Bayesian approaches, has the advantage that any data updates can result in smoother confidence assessments. There is no need to jump between discrete confidence categories, which as discussed in chapter four in regards to the use of risk matrices, can be problematic as a basis for decision-making.

This graph tells us that analytical efforts, and the associated methodological debates, should always be calibrated against a 'map' of the specific levels of confidence that a decision-maker should require in order to make a decision. These confidence levels will, and should, differ according to the type of decision(s) to be made, i.e. risks of unintended consequences, the potential impact of these consequences, the ramifications for the decision-maker etc. In the above graph that uses UK defence intelligence categories (formerly known as the 'Admiralty Scale') a military commander will require these evidence confidence assessments in order to decide on the most appropriate courses of action, and in the light of the specific rules of engagement that apply to these circumstances. There can be legal ramifications to these choices, hence it is important to be clear about these evidence confidence issues.

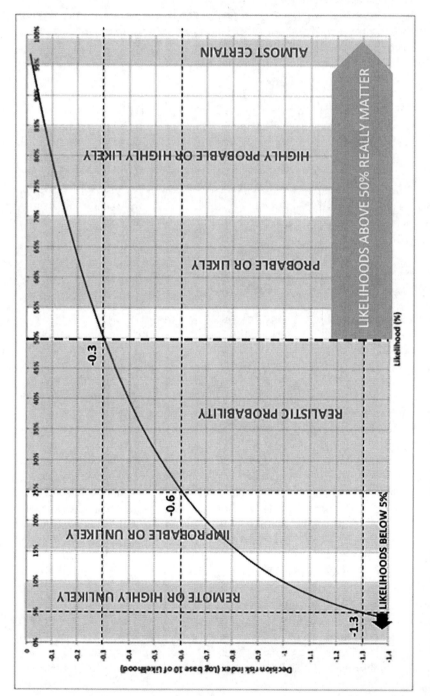

Figure 5.9 Aligning the risk curve and defence intelligence categories

Implementing the transition   151

Given the shortcomings of risk categories (as manifested so clearly in the use of risk matrices), it is preferable to use a continuous visual spectrum of likelihood regions in order to make clear how important, or unimportant, issues of test and evaluation accuracy actually are. For example an evaluation of an innovation support programme should specify at the outset what the degree of precision required to make a decision will need to be. This specification then allows the evaluation process to make design choices that aim to minimise the costs to be borne in order to meet this decision precision objective.

This end-user focus can be augmented by the pragmatic approach taken to assess the rate of return on public spending by some central economic ministries based in pre-defining a politically acceptable threshold rate of return on the public investment and then looking at whether the most credible and reliable evidence supports the test that this threshold has been reached. This threshold test method allows the contamination of evaluation results by unreliable evidence to be minimised (economic impact estimates usually involve a tail of increasingly less reliable evidence) – so it is preferable simply to test whether the best-quality evidence supports a hypothesis of the threshold ROI rate being achieved by the intervention. Too often, complex economic impact studies can unravel simply because they have incorporated this tail of lower-confidence estimates in an effort to maximise the estimate of the ROI. In effect, resulting in false positive test results for high ROI values. These false positive rates can be high – and too high to inform evidence-based decisions.

This is a different approach to the way in which conventional frequentist tests of statistical significance are used. These tests calculate the likelihood that the data observed could have been generated by random behaviours in a manner that prioritises precision in rejection of a null hypothesis of no treatment effect. Methods that simply apply the 0.05 probability threshold do not consider whether or not that degree of precision exceeds that required *in practice* by decision-makers given time pressures and the risks of delaying a decision in real policy conditions.

As noted earlier, the recommended Boolean approach to assessing different evidence sources and types is compatibility with the Qualitative Comparative Analysis (QCA) method developed by Charles Ragin in the mid-1980s (Ragin, 1987). QCA is a Boolean evaluation methodology (i.e. it is based on variables having the two states: true or false) and seeks to bring greater rigour to complex causal relationships. The approach was originally developed in an attempt to deal with the challenges in sociology and political science that stem from the division of research expertise between country and area specialists, who conduct case studies (often qualitative), and quantitative specialists who study patterns in cross-country phenomena (Ragin, 2008). This bridging aspect makes QCA particularly interesting from a public policy perspective. Detailed case studies are very useful in informing us about how specific economic, social, political and environmental circumstances interact to shape outcomes and future options. Such case studies give decision-makers a concrete expression of the messy real circumstances against which options to intervene will have to be assessed. These case studies also lend themselves to narratives well positioned to communicate how specific manifestations of these complex circumstances function. In contrast, quantitative studies focus on

152   *Implementing the transition*

identifying general patterns in circumstances and behaviours that, in effect, link what case studies pick up as specific (perhaps unique or unusual configurations), but draw out the cross-cutting dimensions. Consequently, any analysis that is able to integrate the qualitative understanding gleaned from case studies and the quantitative understanding obtained from cross-cutting analyses of general patterns can be very valuable in a governance context. Many policy interventions will need to be able to cope with the specific circumstances found 'on the ground' in particular locations (the qualitative) but will tend to be defined around quantitative parameters (as reflected in the theory of change). At a detailed level, specific circumstances are unusual in statistical terms whereas the cross-cutting factors that impact on these specific circumstances can be handled statistically with greater ease.

QCA approaches this methodological challenge by using Boolean methods to examine the nature and extent of the causal links between a wide range of variables based around identifying conditions in which expected outcomes did and did not occur. This approach is in fact similar that used in some types of security intelligence analysis which use a type of Boolean evidence assessment based on determining whether the currently available intelligence supports or contradicts a set of competing hypotheses (CIA, 2009). The CIA 'tradecraft' guidance recommends that hypotheses are favoured that have the least number of negative assessments against them – rather than the highest number of positive assessments. This cautionary principle reflects the philosophical assumption in science that nothing is ever proved 'true' – all theories are only as yet un-falsified.

In QCA 'truth tables' consisting of these Boolean maps of causal factors and relationships are constructed in an effort to identify the conditions under which expected outcomes did occur and the conditions under which they did not occur. These truth tables also cover situations (combinations of these binary codings) that may not have been observed to date. QCA can be particularly useful as a risk assessment method because it helps to shed light on how prevalence of certain factors found in different circumstances (as picked up in detailed case studies) are associated with success and failure in interventions. See Ton (2015) for a recent example of QCA applied to support for farming organisations in Bolivia.

Criticisms of QCA highlight the ways in which, in this small sample size environment, random patterns (i.e. noise) exhibited in the Boolean variables can be misinterpreted as signals of causal relationships, see Krogslund et al. (2015). This is of course a risk with any small sample approach. However, from a practitioner's perspective rather than an academic perspective (i.e. the need to make decisions quickly with only spare and ambiguous information to rely on), this objection to QCA must be balanced against the benefits of having access to a means of extracting information from a small sample size with complex configurations of circumstances. As stressed at various points in this book 'weak signals', small sample size indications of looming problems, are important in governance (and particularly in regulation and national security). From this

Implementing the transition 153

pragmatic angle QCA is a useful means of contributing to odds-based hypothesis tests. It is Boolean in nature, hence interfaces well with binary (true or false) hypothesis testing methods and is specifically designed to examine the complex configurations found 'on the ground' when designing and implementing interventions. Whilst QCA guidelines note that the use of Boolean logic as an analytical method for making sense of qualitative evidence is derived from electronic engineering, QCA does not (to the author's knowledge) try to exploit the useful analytical advantages of using signal processing methods (notably entropy measurements). QCA is therefore compatible with the more general class of Boolean analyses used in signal processing, but still stands to benefit from the use of these signal processing methods (not just entropy but the ROC/ diagnostic capability plots discussed in chapter four), plus of course the binary application of Bayesian inference discussed in this book.

Hence, in both QCA and security intelligence analysis the emphasis is on looking for patterns in complex data that can support or refute a set of hypotheses using binary characterisation methods (i.e. true or false). Whilst binary test results are deliberately limited in scope because they do not capture the magnitude of an impact, magnitude can be captured by using a set of competing hypotheses – each of which asserts a particular range of impact magnitude. In this way, it is possible to address (but separately) two key types of information useful to decision-makers: (a) the likelihood that an assertion is true or false given the available evidence and (b) the magnitude of an impact. Whilst in practical terms (b) is far more interesting and important in political terms than (a), there are many circumstances in which policymakers do highly value simple binary answers, for instance is there or is there not a credible threat of some type? In such cases, commonly found in national security, decisions may not always be based on graduated degrees of harm reduction – they aim for complete harm reduction (i.e. aim for threat *elimination*). The decisions made will, wherever possible, seek to avoid benefit–cost trade-offs. It is therefore important to be clear at the outset, if this is possible, which type of decision will be made. If a binary answer is sought then the analysis should focus on simply producing that binary result. If a *magnitude* answer is sought then the analysis should focus on producing a magnitude result.

For example a policymaker may be interested in whether or not a programme that has been subsidising R&D performed by SMEs (in order to create employment) has, on the basis of currently available evidence, created either more jobs or reduced losses of jobs. This can be evaluated by testing hypotheses relating to job creation vis-à-vis a counter-factual of no intervention of this type. A useful example of the use of QCA in industry performance can be found in Greckhamer et al. (2008).

Given that the binary representation lends itself, in principle, to the use of Shannon's framework – including the calculation of information entropy – this opens up options to apply non-frequentist statistical approaches to distinguishing between signals and noise in QCA analysis. QCA is also useful in a national security context as a means of analysing challenges such as 'attack paths' – the chains of causality

154 *Implementing the transition*

involved in delivering and attempting to foil an attack. See Valeriano and Marin (2010) for an application of QCA to historical experience of the different pathways to war between nations.

In general terms, and using a Boolean approach based upon QCA but benefitting from signal processing methods in analysing evidence from multiple sources (quantitative and qualitative), relevant information can be collated in a matrix that relates the range of evidence (in rows) to the range of situations that can be related to hypotheses (in columns). Frequency of occurrence data is then added for each configuration of conditions mapped. A binary test result is then derived for each item of evidence (e.g. different statistical studies and/ or discrete performance measures), indicating a positive, negative or null alignment with each hypothesis. Weightings to reflect the differential credibility of these different evidence sources (degrees of confidence in the accuracy of the data) can then be applied (weightings which, as has been suggested, can themselves be calculated using data on revealed diagnostic errors in the past for different types of evidence).

This analysis easily yields a weighted count of the number of cases in which the available evidence supports or contradicts competing hypotheses (generating odds of the form $x{:}y$ in favour of a positive test result). Figure 5.10 illustrates how this binary/Boolean approach to evidence assessment works. Figure 5.11 illustrates the similar manner in which security intelligence assessments are sometimes carried out, see CIA (2009) and also Heuer (1999).[4]

This approach also facilitates using evidence updates to assess the incidence of false positive and false negative test results – situations in which accumulating evidence demonstrates that an earlier diagnosis turned out to be false or was missed. In addition to providing the basis for an index of evidence credibility by evidence type, that information can be very useful in a forward-looking sense by calibrating new discrete test results via giving a sense of the likelihood that this initial test may eventually be revealed to be a false result.

		Characterisation of cases by variables						Assessment		
		A	B	C	D	E etc	Frequency of cases	With	Without	Consistency Coefficient
Cases/situations	1	0	1	1	0	0 ...	8			
	2	1	1	0	0	0 ...	12			
	3	0	1	1	0	1 ...	10	*Technical details of QCA approaches to assessment available in the literature*		
	4	0	1	0	0	0 ...	7			
	5	1	1	1	0	0 ...	4			

Figure 5.10 The Boolean approach to evidence assessment

JUDGE HYPOTHESES BY THE LEAST NUMBER OF NEGATIVE ASSESSMENTS AGAINST THEM	COMPETING HYPOTHESES			
	A	B	C	D
EVIDENCE (MULTI-SOURCE)				
X {implications for hypothesis tests}	+	+	+	-
Y {implications for hypothesis tests}	-	-	-	+
Z {implications for hypothesis tests}	-	-	-	-
Ψ {implications for hypothesis tests}	+	+	+	+

Figure 5.11 Analysis of competing hypotheses in security intelligence analysis

As such, the approach allows for systematic tests of evidence that yields direct tests of the odds of competing hypotheses being correct, rather than (as is conventionally done in non-Bayesian statistical work) basing tests of statistical significance on the probability that observed data is a signal compared to background noise (the null hypothesis/placebo). These conventional sampling theory–based tests of statistical significance prioritise precision in sampling accuracy over the magnitude of the observed treatment effect. This can result in beneficial treatments (those with large impacts) failing to achieve conventional statistical significance and treatments with lower impacts achieving statistical significance simply due to sampling characteristics (Ziliak and McCloskey, 2014).

The approach recommended here is far simpler to use than modern forms of Bayesian inference that require complex mathematical models and advanced simulation modelling. In effect, the security intelligence method substitutes an 'extrinsic' breadth and variety in the evidence used for the 'intrinsic' set of mathematical permutations used to determine the sensitivity of hypotheses tests to data characteristics.

156 *Implementing the transition*

Implementing a Bayesian expression of the policy learning cycle

Chapter four used a circular learning loop diagram to illustrate the concept of Bayesian updating. This circular perspective aligns well with the familiar policy cycle (which is also a learning process). Figure 5.12 brings in the weight of evidence factor discussed in this chapter, framed in relation to specific competing hypotheses – treated as radial distance (the stronger the weight of evidence the farther from the centre the trajectory). The diagram illustrates one way of linking Bayesian inference to the policy cycle, framed here using Deming's familiar plan-do-check-adjust loop.[5] This illustrates the way in which learning by doing (and its analysis) can lead to updated odds of different hypotheses being correct. In this illustration, Hypothesis/intervention 1 (H1) exhibits an increasing Weight of Evidence over the policy cycle whilst Hypothesis/intervention 2 (H2) does not – and is abandoned early as a result.

One advantage of expressing the weight of evidence measure in this visual (and cyclical) manner is that it facilitates scrutiny of relative rates of change over time in the weight of evidence in favour of competing hypotheses. This is particularly useful as a means of communicating Bayesian inference as decision-support information to non-specialists. In this approach 'evidence' (a term used so frequently now but with so little epistemological precision) is treated as the Bayesian pathways followed by competing hypotheses in the policy learning cycle.

The basic Bayesian learning cycle in the previous diagram (figure 5.12) can be modified to reflect different types of Bayesian applications. For example a physician may use Bayesian inference in a diagnostic manner (as follows):[6]

- take patient case history (specific conditions);
- relate the specific patient case history to general statistical likelihoods using the broader evidence base in order to generate the most plausible hypotheses to test;
- use diagnostic methods to test the most plausible hypotheses induced from the evidence base (often by a process of successive elimination of competing hypotheses);
- Arrive (if possible) at a conclusion as to the most plausible explanation and, on that basis, recommend the most suitable treatment options.

In this physician's diagnostic application of Bayesian inference, hypotheses of diminishing plausibility are generated by relating the specifics of a case to the general statistical evidence ('priors') – in essence a pattern recognition exercise that suggests hypotheses. This can be characterised as the *induction* of hypotheses from available evidence leading to hypothesis testing in order to recommend treatments. This is different from a pure hypothetico-deductive implementation of the Bayesian policy learning cycle (but just as relevant to public policy), a process illustrated in figure 5.13.

This inductive version of the Bayesian learning cycle, a process in which case-specific conditions are used to prioritise diagnostic hypotheses based on the evidence

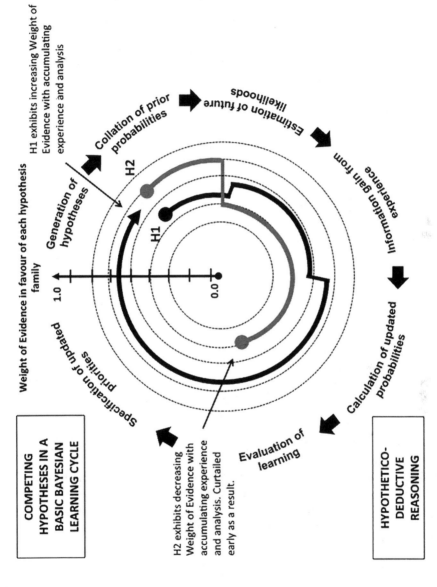

Figure 5.12 Competing hypotheses in the policy learning cycle

158 *Implementing the transition*

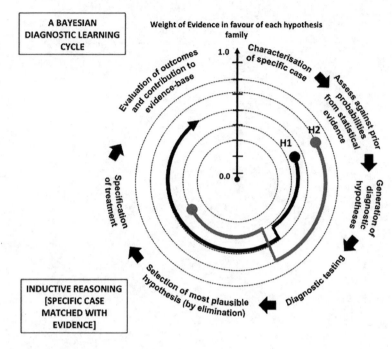

Figure 5.13 A Bayesian expression of the policy learning cycle

available at that time, is compatible with the use of Boolean evidence assessment methods as a means of characterising case-specific factors of relevance. As such, the approach would be particularly useful as a means of informing choices of the most appropriate intervention to attempt given these specific circumstances.

For example in an urban regeneration context with diversity in geographical conditions (environmental, socio-cultural, economic etc.), the choice of the most likely intervention to succeed *given those particular conditions* is best made via an analysis of the inter-play of specific conditions and general influences observed in a wide range of other cities and towns. Boolean evidence assessment provides a means of carrying out this sort of profiling as a means of prioritising the best interventions to attempt. The added advantage from an adaptive governance perspective is of course that the lessons from each attempted urban regeneration initiative are far more easily grasped using the seamless framework that links appraisal and evaluation using hypotheses testing.

A dynamic approach to diagnostic errors

In the discussion so far, diagnostic errors have been treated in a static manner as snapshots of the situation. False positive and false negative test results are only revealed by subsequent and more accurate tests (including results from monitoring prior to full-scale evaluations) – although a sense of the likelihood that a particular initial test may turn out to be a false result can be gained from statistics on the prevalence of these diagnostic errors.

The way in which appraisal, monitoring and evaluation have been approached using explicit hypothesis tests allows for a more dynamic approach to be adopted. As the odds in favour of the various hypotheses are updated (and particularly if this takes place via regular monitoring), then it is possible to examine the trajectories exhibited by each hypothesis test with each data update. These trajectories may exhibit random movements (which tells us that we can't understand what is going on using this hypothesis). But, of course, the trajectories may also exhibit a clear direction via repeated updates resulting in a consistent pathway emerging (e.g. decreasing odds with growing implementation experience). Figure 5.14 emphasises this point by showing how an initial odds specification can, in principle, end up going in any direction. In this case, with even starting odds (a standard Bayesian response to uncertainty that hedges its bet).

From this dynamic perspective, diagnostic errors reveal themselves as 'weak signals' – indications that what was previously assumed to be true may turn out to be less reliable and possibly distinctively untrue. In this framework, these weak signals emerge visually (in the test odds trajectories) and can therefore

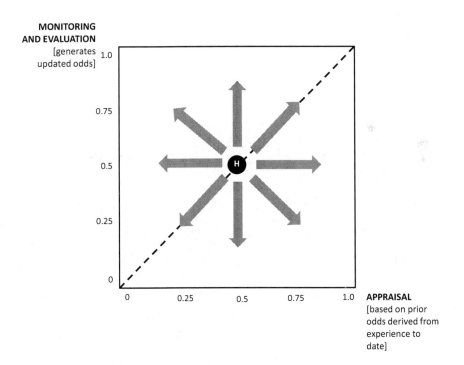

Figure 5.14 Possible pathways when linking appraisal to evaluation

160   *Implementing the transition*

serve as a basis for resource allocation decisions aimed at finding out more about what is going on.

This dynamic approach to diagnostic errors, especially the weak signals dimension, has the advantage of creating a conceptual space for decision-makers to apply judgement, and learn-by-doing in getting better with experience in using judgement, in response to uncertainty and risk. Given the importance, as stressed throughout this book, of fostering this type of learning-by-doing in coping with uncertainty and risk via testable conjectures about future as-yet-unobserved 'valleys' of evidence, this weak signals aspect is particularly important.

Security intelligence uses a discovery process referred to as the 'intelligence cycle'. In this process, policymakers on reviewing intelligence assessments and other relevant information (and ideas) can request specific information and analyses from the intelligence services. These requests then set in motion specific intelligence collection activities, information that is then analysed and fed back to policymakers. In the broader governance domain this ability to request 'bespoke' analyses involves less well-developed and structured processes. For instance, civilian analysis is more often single source (based on a particular report and type of analysis) and places a lower emphasis on assessing correlated intelligence (i.e. the extent to which the same conclusions can reasonably be drawn from diverse sources of evidence). The ways in which the security intelligence community applies formal approaches to assessing the nature and the extent of correlated intelligence and uses uncertainty-based classifications of the reliability of that intelligence to inform decision-makers provide a useful basis for civilian processes. In effect, security intelligence strives for diagnostic accuracy via the analysis of sparse and ambiguous information whereas the civilian policy community (emphasising recent trends) favours RCTs – effectively a delegation of diagnostic accuracy to the experimental realm.

The approach articulated here seeks to provide the civilian policy community with an alternative and potentially more 'fit for purpose' approach. In particular, it provides a practical basis for identifying weak signals of potential changes in policy circumstances that require further investigation – and creates the methodological environment (via structured hypothesis testing) for the sort of formalised synthesis of evidence used in the security intelligence community. This approach can be done quickly, cheaply and in a manner that facilities learning and adaptation.

Implications for cross-sectoral collaboration over public policy

The approach to delivering adaptive governance articulated here has some specific implications for collaboration and liaison between sectors, specifically in regards to how governments work with academia, civil society organisations (including policy think tanks) and the business sector.

Academia is well placed given the mix of subject matter and methodological expertise to take the lead in developing and refining a signal processing–based approach to assessing diverse sources of evidence (in effect the technical matters covered in this and the preceding chapter). Academia is also ideally placed to carry out the systematic reviews of the evidence base that both populate the signal processing framework with information and provide the all-important measures of the credibility of different types of evidence based on diagnostic error rates. Academia is also very well placed to drive the necessary capacity-building work associated with effective hypothesis formulation (not a strength in government departments at present).

Civil society organisations are well placed to use their on-the-ground understanding (mainly reflected in place-specific tacit knowledge) to contribute to new hypothesis formulation. This opportunity to introduce new hypotheses into the policy framework is especially useful given the different insights and experiences of those delivering public service 'on the ground' (whether as government employees, contactors or civil society actors). This place-based understanding can be an especially rich source of new ideas – concepts that this framework allows to be thrown into the mix of options for potential pilots and experiments. For example positive unintended consequences can be spotted quickly, investigated and used to generate new pilot concepts when civil society actors are engaged fully in this sort of policy experimentation cycle. Consequently, if a standard framework for linking QCA to odds-based hypothesis tests in an easily grasped manner could be developed it would facilitate civil society engagement in the policy cycle.

Conclusions

All the benefits summarised above are made possible by combining two basic principles: (a) the use of formally specified hypotheses to define, appraise, monitor and evaluate interventions, and (b) the use of odds-based binary (true or false) evidence assessments to measure the weight of evidence in favour and against these hypotheses. The result is a means of creating a seamless connection between appraisal and monitoring and evaluation – a seamless connection that does not currently exist.

Notes

1 Sabel and Zeitlin (2012) consider the potential of 'experimentalist' governance as an explicit approach to learning-by-doing that allows for very general outcomes to be set at the outset of an intervention followed by refinement via implementation.
2 See Althaus et al. (2007) for a discussion of the policy cycle.
3 This issue was discussed in a workshop entitled *Supporting risk-aware research* held on 11 July 2008 at the Australian National University. At this workshop Steve Dowrick used a presentation to suggest this particular solution to the need for less risk-averse research funding models.
4 Schweitzer (1978) and Wheaton and Deshmukh (2009) discuss experimental applications of Bayesian methods within the CIA.
5 There are other more specific models of the policy process, see for example Althaus et al. (2007), however the Deming model is used here to avoid complicating the picture. Most if not all specific versions of the policy cycle align with Deming's broad stages – but with differing flourishes and levels of detail.
6 I am grateful to Dr Robert Greenough (a physician) for stressing this diagnostic application of Bayesian inference in this policy context.

162 *Implementing the transition*

References

Althaus, C, Bridgman, P and Davis, G 2007, *The Australian Policy Handbook*, 4th edition. Allen & Unwin, Sydney.

Central Intelligence Agency 2009, *A Tradecraft Primer:Structured Analytic Techniquesfor Improving Intelligence Analysis*. CIA, Virginia.

Fenton, N and Neil, M 2013, *Risk Assessment and Decision Analysis with Bayesian Networks*. CRC Press, Boca Raton.

Good, I J 1979, Turing's statistical work in World War II. *Biometrika*. vol. 66, no. 2, pp. 393–396.

Greckhamer, T, Misangyi, V F, Elms, H and Lacey, R 2008, Using qualitative comparative analysis in strategic management research: An examination of combinations of industry, corporate, and business-unit effects. *Organizational Research Methods*. vol. 11, no. 4, pp. 695–726.

Heuer, R J Jr. 1999, *The Psychology of Intelligence Analysis*. Center for the Study of Intelligence, Virginia, USA.

HM Treasury 2011, *The Magenta Book: Guidance for Evaluation*. HM Treasury, London.

Krogslund, C, Choi, D D and Poertner, M 2015, Fuzzy sets on shaky ground: Parameter sensitivity and confirmation bias in fsQCA. *Political Analysis*. vol. 23, pp. 21–41.

Meehl, P E 1978, Theoretical risks and tabular asterisks: Sir Karl, Sir Ronald, and the slow progress of soft psychology. *Journal of Consulting and Clinical Psychology*. vol. 46, pp. 806–834.

National Audit Office 2013, *Evaluation in Government*. National Audit Office, London. Ragin, C C 1987, *The Comparative Method. Moving Beyond Qualitative and Quantitative Strategies*. University of California Press, Berkeley, Los Angeles & London.

O'Hagan, A and West, M 2010, *The Oxford Handbook of Applied Bayesian Analysis*. Oxford University Press, Oxford.

Ragin, C C 2008, *What is Qualitative Comparative Analysis (QCA)?* Presentation Slides. Department of Sociology and Department of Political Science University of Arizona Tucson, Arizona.

Sabel, C and Zeitlin, J 2012, Experimentalist governance, in D Levi-Faur (ed.), *The Oxford Handbook of Governance*, Oxford University Press, Oxford, pp. 169–183.

Schweitzer, N 1978, *Bayesian Analysis for Intelligence: Some Focus on the Middle East, Note on Analytical Techniques (Declassified Without Redaction)*. Central Intelligence Agency (CIA), Virginia.

Ton, G 2015, *Using Qualitative Comparative Analysis to Explore Outcome Patterns of Grant Support to Farmer Organisations in Bolivia*. Working Paper 2015–82. Agricultural Economics Research Institute LEI Wageningen UR, Netherlands.

Valeriano, B and Marin, V 2010, Pathways to interstate war: A qualitative comparative analysis of the steps-to-war theory. *Josef Korbel Journal of Advanced International Studies*. vol. 2 (Summer), pp. 1–27.

Wheaton, K J, Lee, J and Deshmukh, H 2009, Teaching Bayesian statistics to intelligence analysts: Lessons learned. *Journal of Strategic Security*. vol. 2, no. 1, pp. 38–58.

White, G and Matthews, M 2016, An 'odds on' approach to evaluation. *Evaluation connections. Newsletter of the European Evaluation Society* (February), Prague, pp. 10–11.

Ziliak, S T and McCloskey, D N 2014, *The Cult of Statistical Significance: How the Standard Error Costs Us Jobs, Justice and Lives*. The University of Michigan Press, Ann Arbor.

6 Conclusions
Lower entropy governance

The core argument

This book has argued that governments' ability to deliver cost-effective public policy is being held back by a reluctance to think about some of the fundamental conceptual and methodological issues raised by the process of governing. Some of these methodological issues are concerned with what the concept of 'evidence' means and, in particular, an over-enthusiastic focus on facts (detective work on the past) that has been de-coupled from the conceptual thinking and the testable hypotheses that are better positioned to help us grapple with what the future may have in store for us. Some of these issues are concerned with how well (or badly) governments cope with uncertainty and risk and also with how well (or how badly) learning and adaptation take place.

An important aspect of the latter issue is the extent to which a direct connection between intended outcomes and actual outcomes is established. As the book has argued, this connection can be strengthened if uncertainties and risks are explicitly identified via Bayesian tests of hypotheses used to define interventions at the outset and then linked directly to the measured outcomes.

From the perspective laid out in this book, public policy can be thought of as an iterative process of investing in increasing the odds of things occurring that we want to occur and decreasing the odds of things occurring that we don't want to take place. But, these outcomes are all odds – not the certainties, objective facts and evidence that currently pervade contemporary discourse in public policy. The more we focus on 'robust' evidence the more we focus on experience to date from a quasi-legalistic perspective of 'proof', rather than the odds-based perspective that aligns more easily with governments' role in trying to cope with the uncertainties and risks that markets cannot handle effectively (or indeed not at all). In contrast, an odds-based approach does not rely on evidence as proof of cause and effect – and of outcomes and impacts. Rather, it focuses on the more realistic and more forward-looking issue of whether or not what governments have done (or plan to do) may have increased the odds of things occurring that we want to occur and decreased the odds of things occurring that we don't want to take place. These odds can be calculated using the available evidence, but the conceptual space created in linking testable hypotheses

164 *Conclusions*

to the calculated odds that these hypotheses are correct does not limit governance to the evidence. It allows for judgement and beliefs, not least because judgement, beliefs and the associated creativity is key to generating the hypotheses that drive knowledge – and practice – forward.

The argument is that an evidence-obsessed policy stance can amplify risks by increasing the potential for nasty surprises to occur over and above unavoidable levels. Practices and procedures within government that drive a disjuncture between a stochastically influenced reality and a 'good governance' misrepresentation of that reality that attempts to marginalise and downplay this stochastic aspect can result in an amplified potential for nasty surprises. This amplified potential for nasty surprises can drive up public sector debt. This is most recently demonstrated by the global financial crisis in 2008 and 2009 and also in the ways in which large-scale military interventions, and wars, can be driven by inaccurate information and misleading assumptions. In effect, increased public debt becomes a manifestation of this attempt to pretend that uncertainty and risk are avoidable problems – problems that prudent and sound risk management that complies with fixed standards and guidelines can minimise. We can only transition to ways of governing with a reduced potential for nasty surprises if we abandon the pretences that: (a) substantive uncertainty can be treated as if it is quantifiable risk, and (b) we bring the consideration of uncertainty and risk centrally into how we frame, implement and learn from interventions.

The knock-on effect of bearing high levels of public debt is that the resulting austerity measures, in turn, limit governments' capacity to minimise the potential for nasty surprises. This creates a vicious circle with the potential to exacerbate fiscal problems. The bottom line of this argument is that a transition in public policy to a more realist 'odds-based' approach could contribute to fiscal stability by reducing the potential for nasty (and costly) surprises. Whilst we cannot avoid the unavoidable we can avoid making these unavoidable nasty surprises even worse than they would otherwise be.

These arguments stem from applying the logically coherent framework developed in the Second World War, i.e. a policy and decision-making context in which to minimise the risk of nasty surprises was a matter of existential importance. As reflected in the elegant Bayes-influenced mathematics of information pioneered by Claude Shannon, governance is an entropy-minimising process. The costs of governance are therefore strongly influenced by the costs of coping with entropy: the greater the reduction in entropy over unavoidable levels the lower the costs of governance. Hence, attempting to govern as if entropy can be assumed away (as modern risk management frameworks tend to in effect assume) can only increase the risk of exacerbated public debt.

The implications of these arguments for regulatory stances may be particularly useful at a practical level. As the various examples of risk amplification noted in this book have illustrated, the specific methodological choices and assumptions made have the potential to amplify risk by increasing the potential for nasty surprises. The choices made over which statistical data to rule in and rule out of bounds, the choice of analytical and risk management methods, assumed statistical distributions – all have the potential to amplify risk by increasing the potential for nasty surprises to take place. Consequently, regulatory stances that reduce this risk of nasty surprises by being strongly adaptive can be especially useful. In practical terms this means allowing learning and the resulting adaptation to modify boundary assumptions rather than work only *within* those assumptions. 'Red teaming', i.e. efforts to break a defined regime and framework, should be allowed to question all the fundamental assumptions made in a regulatory framework – and especially as regards assumed statistical distributions, data points ruled in and out of bounds and the methods used to analyse data and make key decisions. Compliance with the status quo in these terms can be very dangerous. A minimised risk amplification ratio, framed as the ratio of the achieved potential for surprise over the unavoidable potential for surprise, can provide the rationale for such red teaming exercises, and a range of other efforts to minimise governance entropy.

From this perspective, the most important thing to comply with is a requirement to consider and to seek to reduce this risk amplification ratio. This means that public sector organisations need to be able to grasp this entropy-based concept, understand its implications for practices and procedures and to act with the objective of minimising the amplification of risk.

In each of the examples used to illustrate these issues there was a false negative conclusion to the test for system failure risk. In the case of the space shuttle the false negative was caused by methodological restrictions imposed by NASA on itself that constrained risk assessment as regards prior data on failures in similar systems and avoided a probabilistic approach to risk management in preference for engineered safety margins (a methodological choice that impacted upon decision-making over risks). In the case of the Hoover Dam, design tolerances and operational guidelines that impact on risk were based on biased statistical data on rainfall patterns. In the case of the Australian home insulation scheme false negatives arose because risk management was treated as a compliance ritual and an impediment to rapid programme delivery (rather than being placed at the centre of the design and delivery of the intervention). In the case of the global financial crisis part of the problem lay in the shape of the assumed statistical distribution used to define risk measures in the regulatory framework – leading to a false negative risk assessment. These false negatives amplified the potential for nasty surprises above unavoidable levels. In other words, risk was amplified because organisations made choices over risk management that increased the likelihood of false negatives for tests of potential system failure – amplifying risks by increasing the potential for nasty surprises.

Use of the risk amplification ratio can also assist in balancing short- and medium-term gains against longer-term concerns. One feature of modern public policy that stems from the high priority placed on how announcements will play in the media is a tendency towards myopia. Announcing policy stances that may have a more immediate beneficial impact but that can drive less beneficial or even harmful impacts over the longer term through negative consequences that are overlooked as they are too far away in the future. This is a tricky area because

166 *Conclusions*

some policy initiatives may have their effectiveness compromised by unforeseen developments that are genuine nasty surprises. However, there are cases in which these less beneficial or even harmful impacts could, reasonably, have been foreseen but were overlooked or ignored due to high discount rate thinking and policy frameworks that place an especially low value on events a few decades hence. Indeed, as stressed earlier, one outcome from effective public policy is the reduced social rate of discount associated with enhanced prescience.

In both situations, an over-arching focus on considering the implications for the risk amplification ratio will tend to decrease these risks of shortcomings in policy delivery. Furthermore, a greatly strengthened capacity to learn and adapt will increase risk mitigation effectiveness by allowing emerging understanding of unforeseen problems to drive evolution in policy. The risk amplification ratio provides a useful tracking measure of progress (or lack of it) in this regard.

From a Bayesian angle, these longer-term unforeseen and 'discovered' problems in policy delivery are false negative test results – what originally appeared to be a true positive turns out to be a false negative. These experiences tell us that using (Bayesian) signal processing methods that focus attention on the likely incidence of false negatives and false positives in risk assessments in governance in general, and regulatory stances in particular, are an important methodological consideration. From this perspective, the 'confusion matrix' that summarises the incidence of the four permutations possible (true positives, true negatives, false negatives and false positives) should be a familiar diagnostic tool in governance. Use of the confusion matrix in efforts to grasp and easily communicate the ways in which the potential for nasty surprises is subject to amplification could have a useful impact on the effectiveness of governance.

If we avoid drawing upon insights from Bayesian inference, and the tools from signal processing derived from those insights, we risk basing policy decisions on false positives or false negatives. These tend to be counter-intuitive results from 'commonsense' analyses. The concept of the 'weight of evidence', expressed as the odds in favour of competing hypotheses, provides a suitable and easily grasped means of measuring the extent to which the experience gained from policy delivery is changing the odds in favour of the hypotheses that these policy interventions are testing. Using a simplified and standardised Bayesian approach to assessing how policy delivery impacts upon the weight of evidence supporting different hypotheses may provide the basis for an open and collaborative approach to public policy that is likely to be more effective than the current stance. In the approach advocated here, evidence is treated as the Bayesian pathways that are followed by competing hypotheses in the policy learning cycle.

Using Shannon's concept of entropy (the less likely the *assumed* likelihood of observing information, the greater the information gain if we do observe it), then governments can play their distinctive role effectively if:

- they seek to maximise the set of assumed likelihoods (especially low likelihood – large consequences events), *and*

- maximise the information they are able to access about evolving experiences, *and*
- adopt analytically tractable (that is to say simplified and standardised) Bayesian methods.

Collaboration with academia and with civil society provides the key to achieving all three of these capability objectives. Civil society organisations are especially well placed to accumulate and use tacit knowledge on strengths and weaknesses in service delivery (generating new intervention concepts and assessing delivery effectiveness) and universities are well placed to deploy analytical methods to design, develop and demonstrate the advantages of a standardised Bayesian approach to the policy innovation cycle. Consequently, a trilateral partnership between government, civil society and academia has the potential to catalyse this sort of transformation in ways that are less likely than with government acting alone.

One useful aspect of future work in this area will be to develop 'value for money' estimates based on the cost of achieving advances in understanding as reflected in updated odds of competing hypotheses being correct. This will have the advantage of reflecting decreases in uncertainty as improved odds of certain hypotheses being true – in so doing allowing a return-on-investment calculation ('truth comes at a price': public investment is a means of buying more favourable odds in the future). This sort of approach would be particularly useful in providing a basis for expressing the return on investment in academic research rather than relying too narrowly on research commercialisation concepts.

Within government, and in the ways in which government uses external consultants to conduct independent evaluations, we currently face the challenge that the more rigorous we are in methodological terms when conducting evaluations, the lower the calculated return on public spending. We need to transition from this state of affairs to a trajectory in which the cumulative experience gained from each year's spending on appraisal and evaluation (the book has argued that these should be two sides of the same framework not separate activities) is reflected in improved diagnostic capabilities associated with lower false positive and false negative test results. At present, this spending and cumulative experience appears to be resulting in a growing awareness that false positive test results for additionality are far more prevalent than has been apparent. Indeed, one major benefit of the emphasis on evidence-based policy has been an increased attention paid to methodological robustness and a reduced tolerance for dubious and positively biased evaluation results – especially when these are produced by independent consultants pressured to come up with 'strong' return-on-investment figures.

Implications for developing economies

On a global scale, one of the assumed differences between governance in developed and developing countries is the demonstrated capacity to abandon policy

168 *Conclusions*

interventions that are not working well. Indeed, in diagnostic terms, failures to learn and adjust in policy implementation are a key indicator of low capability levels. Efforts to foster this adaptive capacity in governance are driven by a mix of political will and by the technical capability of governments to monitor, evaluate and learn from past and current interventions. It therefore makes sense for governments actively seeking to build-up their policy capacity capability to consider the extent to which their capacity to learn and adapt is as good as it could be – and how this capacity could be improved. This requires diagnostic tools that are 'fit for purpose' and the ability to use such tools effectively within the public sector.

As stressed earlier in the book, in OECD countries, the formal monitoring and evaluation frameworks that are, in theory, a key driver of policy learning can be excessively 'administrative' and focused on compliance with funding contracts and/or standards and guidelines rather than on maximising opportunities to learn-by-doing in policy implementation. This disconnect means that the ways in which OECD governments handle evaluation (and use evidence more generally) in the context of their broader public sector reform agendas is not necessarily a capability that other nations are wise to emulate. It would be wiser to explore capacity-building approaches with the potential to jump beyond current 'best practices'. A focus on the risk amplification ratio as a diagnostic tool and on using Bayesian inference, framed in signal processing terms, is one potential approach to articulating this sort of capability 'leap-frog' strategy.

Conclusions on the set of propositions tested

Chapter one listed five propositions to be tested in this book. The conclusions reached on each of these propositions are as follows.

1 *It is useful to analyse the effectiveness of governance from the perspective of attempts to minimise the potential for surprise.*

Examining the effectiveness of governance from the perspective of attempts to minimise the potential for surprise, especially nasty surprises, does provide a useful basis for moving forward. This is because it establishes an over-arching framework able to counter-balance tendencies for risk management to be treated as compliance ritual that is, in effect, bolted on to appraisal and evaluation processes rather than being central to these functions. Experience demonstrates that this tendency to treat risk management as an impediment to delivery can be very damaging to the performance and the credibility of government.

2 *An equation linking the amplification of risk to the ratio of the actually achieved potential for surprise over the unavoidable potential for surprise provides a practical and conceptually robust method for implementing this focus on the potential for surprise.*

The concept of a risk amplification ratio based on the ratio of actually achieved potential for surprise over the unavoidable potential for surprise has the potential to be a generally applicable concept that is grounded in signal processing and information theory approaches. However, the ratio is most attractive as a heuristic for guiding organisational approaches that integrate the management of uncertainty and risk with the appraisal and evaluation of interventions.

The ratio can be used to highlight the way in which a range of cases in which the methodologies and statistical data used to assess risks have amplified risks by increasing the potential for nasty surprises to occur. This takes place because of what is *ruled out of bounds* in risk assessments. This can be:

- an assumed statistical distribution that is biased (e.g. the assumed distribution has a fatter tail than the real distribution);
- an approach to decision-making that down-grades the room for risk-mitigating decisions in preference to assumed risk elimination;
- approaches that don't allow for subjective judgement in the face of uncertainties about the future not justified by 'hard data'; or
- approaches to risk management that are primarily treated as compliance rituals that are impediments to getting on with delivering policy.

These are all documented situations in which risk management in public sector activities is found wanting because of the rigidities associated with not approaching uncertainty and risk as opportunities to be creative.

As such, it is unlikely that there will be a single dominating technical method for calculating this ratio and more likely that its diffusion and use will encourage the development of a family of specific implementations aligned with this ethos – each with particular strengths and weaknesses in specific governance contexts.

3   *The concept of governance entropy, defined as the extent to which the unavoidable potential for surprise is increased by mind-sets, practices and procedures (resulting in amplified risk), provides a useful analytical contribution to the public sector reform process.*

Coping in times of austerity in the public sector can be very challenging for those involved (and those seeking to access government services). This ability to cope can be made even harder if we avoid focusing on the various ways in which the ways we approach decisions, and evidence we draw on to support those decisions, neglects the risk of increasing rather than decreasing entropy. As such, an emphasis on the concept of governance entropy, as reflected in information theory, can play a useful role in encouraging officials to consider the possible unintended collective consequences of specific decisions. It provides a basis for challenging classic bureaucratic behaviours that support the narrow interests of a particular cog in the government machine and location in the hierarchy,

170 Conclusions

by focusing attention on indirect knock-on effects in a manner that relates closely to the potential for wasted efforts (increased entropy is associated with increased waste).

4   *A simplified and standardised Bayesian expression of the policy learning process has the potential to support efforts to minimise the potential for surprise.*

As articulated in chapter four, it is feasible to develop a simplified and standardised Bayesian expression of policy learning if a binary test approach linked to the use of data expressed as natural frequencies is used – and this expression is able to benefit from some useful technical methods developed in signal processing work notably in the ROC diagnostic.

5   *Testing competing hypotheses using the simplified and standardised Bayesian decision-support framework expression provides a practical and conceptually robust means of minimising the potential for surprise by creating a seamless integration of the currently distinct appraisal, monitoring and evaluation and risk management functions.*

The framework proposed in chapter five is a logically coherent means of articulating and implementing a seamless integration of appraisal, monitoring and evaluation and risk management functions. The key enabler of this method is the use of structured hypothesis tests to directly link appraisal, monitoring and evaluation and risk management functions and the use of odds-based tests of these hypotheses based on the relative weight of evidence for and against each hypothesis to provide a nuanced yet easily updated and therefore dynamic and timely picture of what is going on.

From the perspective articulated here, the dominating emphasis on 'evidence' provision as a basis for constructive engagement between government and academia, and government and policy think tanks, should be counter-balanced with greater recognition of the potential for nasty surprises that this evidence cannot reduce. This creates a role for judgement and conceptual thinking that encourages a more creative and innovative approach to leveraging the advantages of collaboration between these sectors. Recognising that governments are the uncertainty and risk managers of last resort helps to focus attention on the limitations of evidence and on the importance of more forward-looking approaches.

The use of simplified and standardised Bayesian approaches to hypothesis testing, with all interventions treated as sets of hypotheses being tested via implementation, provides both a means of explicitly encouraging this creativity (new hypotheses are measurable outputs of creativity) and a basis for collaborating in monitoring and learning as policy is being implemented. This focus on hypothesis *generation* would be particularly useful as a means of encouraging efforts to reduce the potential for nasty surprises by proposing hypotheses able to test for early 'weak signals' of potentially major shifts in circumstances. These weak signals characteristically signal threats before conventional statistical significance can be achieved (by which time it can be too late). This aspect adds further support to the use of Bayesian signal processing–based methods because these are, by design, intended to alert us to these weak signals.

Scope for enhanced international cooperation

The next step in the capacity-building agenda framed in this book would be to implement a simplified and standardised Bayesian approach in systematic reviews (meta-studies) of how effectively policy learning has been taking place in similar policy areas in different countries. The use of ROC based DCPs (Diagnostic Capability Plots) would provide a useful way of summarising differences in diagnostic capability between countries and policy domains, and would provide a practical yet theoretically robust means of tracking the success of future capacity-building efforts in evidence-based evaluations. This sort of bird's-eye view could be particularly useful for senior officials seeking an easily grasped summary of diagnostic capabilities in policy formulation and delivery, and a useful performance benchmarking tool for identifying and understanding better practices.

As regards the key technical challenge of calculating likelihoods of test inaccuracies it is important to recall that, in clinical diagnosis, the estimated likelihood of true and false positives and true and false negatives in test results is a function of the overall prevalence of measured test accuracies (as the context against which the likely validity of a specific test result is judged). Consequently, a collective international systematic review process would provide a means of calculating the overall prevalence of test inaccuracies for particular types of evaluation in particular public sector activities.

In other words (and just like in clinical diagnosis), we should seek to develop an integrated dataset that allows practitioners in government, and their professional advisors, to calibrate specific test results against the overall prevalence of test inaccuracies. It is important to note that these test inaccuracies are the combined result of methodological shortcomings *and* emerging events and outcomes.

With sufficient international cooperation, perhaps facilitated by the Organisation for Economic Co-operation and Development (OECD), such a global dataset could be developed by tracking of the relationships between sequences of programmes and project-specific evaluations (the best way of measuring false positive and false negative test results is by using successive tests as these can reveal shortcomings in previous tests). The more comprehensive grasp of the worldwide patterns in false positive and false negative test results for appraisal and evaluation studies would, in turn, provide a useful resource for policy design. This systematic review work could assist in judging risks at this initial stage much in the

172   *Conclusions*

same way that similar data assists in judging the risks associated with the choice of a medical intervention. At present, this risk assessment process is not especially rigorous in methodological terms or robust in empirical terms.

This process highlights the potential benefits of collective action at an international level aimed at sharing information and insights with the potential to reduce the potential for nasty surprises. Indeed, it may be possible to develop high-level estimates of the risk amplification ratio using such data. This would provide a useful bird's-eye view of how well (or not) governance entropy is being managed.

Adopting an open innovation approach

This book has laid out an agenda aimed at working out how we can translate our well-meaning intentions to govern effectively by getting better at learning and adaptation into the practical tools and techniques that will help us to do this.

The main focus in exploring these possibilities has been a fairly detailed and methodologically oriented look at what it means to govern in an uncertain and risky world – a world especially well configured to throw up nasty surprises. These nasty surprises are manifested in many ways, including high levels of public debt. Within this broad theme, particular attention has been paid to the ways in which the choices we make over how to govern can increase rather than decrease this potential for nasty surprises. The proposed risk amplification ratio that explicitly seeks to focus attention on this potential to increase rather than decrease this potential for nasty surprises, the use of signal processing concepts and diagnostic tools together with the development of a simplified and standardised Bayesian approach to testing competing hypotheses (hypotheses that are used to define policy interventions) are all put forward as areas for future work aimed at assisting practitioners.

This is an ambitious agenda for assisting the process of public sector reform. As such, the best approach to making progress is likely to lie in encouraging an 'open innovation' effort. This involves government soliciting creative solutions able to contribute to these aspects of public sector reform via discrete contributions and advances that feed off each other – each standing to benefit from progress made by others. For example there are a range of ways in which the risk amplification ratio can be calculated. Rather than selecting one method and complying with that, it would be preferable to encourage the development and use of a range of methods and for users to select those that seem to be most appropriate and then 'triangulate' their results in order to inform decision-making.

The Expected Value (EV) model of the innovation process introduced in chapter two and drawn upon at subsequent stages in the argument highlights the ways in which this open innovation effort will itself involve investment risks – and will be expected to cross the so-called 'valley of death' in the innovation process (the region in which the EV trajectory goes negative and gets worse before it gets better). This investment risk trajectory requires risk-taking

Conclusions 173

investments that would be best achieved using an open innovation model because this provides a good basis for mitigating risk by maximising the sharing of collective benefits (engendering a positive sum game).

One first step in fostering this open innovation approach to lower entropy governance could be to focus on the entropy dimension. Entropy is measured by observed randomness – it is greatest when there are even odds that a particular event will be observed in the future (labelled 'noise'). Entropy decreases as these odds diverge from even and is zero when there is a probability of zero or 1.0. As a practical tool, it can be useful to test for randomness in a manner that assumes this is to be expected and, thus, highlights the relevance for decision-making of non-random behaviours. This is the principle behind the diagnostic use of the ROC curve used in electronics, re-framed in this governance context as a Diagnostic Capability Plot (DCP). If we find random behaviour then we react in a way designed to reduce that randomness. Of course, one strength of robust evidence-based methods is that they do test for significance (information) against randomness (noise).

It would therefore be useful to develop a means of testing against randomness without the need for RCTs (as the most reliable means of doing this) – in so doing providing a useful baseline assessment of the current state-of-play. Systematic reviews could be used to test for the extent to which the data on policy formulation and delivery can best be explained as random behaviour – or, of greater concern, 'worse than random' behaviour in the sense that the decisions made and actions taken are correlated with what is taken to be reality (on the basis of the evidence we have) but in a negative manner.

For example consider a government programme seeking to support innovation in SMEs. If it is found to have followed risk-averse grant allocation procedures that have resulted in projects being supported that would have gone ahead anyway without a public subsidy whereas projects that would not have gone ahead without a public subsidy were not supported, then this is effectively a programme that should be located below the (random) diagonal line in the DCP framework. Resource allocations are correlated with the conditions in SMEs assumed to warrant the government intervention – but correlated in an inverse manner and against the rationale for such an intervention. Such situations are in fact less rare than those unfamiliar with the details of evaluating government support may assume. It is not unusual for programme funding guidelines to actively favour projects relating to innovation that have a low risk of failure – a risk sufficiently low that private sector funding would be likely to be forthcoming anyway. This is one way in which concerns within government over accountability and transparency that are framed as risk avoidance can result in what are effectively corporate welfare payments.

Another illustration of this sort of problem is the way in which applications for public support for private sector innovation projects can sometimes be made precisely because a corporate board has rejected a project proposal as being

174   *Conclusions*

driven by the interests of those intending to do the work rather than by the company's overall strategic priorities. In such cases, if the project goes ahead because public funds are accessed (the project may be low risk in technical terms and thus receive public funding if risk-averse procedures are followed), then it is likely to meet its technical objectives but will still not be adopted because it does not align with board priorities.

Consequently, it can be useful to have access to an analytical framework for use in public sector evaluations that is based on signal processing methods designed to highlight better than random, random and worse than random situations. As the illustrations above highlight, public spending that exhibits the worse than random characteristics associated with the region below the diagonal in a diagnostic capability plot helps to drive up public debt. This is because the decisions made over the use of public funds tend to result in wasted expenditure – the collective public benefits intended for the intervention fail to materialise. In general terms, the greater the proportion of public spending that lies below the diagonal in this diagnostic framework, the greater the potential for increased public debt. From this perspective, it is not governance entropy that drives up public debt but something of greater concern: a form of negative entropy (configurations of test result inaccuracies that reverse the truth). One way of thinking about this is to compare expected outcomes from random resource allocations with the outcomes when this negative entropy exists.

This characterises the human condition. Beliefs and judgement have the potential to reduce entropy (placing behaviours towards the ideal spot as regards the incidence of true positives and true negatives in hypothesis test results) but they can also result in behaviours that are worse than random – generating hypothesis test results that correlate negatively with reality. To use an illustration from the activities that led the ROC curve to be developed in the first place (interpreting blips on a radar screen) – it is the radar operators who consistently misinterpret the data they are presented with that should be our greatest worry: deeming a contact when there is no contact and missing the real contacts. From a governance perspective we would be better off with decisions that are made randomly than attempt to cope with such situations of worse than random decisions (such decision-making would, after all, be far less costly to deliver!). Consequently, this sort of signal processing framework could provide a sobering diagnostic and capability benchmarking tool.

The recommended approach based on these signal processing concepts is compatible with existing economic concepts used in public sector evaluations but has the advantage of making it easier to compare the results of a disparate range of evaluations by creating an analytically coherent space in which to measure their characteristics from a signal processing perspective. The potential for observed behaviours to be better than random, random or worse than random is key to this measurement space. This stochastic aspect makes it much easier to handle the inevitable 'noise' (entropy) found in reality. This contrasts with the rather mechanical nature of some evaluation approaches that are less well equipped to handle stochastic behaviour.

This open innovation process would provide universities and research institutes with an opportunity to demonstrate research impact by virtue of the ways in which they are especially well positioned to use advanced research methods, create advances in these methods, and apply these methods to complex and hard-to-analyse data. The results obtained by using such methods can be framed as measures of research impact that go to the heart of governments' role as uncertainty and risk managers of last resort. It would be useful to pay particular attention to trying to identify situations in which public spending exhibits worse than random characteristics of the type illustrated in the SME innovation support example.

Whilst we can, of course, never be sure that the evidence we are using to make important decisions is totally accurate we can, at a practical level, assess the extent to which the decisions we make are better or worse than randomly made decisions. This approach is well suited to academic mind-sets and less well suited to bureaucratic mind-sets. It is this difference that generates the potential to advance evidence-based policymaking in a manner that will remain compatible with the emphasis placed on robust test results in RCTs but not be restricted to the use of RCTs.

To return to the metaphor of the observed and the unobserved valleys (about which we can only conjecture) with which this book opened, as uncertainty and risk manager of last resort governments should continually strive to develop better ways of interpreting the evidence we have (for the valley we are currently in) in a manner that helps rather than hinders the ability to conjecture about the as-yet-unseen valley that we may have to deal with in the future. Beliefs and judgement are not factors to be eliminated in evidence-informed policy – they are critical to this process – and are best assessed with reference to random decision-making rather than harder-to-justify legalistic notions of 'truth' and 'proof'. Signal processing concepts and methods provide us with a coherent framework for articulating this perspective on governance.

One step forward in this process of delivering a transformation in how governments cope with uncertainty and risk would be for governments to encourage international cooperative work aimed at developing tractable methods for implementing these signal processing methods and to test the relative strengths and weaknesses of these methods against a wide range of policy interventions. As the book has demonstrated, a natural frequency-based expression of Bayesian methods makes it far easier to implement this practical approach to learning and adaptation in the public sector by avoiding the highly complex mathematical approaches necessitated by the use of conditional probability–driven versions of Bayes Rule.

Towards a compromise-based solution to tests of statistical significance

Currently, we face a situation in which the (classical) statistical methods used to deliver evidence-based policy treat model parameters as fixed and the observed data as a sample from a random but unknown set. The objective of analysis in that approach is to calculate the probability that the data observed could have

176 *Conclusions*

been generated by random processes. If this probability is low then the observations are deemed to be statistically significant. This approach aligns rather well with an ethos in which public policy sets well-defined objective measurable targets that the intervention then seeks to meet. In other words, the parameters are fixed and the question of whether or not the intervention has been successful amounts to the calculated probability that random factors could have generated the observed measures applied to evaluate the intervention. This is precisely what an RCT seeks to measure. It is also a stance that encourages an intervention to pre-define a 'theory of change' in some detail in order to justify an intervention – a process that requires rather heroic assumptions to be made about complex systems of cause and effect in which actors are able to react to an intervention – perhaps in unexpected ways.

The inverse of this classical approach is to treat model parameters as a random but unknown set (we are uncertain as to complex cause-and-effect relationships) and the observed data as fixed (rather than a sample of unobserved data). This aligns with an approach to interventions that reverses the current logic: interventions are experimental tests of how these complex cause-and-effect relationships are operating and, as such, do not require clearly defined targets in order to be effective. From this 'inverse' perspective if clearly defined targets are assumed to be effective then we are certain rather than uncertain about the complex cause-and-effect relationships that characterise reality – we do not need to use an intervention to discover new information about these complex cause-and-effect relationships.

From this methodological angle, the challenge of how best to govern involves balancing two fundamentally different, but not necessarily incompatible, approaches – each of which reflects initial assumptions made about whether the data we actually have is treated as fixed or a sample from an unknown random domain and whether the parameters we use are fixed or are treated as random and unknown processes to be discovered. This correspondence between classical versus Bayesian statistical methods and approaches to governance in an uncertain and changing world is striking.

A pragmatic response would be to move beyond a zero sum stance that requires the choice of *either* classical statistical analysis or Bayesian methods to support *either* target-delivery *or* discovery-based approaches to interventions. This zero sum approach encourages doctrinal arguments between statisticians that don't seem to take us forward and doctrinal arguments in public policy that don't take us forward either. As with any negotiation with conflicting preferences the solution lies in compromise. It lies in both camps recognising that each approach has strengths and weaknesses and that the complexity of modern governance creates a space for both approaches to be complementary to each other. Target-delivery approaches to interventions using classical statistical methods to evaluate them have their place. Discovery-based approaches to interventions using Bayesian inference (albeit simplified and if possible standardised) also have their place.

In broad terms, target-delivery approaches are the most suitable when the situation is simple and not thought to change or evolve (including as a result

Conclusions 177

of responses to an intervention as it is being implemented). In other words when the potential for surprise is low. Discovery-based approaches are the most suitable when situations are complex and subject to change. In other words when the potential for surprise is not low (though it may not be particularly high). The risk amplification ratio based on the achieved over the unavoidable potential for surprise therefore provides a useful tool for helping to arrive at this sort of compromise arrangement. When the ratio is assumed to be low then classical target-delivery approaches are appropriate. When the ratio is high then discovery-based Bayesian approaches are appropriate. In addition, this ratio can be used to monitor and evaluate the extent to which the decisions made over which method should be used are effective. As the intervention cycle proceeds it will be possible to track the extent to which the initially assumed potential for surprise proved to be realistic. In cases where the potential for surprise is initially assumed to be low (hence classical target-delivery interventions are used) but turned out to be higher, then a lesson has been learned for the future. Similarly, when the potential for surprise is initially assumed to be fairly high (hence discovery-based Bayesian approaches are used) but turned out to be exaggerated, then another useful lesson has been learned. These adjustments are represented in the following diagram (see figure 6.1).

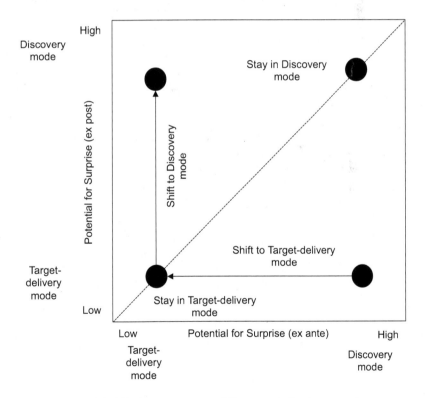

Figure 6.1 Potential shifts between target-delivery and discovery mode

178   Conclusions

Over time, this ability to switch methods should facilitate more effective policymaking. This is itself a process of learning and adaptation via which governments can improve how well they judge which approach to adopt as well as how well they learn and adapt to surprises.

One pragmatic way forward in such a composite approach stems logically from the current dominance of classical target-delivery interventions using classical statistical tests for treatment effectiveness. Given this dominance, all that it is necessary to put in place is a process for evaluating how well target-delivery approaches are working and to select cases in which the potential for surprise was under-estimated and, therefore, to shift, in future interventions, to the discovery-based architecture.

In practical terms this requires that the evaluation function (a) works with a reduced rate of diagnostic errors (given the high rates presently), and (b) is designed in such a way that learning about the potential for surprise can be captured. This latter aspect is most easily achieved if appraisal is closely coupled to evaluation in methodological terms. In principle, both classical and Bayesian statistical methods are well suited to capturing the potential for surprise provided that assumptions are specified at the outset.

In a classical statistical approach used to support a target-delivery intervention mode the potential for surprise can be defined as the extent to which the theory of change turns out to be accurate (i.e. the specified theory of change is a set of testable hypotheses). The use of this hypothesis-based specification (if done in a competent manner) makes it relatively easy to link appraisal to evaluation (simply because appraisal defines the hypothesis and evaluation tests them). When an evaluation reveals that the theory of change, as reflected in the hypotheses used in the appraisal, turns out to be unrealistic (i.e. things did not work as expected) then the degree to which these hypotheses are tested as being untrue provides the measure of surprise. In other words, all that is required to measure the degree of surprise is (a) to be clear in the appraisal what the hypotheses that express the theory of change are, and (b) to be able to measure the extent to which these hypotheses are supported (or not). It is in this latter respect that some methodological challenges arise. In classical statistics competing hypotheses (or a single hypothesis) are not tested directly, they are each tested relative to the null hypothesis of no treatment effect (including a placebo effect). The simplest response is to adopt a 'dual use' approach in which the set of hypotheses used in a classical statistical and target-driven intervention design are also tested in a Bayesian manner (in terms of the odds for and against each hypothesis being correct).

For example an intervention seeking to help long-term unemployed to re-enter the workforce by providing face-to-face mentoring and encouragement might be defined in classical terms with clear targets for the number of people who were unemployed for five years or more that remain employed five years after the one-month-long coaching service was delivered. These targets will have been set on the basis of some kind of understanding of the reasons why people find it hard to re-enter the workforce and will define a theory of change

Conclusions 179

covering how these impediments are to be overcome. The theory of change can be expressed as a set of linked hypothesis (linked in a chain of causal relationships) and the extent to which the targets have been met is easily measured. The potential for surprise arises because targets may not be met because the theory of change turned out to have been unrealistic (an intrinsic effect) and/ or other unexpected things happened that disrupted the effectiveness of the intervention (an extrinsic effect). It is necessary to strip out any extrinsic effects in order to isolate the intrinsic effects – we are interested in the extent of surprise within the definition of the intervention.

Whilst there are complex matters to consider here in methodological terms, the basic point is that there is little hope of making useful estimates of the nature and extent of surprise if appraisal and evaluation are de-coupled – as they currently tend to be. The first step is therefore to ensure that monitoring and evaluation and appraisal are just two (or more) phases in a unified methodology, rather than evaluation being bolted on (at a later date) to a separate appraisal method. This process can be kicked-off simply by making the effort to define all interventions using a set of hypotheses covering what the intervention seeks to achieve and how it will achieve this. Once this has been done, the basic platform upon which these more sophisticated investigations can take place has been established.

As political imperatives drive a devolution of policy capacity to the regional level (as in the UK at present) this will place a great emphasis on building new policy capacity at the local and regional government levels. Because there is a lower likelihood that entrenched ways of doing things already exist, this opens up a useful 'greenfield' opportunity to develop faster and cheaper approaches. These new approaches can seamlessly integrate appraisal and evaluation within an uncertainty- and risk-based framework – without the impediments created by established old ways of doing things. The signal processing–based methods discussed in this book could provide the architectural principles for this developmental work.

Next steps

The following next steps have emerged from this discussion of practical tools and methods for delivering adaptive governance.

1   Start to implement this standardised and simplified method able to assign odds for and against a set of competing and complementary hypotheses being true on the basis of available evidence – both qualitative and quantitative. This framework would provide a unified approach to both appraisal and monitoring and evaluation that is able to make use of a broad range of evidence during the appraisal phase and then move seamlessly to monitoring and evaluation activities using the same framework. Uncertainty and risk are addressed directly via the odds-based assessment of hypothesis validity (the greater the substantive uncertainty to lower the odds of any

180 *Conclusions*

hypothesis being correct). Gains in understanding achieved via better evidence and learning-by-doing would be reflected in updated odds. Ideally the framework would combine a Boolean approach to the analysis of evidence of the type pioneered in Qualitative Causality Analysis (QCA) with credibility weightings able to reflect differential credibility of evidence sources and yield a clear traceable connection between diverse sources of evidence and the odds assigned to hypothesis tests. In technical terms the main challenge (which is always a challenge) is to agree on a protocol for handling the all-important credibility weightings. The rest of this framework is not especially hard to implement. The specific suggestion made in this book is that these credibility weightings should be based upon the use of the simplified 'natural frequency' expression of Bayes Rule (the ratio of true positive test results to the sum of true positive and false positive test results) and should be based upon systematic reviews of the diagnostic accuracy of all available studies. This diagnostic accuracy can only be measured *ex post* and in cases in which more recent tests reverse earlier diagnostic conclusions (e.g. what was previously thought to be a true positive turns out to be a false positive and vice versa). In this approach, credibility weightings for different types of evidence are not assumed as parameters, they are measures driven by cumulative experience of diagnostic errors to date. For example expert opinion will only be given the lowest rating and ranking if the evidence tells us that it has a higher diagnostic error rate than other forms of evidence. Most usefully, the recommended approach is able to use a measure of relative credibility (as measured using Bayes Rule) that could result in graduated distinctions between the credibility of different evidence sources rather than a simple rather arbitrary ranking. Academia is of course well placed to perform these signal processing method–based systematic reviews of evidence credibility (see the following item).

2   Commence systematic reviews of diagnostic performance in appraisal and evaluation activities aimed at generating data on the prevalence, in particular, of false positive and false negative test results. This work would aim to classify collective experience in appraisal and evaluation by policy area in such a way that work on specific appraisals and evaluations would be able to consider the broader prevalence of diagnostic errors against which these specific results should be calibrated. For example if intervention appraisals in relation to support for strengthened innovation in SMEs exhibit in general terms a 35 per cent rate of false positives (i.e. that proportion of appraisals that falsely identify treatment requirements in the sense that no intervention is in fact required), then that information provides a useful incentive to maximise diagnostic effectiveness by using best practice methods whilst also providing senior decision-makers reacting to specific appraisals with an evidence-based resource for querying the assessments they are presented with. This metadata on the prevalence of diagnostic errors in particular government departments would also provide a useful basis for performance benchmarking by allowing specific performance to be compared to general

performance in relevant policy areas. It is anticipated that the main technical challenge would be in how to accurately normalise for variations in the details of appraisal and evaluation contexts within the same policy domain. This systematic review work would provide a key data input to the evidence credibility measures to be used to implement the odds-based hypothesis testing framework outlined in item 1 above.

3   Develop and pilot a variant of the Capability Maturity Model (CMM) based upon the use of Diagnostic Capability Plots using signal processing concepts. This framework would aim to use measurements of the ability to manage false positive and false negative diagnostic test results to determine capability levels in a governance context. This diagnostic should also address 'worse than random' performance (diagnostic errors that are negatively correlated with reality) and extend the characterisation of capability levels 'downwards' to address this dimension – effectively adding negative capability levels of the form suggested by Schorsch (1996) building upon Finkelstein (1992). One example of a worse than random intervention pattern would be a prevalence of cases in which subsidies for business activity (innovation for example) turn out to favour companies more likely to perform well in any case – rather than helping companies less able or likely to perform well to learn how to perform better. These situations can arise when funding guidelines are sufficiently risk averse that the only companies supported could have obtained private sector funding – the public funding simply displaced private sector funding. Whilst there is a tongue-in-cheek aspect to these ideas in a software engineering context (e.g. an emphasis on producing excessively detailed process-dictating manuals that are too complex to use), the characterisations of how government departments manage themselves are rather accurate. This approach would bring precision to organisational capability assessments by examining matters from the specific lens provided by diagnostic accuracy in appraisal and evaluation – key functions as regards when governments decide how to intervene and how they learn from those interventions. If such an initiative is successful then it would provide a basis for assessing adaptive governance capacity in different government departments. The pilot would require access to the results of the comparative study of diagnostic error rates in appraisal and evaluation outlined above. The objective will be to develop a mapping between levels of capability maturity and the DCP framework in figure 6.2 below.

4   Develop an integrated approach able to combine target-driven interventions using classical statistical significance tests of effectiveness and discovery-based interventions using Bayesian tests of learning gains. This would involve developing a framework able to determine the most appropriate type of intervention to launch in response to a challenge and also able to guide any shifts between intervention modes (from target-driven to discovery-based or vice versa) as appropriate. A project of this type would be useful in moving beyond an adversarial relationship between frequentist and Bayesian approaches to the analysis of evidence in a policy context. It would also

182 Conclusions

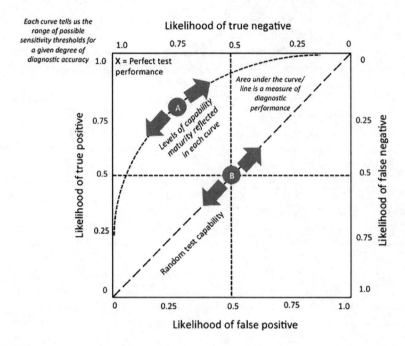

Figure 6.2 Using Diagnostic Capability Plots to inform capability maturity assessments

shed more light on the connections between the choice of statistical method used to assess evidence and the approach taken to policy interventions – an important but perhaps under-explored aspect of public policy.

5   Once results from both the systematic review work and the related diagnostic capability assessments start to emerge it would be useful to investigate the feasibility of measuring the costs of poor diagnostic performance. In other words, the costs associated with producing and making decisions on the basis of false positive and false negative diagnostic test results. As such, this signal processing perspective provides a means of assessing wasted expenditure in governance: appraisals that lead to unnecessary interventions and evaluations that misrepresent the benefits created by interventions. In combination, these are costly consequences of diagnostic errors that restrict the ability to learn and adapt. Figure 6.3 illustrates the patterns of synergy targeted in this approach.

The aim of these linked initiatives would be to raise awareness of the advantages of approaching adaptive governance as a matter of fast and effective diagnosis and treatment evaluation by using signal processing methods.

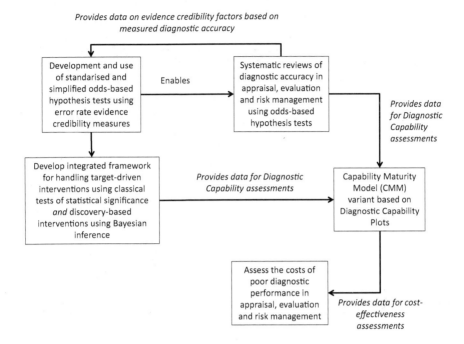

Figure 6.3 System of synergies to be exploited

Diagnostic accuracy should become a high-profile objective able to counterbalance the imposition of authority irrespective of diagnostic accuracy. In those 'discovery-based' situations in which learning and adaptation are important, the targets used should not be fixed performance targets but (if targets are necessary) dynamic learning targets as captured in changes in the odds of the hypothesis that define an intervention being true. These revised odds measure what we have discovered about what we were less certain about in the past (or indeed know nothing about). In this way, governance can transition to a mode that combines a more scientific approach to appraisal and evaluation with a greater recognition of the importance of creativity in formulating potential solutions – creative processes that can be understood and tracked via the 'churn' in the hypotheses they yield (churn in the sense of adding new and revised hypotheses and eliminating ineffective hypotheses). This type of measure will help to draw attention to the important role of creativity in governance and provide a basis for actively managing this creativity. Potential new and revised hypotheses will tend to require collective scrutiny and selection – much in the way that an industrial corporation manages its innovative activities via the structured competition between alternative concepts with those that prevail in these selection rounds attracting more funding (funding freed up from the concepts that have been eliminated).

184   *Conclusions*

In this vision, uncertainty and risk management cease to be 'add-ons' to formulating and delivering public policy – these considerations become the basis upon which policies are formed, delivered and adjusted based upon the experiences gained. To re-visit current general thinking on 'adaptive governance' as a networked activity associated with common pool resources and other collective challenges, the recommended integrated approach would remove, or at least greatly reduce, the impediment to networked and collaborative activities. A seamless integration of appraisal, monitoring and evaluation and risk management based on odds-based tests of structured hypotheses would create a space in which diverse actors (including civil society) can become more actively involved in the policy process. Without this seamless integration the traditional, cumbersome and uncertainty- and risk-averse nature of how governments organise themselves will make adaptive governance hard to achieve.

Finally, one striking aspect of the intellectual history of mathematical inference in astronomy is the information gain made possible by *circularity*. The repeated orbits of planets, their moons, comets and observable asteroids follow elliptical paths that interact with each other in complex ways. It is the empirical measurements of these orbital irregularities and displacements that provides the evidence against which competing hypotheses can be tested mathematically. Astronomers conjecture about as-yet-unobserved objects (including planets) on the basis of the odds that the measured orbital displacements for the objects we can observe could, potentially, be explained by the hypothesised object or objects not yet observed. Laplace's development of the mathematical framing of these hypotheses (the work that really kicked off what we know call Bayesian inference) was founded upon calculating the odds that a conjecture would provide a simple explanation for complex observed phenomena. As such, this approach provides the bridge between the evidence we have and the evidence we *might* be able to have in the future (i.e. the valley we can see and the valley we cannot yet see) *once we have set about discovering it*. It is these types of conjecture that posit the existence of the as yet unknown as potential explanations of the known that provide a better ethos for doing public policy than an excessive emphasis on scrutinising all the evidence we currently have and avoiding conjectures and speculation over what the future may have in store.

The emphasis on strengthening circularity in the policy process in this book (by integrating appraisal, evaluation and risk management) would provide a basis for applying the Laplacian/Bayesian focus on calculating the odds that conjectures are true in the policy process. The resulting cycles of planning, doing, checking and adjusting, expressed via the odds that competing hypotheses (including speculative conjectures) are true, would provide a firmer basis for doing public policy. This integrated approach, if implemented using the diagnostic power of established signal processing methods, would allow us to cope with the uncertainties and risks created by changes in the conditions under which decisions must be made by focusing on changes over time in the diagnostic accuracy of the policy process. The lower this diagnostic accuracy the greater the confusion we face over what to do, and the more likely it is that the ways in which we govern will amplify the potential for nasty surprises and consequently drive up public debt. From this perspective, the high levels of public debt we try to cope with are a symptom of our demonstrated capacity to govern using techniques that amplify rather than reduce the potential for nasty surprises. The unavoidable potential for surprise is made even worse by our risk-averse compliance ethos in governance that scorns ambiguity, subtlety and agility in preference for rigid inflexible targets, our myopic 'proof'-based approach to the use of 'evidence' and a well-cultivated fear of speculation and conjecture in the policy process (i.e. trepidation in moving beyond the evidence). Governing in a 'worse than random' manner (uncertainty- and risk-averse problem diagnoses and resulting decisions that are negatively correlated with reality) is an especially strong foundation for building public debt.

Getting policy wrong more than half of the time(worse than randomly), and the public debt this creates, is a luxury that taxpayers should not be willing to tolerate. At present, however, the way in which we frame, analyse and communicate public policy to the electorate obscures these aspects by avoiding the sort of scientific analysis that bases conclusions on the extent to which what is observed is random – or worse than random. The signal processing paradox in governance is that the public sector has funded the scientific and technological advances that are able to learn and adapt to subtle factors quickly, effectively and in a self-governing manner (i.e. machine learning) *yet* has been unable to apply these same advances to the machinery of government. Such an application would provide a compelling new paradigm for public sector reform. The most potent targets to set when governing should encourage efforts to learn how to transition from near or worse than random capability towards greater accuracy in problem diagnosis, treatment development and implementation. This transition requires that rates of false positive and false negative diagnoses, and also their incidence in the assessment of treatment effects, are measured, tracked and communicated in ways that are amenable to target-setting. Each policy cycle should become a demonstration of improved diagnostic accuracy and (as in astronomy) a source of useful conjectures and formal inference on possible causes of the measured displacements in these repeated cycles.

References

Finkelstein, A 1992, A software process immaturity model, ACM SIGSOFT. *Software Engineering Notes.* vol. 17, no. 4 (October), pp. 22–23.

Schorsch, T 1996, *The Capability Immaturity Model* (CIMM). Paper Prepared at the Wright Patterson Air Force Base, Ohio.

Glossary

Abductive reasoning Inducing testable hypotheses from the available evidence.

Achieved potential for surprise The actually achieved potential for surprise over and above the unavoidable potential for surprise.

Analysis of competing hypotheses An analytical technique used within some specialist areas of government (notably security intelligence) to assess sparse, ambiguous and changing evidence. Often used when decisions cannot be deferred, hence a strong emphasis is placed on correlating evidence from multiple sources in an effort to reduce the risks of misdiagnosis.

Appraisal A formal assessment of the benefits relative to costs for potential government interventions (and ideally factoring in risks and uncertainties).

Bayesian inference An approach to statistical hypothesis testing that directly compares the likelihoods that hypotheses are correct given the available evidence – designed to facilitate updated odds when new evidence becomes available.

beta A coefficient used in the Capital Asset Pricing Model to reflect specific investment risks relative to those prevailing in the market as a whole.

Capital Asset Pricing Model (CAPM) A formal model of investment risk that calculates the relationship between levels of risk exposure and expected rates of return to compensate for these risks.

Classical statistical significance Statistical tests of hypotheses based upon estimating the probability that the data observed could have been generated from random processes. Hypothesis validity is judged via comparison with a null hypothesis of no observed treatment effect.

Computational Fluid Dynamics Sophisticated mathematical simulation models of how fluids and gases behave under real complex and changing conditions.

Diagnostic Capability Plot (DCP) A version of the Receiver Operator Curve (ROC) applied to assess an organisation's diagnostic capabilities via the prevalence of false relative to true positive test results.

Double hermeneutic A syndrome via which those whose behaviour it is intended to influence modify their actions in response to their understanding of the theories held about them.

Entropy A measure of the predictability of the elements in a signal based on the balance between randomness and information in past observations – in effect a measure of the potential for surprise.

Glossary 187

Evaluation Studies of the benefits created by a government intervention.

Evidence-based policymaking Efforts to base public policy on robust empirical evidence (usually statistical data of various types). The aim is to avoid subjective and anecdotal dimensions that bias decisions away from objective conclusions.

Expected value (EV) The estimated economic value of an investment option adjusted for quantifiable risks (balances the risk-adjusted value of success against the risk-adjusted cost of failure).

Experimentalist governance An approach to governance in which intended outcomes for interventions are loosely specified at the outset and in which learning and adaptation through experience and in the face of uncertainties are intended aspects of delivery.

False negative A negative test result when the tested condition is present.

False positive A positive test result when the tested condition is not present.

Gaussian copula A multiple variable version of the normal distribution.

International Financial Reporting Standards Internationally agreed standards that seek to create more coherent and less nationally-variable practices in corporate financial reporting, thus reducing risks to investors.

ISO 31000: 2009 The latest published version of the international standard for risk management.

Key Performance Indicator (KPI) Measures used to establish whether or not agreed performance targets are being met.

Learning-by-doing Learning based on actual experiences.

Learning-by-undoing The result of the double hermeneutic in action – resulting in intended outcomes from a government intervention not happening due to learning and adaption by target groups that falsifies the theory of change.

Log-frame A programme and project management methodology based on matrices that link goals, purposes, activities and outputs.

Machine learning A range of automatic techniques via which machines learn and adapt their behaviour based on evolving a set of empirically testable hypotheses in the light of experience.

Monitoring Regular collection and scrutiny of data on the performance of a government intervention (usually focusing on whether targets and milestones have been met).

Monitoring, Evaluation and Learning (MEL) The combined impact of monitoring and evaluation on learning-by-doing.

Net Present Value (NPV) The current economic value of a proposed investment assessed by subtracting the discounted stream of expected costs from the discounted stream of expected future benefits.

Normal distribution A widely used statistical distribution (also known as Gaussian distribution) derived from the averaged behaviour of random events. It has the useful diagnostic attribute of generating estimates of the probability that observed data could have been generated by random effects. The lower this probability the more likely it is that the data observed is of significance (i.e. can be treated as information rather than noise).

188　*Glossary*

Occam's Razor　The philosophical principle that a simple explanation should be preferred to more complex explanations that are otherwise comparable in explanatory power.

Output-outcome budgeting　A structured 'mechanistic' approach to defining how government activities are intended to generate useful outcomes via specific outputs.

Placebo effect　Measured treatment effects even though no real intervention has been attempted (whether or not the intervention has been applied having been hidden from intervention recipients). Commonly encountered in clinical medicine.

Public value　In a democracy, the value placed by the electorate on what governments do.

Qualitative Causal Analysis (QCA)　A Boolean (and/or) method for analysing the characteristics of qualitative conditions and possible explanations. Particularly well suited to case study analyses and with particular prominence in political science.

Quantifiable risk　Risks and measurable uncertainties that can be adequately handled numerically.

Randomised Control Trial (RCT)　An experimental methodology that seeks to minimise the risk of generating false positive test results (including the placebo effect) by randomising as many factors as possible.

Rapid Spiral Development (RSD)　An approach to innovation in complex technical systems based upon rapid learning and adaptation via repeated incremental design improvement and testing cycles. Requires modular designs that allow sub-systems to be modified and tested as part of the whole without major system re-designs.

Receiver Operating Characteristic (ROC)　A diagnostic tool used in signal processing to measure the accuracy of interpretations of data via the incidence of 'true positive' relative to 'false positive' test results.

Research and Experimental Development (R&D)　Activities of a risky nature aimed at advancing knowledge and understanding carried out in universities, research organisations and other non-profit entities, together with businesses. Usually attracts favourable tax treatment in response to the risks faced and, in some cases, also in recognition of the collective but hard-to-appropriate benefits that can result from some types of 'public' R&D.

Risk amplification ratio　The ratio of the achieved potential for surprise over the unavoidable potential for surprise.

Social rate of discount　The declining value that communities of people place on things that may happen in the future – the higher this rate of discount the lower the value placed on future events.

Stage-Gate methods　An approach to managing R&D and innovation in corporations by exploiting the ability to select between competing design concepts, allowing some activities to be curtailed and, as a result, resources to be re-allocated to more compelling design concepts. This provides for

Glossary 189

flexibility in response to learning and exploration and reduces the potential for wasted expenditure.

Substantive uncertainty Uncertainties that are not adequately treated as even odds of occurrence – effectively ignorance.

Systematic review A comprehensive assessment of available scientific evidence that uses robust methodologies applied to a wide range of studies.

Theory of change A technical specification of the relationships between cause and effect that frame and justify a government intervention.

True negative A negative test result when the tested condition is not present.

True positive A positive test result when the tested condition is present.

Truth table A diagnostic framework used in Qualitative Causal Analysis (QCA) to identify patterns in qualitative conditions (e.g. across a set of case studies).

Unavoidable potential for surprise The potential for surprise dictated by circumstances that cannot be controlled (e.g. an earthquake).

Weak signals Subtle and easy to miss indications of emerging threats.

Afterword

The process of researching and writing this book has involved highlighting a problematic aspect of modern governance (difficulties in coping with uncertainty and risk). It has also proposed a theoretical perspective able to drive strategies that could address these problems. This has been a 'developmental' exercise, a formative stage in a longer-term project, rather than presenting a *fait accompli* with all the technical details settled.

Before summarising the lessons learned from subsequent experimental work carried out by the time the book entered the final stage of publication it is worth emphasising the caution I encountered when drawing attention to the potential to use Bayesian inference to improve public policy. When working on the book I recall being approached by a conference organiser over my participation in a capacity-building event for government officials. When I proposed that I talk about the Bayesian perspective on learning and adaptation in governance I received the reply that I could talk about anything else I wanted in public policy '*but not anything to do with the Bayesian stuff*'. There were similar reactions from practitioners. This aversion reflected the understandable reluctance to risk bamboozling busy people with complex technical matters of little practical utility to them in the day-to-day business of working in government.

Consequently, one take home message from this book is that, thanks to the work done in psychology that has developed simplified ways of introducing Bayesian thinking into day-to-day practice in diagnostic activities, this risk of bamboozling practitioners is greatly diminished.

The simplicity engendered by natural frequency approaches to Bayesian inference in psychology, now available to the public policy community, opens up an avenue for governments to develop better ways of coping with uncertainty and risk and for learning and adapting when information is sparse and ambiguous – as it so often is. When combined with the methods used in signal processing and machine learning, which focus on the potential to generate confusing test results and 'worse than random' decisions, a coherent approach to the 'information state' is formed. A basis may exist for driving public sector reform via a refreshing analytical framework that places 'evidence' – its strengths and its limitations – into a more pragmatic context that recognises that, as the uncertainty and risk managers of last resort, governments must make decisions quickly when there is only weak, unreliable and indeed confusing evidence available. The challenge for the 'information state' lies more in how to cope with a dearth of information relevant to the future – not the excess information on the present and the past associated with the information age. To loosely paraphrase the often repeated remark by the science fiction novelist William Gibson ('*The future is here. It's just not widely distributed yet*') when governments are trying to deal with the future they have access to lots of information, but this information it is not necessarily distributed in ways that actually help them to deal with the future.

The experimental work aimed at filling in details of how simplified Bayesian inference and associated signal processing methods can be applied to improve the capacity to learn and adapt in governing in the face of uncertainty and risk indicates the following.

First, it is not hard to retrospectively frame previous intervention rationales as testable hypotheses or to frame potential future interventions as testable hypotheses. This means that it is feasible to transition to ways of defining government interventions that are explicitly 'experimentalist' and able to focus attention to the importance of learning and adapting effectively when delivering public policy.

Second, whilst some senior practitioners in government (and especially those who have since left government) are interested in the possibility of using explicit hypothesis-testing approaches to public policy able to integrate *ex ante* appraisal, in-process monitoring and *ex post* evaluation, others, especially those engaged in specific 'disconnected' functions (such as evaluation as a stand-alone activity) may be threatened by this potential for integration. This is the classic 'disruptive technology' scenario: faster and cheaper methods based on simplifying traditional ways of doing things threaten the status quo and vested interests – and are therefore resisted.

Third, the Receiver Operating Characteristic, framed in a public policy context as a Diagnostic Capability Plot, provides one approach to operationalising the risk amplification ratio (the ratio of the achieved potential for surprise over the unavoidable potential for surprise). The greater the incidence of false positives and false negatives in tests for potential surprises the greater the achieved potential for surprise relative to the unavoidable potential for surprise. Every test error that misses a signal, and particularly a weak signal of a looming problem that may grow exponentially, results in an amplified potential for nasty (and costly) surprises that will be harder to deal with if not nipped in the bud. Indeed, an existing formula used in signal detection analysis may allow the 'expected value' of the range of test sensitivity choices that can be made for a given level of diagnostic accuracy to be calculated (see Appendix). This is based on weighing up the likelihood of receiving the signal to be tested for, the benefit of the unnecessary costs avoided by being correct in not acting (true negative benefit), the costs of a false alarm (false positive cost), the benefit of a valid detection (true positive benefit) and the costs of a missed detection (false negative cost). The use of this calculation in public policy could inform the allocation of risk

192 *Afterword*

management resources for given levels of diagnostic capability – and would draw attention to the net benefits of investing in improving diagnostic capability relative to other calls on resources.

Fourth, and following directly from the above, the proposed approach may have its greatest potential in informing regulatory policy. Diagnostic Capability Plots, and calculations of the expected value of different test sensitivity thresholds, may provide a generic framework for assessing the current effectiveness of different regulatory designs and for setting the objectives for future improvements in these regulatory frameworks. As such, use of these signal detection methods in public policy could make a useful contribution to adaptive regulation – regulatory designs that are able to diagnose their own limitations as part of the monitoring function and evolve through learning-by-doing in such a way that the potential for nasty surprises is lower than would otherwise be the case. This type of 'rapid spiral regulation' could be particularly useful in security risk management contexts that rely on collaborative approaches with industry (and would provide an opportunity for government and industry to collaborate in improving regulatory performance from a public interest perspective).

Finally, there are a range of lower level technical challenges to be overcome:

- modifying existing Qualitative Causal Analysis (QCA) methods to align with Bayesian signal processing methods by exploiting the binary basis of both;
- developing a method to derive replicable odds-based hypothesis test results from a diverse mix of evidence types (both qualitative and quantitative) – using this marriage of QCA with Bayesian signal processing methods;
- re-calibrating hierarchies of evidence by measuring the differences in diagnostic accuracy using the simplified Bayes rule (and factoring-in judgment about the future) rather than simply assuming fixed hierarchies of evidence.

Solving these technical challenges in real public policy contexts requires sufficient collaboration and cooperation with practitioners. These collaborative opportunities are easiest in the 'greenfield' conditions created by policy devolution. The 'brownfield' conditions found in central government (well-bedded down divisions of labour and lock-in to existing methods and mind-sets) limits interest in new methods that may disrupt the status quo. Consequently, the potential to deliver transformational public policy – a means of governing that copes better with uncertainty and risk – rests largely on the extent to which there is an appetite to innovate by the people responsible for delivering the devolution of public policy capacity outside of central government. If the necessary experimentation and innovation is supported as part of the policy devolution process then the lessons learned will have the potential to be applied in central government at a later stage. The potential to explore 'rapid spiral regulation' methods is less likely to emerge from this policy devolution

Afterword 193

opportunity (regulation is a central government concern). However, the potential does exist for the business sector and civil society to drive innovation in this area – as long as this is done from a broad public interest stance and not from 'regulatory capture' stance.

From this perspective, current fiscal austerity will act as a stimulus for this type of innovation in the public sector – but the will to experiment and to innovate as part of the policy devolution process must also be present. This book is an attempt to contribute to this aspect of public sector reform by suggesting a suitable innovation strategy.

Appendix

Natural sampling and natural frequencies

The following diagram (fig A.1) illustrates the analytical issues faced in testing hypotheses using a biosecurity illustration.[1] The underlying challenges are however highly generalisable in public policy.

If trees are subject to a new imported fungal infection then we may observe some trees that appear to be disease free, some trees that appear to be slightly infected, some trees that are heavily infected but don't appear to be dying and some trees that are heavily infected but that do appear to be dying. Of course, there is always the scope for misreading the disease status of each tree examined (whether this is done in a simple visual manner or using technical instruments of various types). If scientific instruments are used then technological progress will tend to improve diagnostic accuracy, yielding lower diagnostic error rates.

If a classical randomised statistical sample is taken (illustrated by the square sampling frame that has been placed randomly in this region) then we are able to count the numbers of cases of each type – but are left with the problem of deciding how statistically significant this sample is likely to be as a basis for inferring the properties of the overall population of trees. The more money we have, the larger these randomised sample frames can be and/or the more of them we can use. As the coverage of our randomised sampling increases the risk of misdiagnosing the situation decreases.

In essence, classical 'frequentist' tests of statistical significance address this challenge by seeking to estimate the probability that the data observed could have been generated randomly – the lower this probability the more statistically significant the results. The conventional threshold used in many situations is a 5 per cent probability (i.e., a 95 per cent probability that the data observed was not generated by random events and processes). This is a mathematically elegant solution that makes good use of assumed but unobserved statistical distributions in order to calculate these levels of statistical significance. For some public policy situations these assumed statistical distributions work well – for others they may be less realistic as assumptions and therefore work less well.

The alternative approach is to use a 'natural sample' that is not randomised, as illustrated by the larger area around the randomly placed box sample. This can be more costly as a basis for obtaining results (more counting activities are

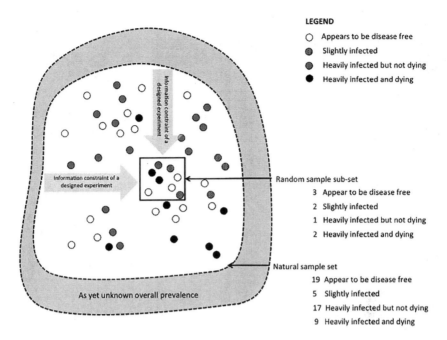

Figure A.1 A biosecurity illustration of natural sampling

required) and can be accomplished as a 'you see what you see' strategy. There is still an unobserved and therefore unknown general prevalence of the tree disease (indicated by the grey periphery in the diagram). However, we do not face the problem of working out how representative our randomly selected sample is – but we still face the problem of estimating the accuracy with which our natural sample is able to infer disease rates in the population of trees as a whole.

One advantage of a natural sample in a public policy context is that the data can be obtained from regular activities that will happen anyway. This can significantly reduce the cost of data collection and, therefore, allow a larger sampling for a given budget – potentially far larger if an extensive program of community engagement is used. Consequently, if natural sampling data collection procedures are built in to normal policy delivery mechanisms then this approach can become particularly cost-effective. It is normal for a range of data to be collected as part of monitoring program delivery, however these date tend to be under-utilised and as a result tend to be viewed as a compliance burden rather than useful information. In contrast, this approach would place this monitoring data at the core of the policy cycle by allowing it to be used to generate the hypotheses test results used to frame and track interventions on a regular basis.

A key issue with both the randomised and natural samples is *diagnostic accuracy*. It is both plausible and, experience tells us, not uncommon for the symptoms we observe to be complex, ambiguous and therefore confusing. This means

196 *Appendix*

that the potential to have miscounted the relative frequencies of disease states is subject to errors. If these diagnostic errors conform broadly to randomised statistical distributions then classical tests of statistical significance can work pretty well as a means of factoring-in this potential for errors into the assessment of statistical significance. Indeed, in research areas such as physics, measurements of the statistical distributions of signals generated by complex scientific instruments (that can be a source of spurious discoveries) can be used as an integral part of these more sophisticated statistical significance tests.

However, there is another approach that can be taken to these diagnostic errors whenever the opportunity exists to update our results, and as a result discover the extent to which these relative frequencies change when we re-examine data and/or use new or improved diagnostic methods that have a lower diagnostic error rate. Indeed, technological advances in scientific instruments are vitally important driver of scientific progress precisely because they can reduce diagnostic error rates: we get fewer cases of false positives and false negatives and more cases of true positives and true negatives. This results in lower levels of diagnostic confusion (as captured in the confusion matrix discussed in the main body of the book).

From this signal detection perspective, we can substitute actual data on diagnostic error rates derived from our updating and calibration processes for the use of assumed stochastic diagnostic error rates (as is done in classical statistical significance tests). Of course, this approach can only work if we are in a position to carry out this updating and calibration work – if not then classical approaches may be preferable.

As stressed above, this emphasis on updating and calibration is the essence of the Bayesian approach. The problem with implementing Bayesian methods in public policy has been that they are mathematically and computationally complex because they traditionally express situations using the mathematics of conditional probability and require what is known as the 'base rate' to be factored into this calculation. The base rate refers to the overall statistical prevalence of a condition, for example, the overall proportion of trees that are infected and dying. This is, of course, what we may be attempting to estimate in the first place if a newly emerging policy challenge is faced.

Luckily, research in psychology has developed a method that eliminates the need for this base rate, and that allows relative frequency of observations to be used in a manner that avoids the need to use conditional probability, Gigerenzer and Hoffrage (1995), Gigerenzer (2002). The result is a far simpler and much easier to use version of Bayesian hypothesis tests – an approach better suited to applications in public policy.

As discussed in Kleiter (1994), Aichtison and Dunsmore (1975) drew the important distinction between two types of scientific experiments: experiments that have been designed and experiments that are naturally informative but not designed.

In a *designed experiment* (which characterises the RCTs currently being used in public policy) the sample size(s) are fixed by the experimenter and, as a result, don't tell us what the base rates are. A fixed sample size imposes a restriction on what we observe – a restriction that means that what we observe is an unreliable means of estimating base rates. In contrast, in a *naturally informative experiment* ("we see what we see") the sample sizes are effectively a set of classes of random variables. By avoiding a fixed sample size we allow the phenomena being observed to reveal information about base rates. This means that unlike in a designed experiment they *do* tell us about the base rate.

This distinction can be grasped by looking at the disease status patterns in figure A.1 (above). In the randomly set box we have selected a sample that allows us to produce counts of disease states that may be representative of the actual conditions – but may not, depending on the 'luck of the draw'. In contrast, in the natural sample set the avoidance of fixing the sample size means that the relative frequencies of disease states that we count *do* give us a more confident indication of the base rates as we currently understand them.

This distinction between *designed experiments* and *naturally informative experiments* is of central importance to the potential to use Bayesian inference in the policy cycle. This is because it allows us to simplify Bayes rule to such at extent that it is readily understandable by anyone (and using simple numerical examples rather than mathematics). Whilst the technical details of how this is achieved are complex and hard to grasp unless one is an expert in mathematical expressions of Bayesian inference, see Kleiter (1992), it turns out that when Bayes rule is expressed in terms of relative frequencies of observations (the preferred formulation used by Kleiter) then the base rate lies in both the nominator and the denominator and therefore is cancelled out. This generates the simple formula discussed in chapter four, in which Bayes rule becomes simply the true positive frequency divided by the sum of the true positive frequency and the false positive frequency. This means that the familiar (and rather complex for non experts) expression of Bayes can be transformed into the simple ratio.

As Kleiter stresses, eliminating the need for normalisation using these base rates aligns better with human cognition and is a counter-posing view to that of Tversky and Kahneman (1974) – who argue that humans are subject to the 'base rate fallacy' of not normalising what is observed by an understanding of broader statistical prevalence. Kleiter's point is that we only need to normalise observations using base rate date if our samples are randomly selected and expressed in relative proportions. In human (and more general mammalian) cognition we think in terms of absolute relative frequency *counts* and not percentage *proportions*, and random sampling is a special case rather than the general rule. This means that we are able to learn and adapt quickly and effectively on the basis of these relative frequency counts.

This natural frequency approach helps us to grasp the significance, for public policy, of the equivalent the 'tug of war' that takes place within the brain between the left hemisphere, which sets up rules based on experience and ignores details (in order to react quickly) and the right hemisphere which avoids these rules in order to detect details and identify novel features – driving learning that may lead to the left hemisphere's rules for ignoring details being updated.

198 *Appendix*

Imbalances in this creative tension can lead to an excessive interest in details and data ('spectrum disorders' in clinical psychology) at the expense of using the 'short cut' rules that allow rapid pattern recognition and associated decision making – especially useful in identifying and responding to threats.

If we can use the simplified form of Bayesian updating made possible by the natural frequency method to inform learning and adaptation in governance then we can improve our ability to generate and quickly update the rules via which we look for the patterns that may signal nasty surprises. This approach reduces the risk that evidence-based policymaking leads to an imbalance between our ability to set up rules based on experience (that allow us to ignore details in order to act quickly) – and our ability to avoid these rules in order to detect details/anomalies that may lead us to update the rules that allow us to ignore details. The better we get this balance the more effectively we can govern in the face of uncertainty and risk.

How Receiver Operating Characteristic (ROC) curves are calculated and interpreted

Receiver Operating Characteristic (ROC) curves provide a means of assessing how we balance the sensitivity of the thresholds that we use to decide whether or not something is happening (such as a threat) against the risk of a false alarm and other signal detection problems. The more sensitive we make this threshold the greater the risk of a false positive test result. The less sensitive this threshold the greater the risk of a false negative test result. In other words, the nature and extent of the confusion that we may face (summarised in the confusion matrix discussed in chapter four) is in part a *choice* that we can make. Signal detection theory is a way of understanding this choice and informing us how best to proceed.

Figure A.2 shows how two frequency or likelihood distributions may relate to each other. If historical observations are available then this would be frequency data, if these data are not available then this could be *assumed* likelihoods. As Bayesian inference tells us, both can play a role and need not be exclusive of each other. One distribution describes a normal state of affairs (with more frequently observed events or assumed likelihoods forming a bell curve) whilst the other curve describes the distribution that we are interested in testing for – which can also be either hard data or assumed likelihoods (the latter is especially important if we are using conjectures to look for weak signals). Our choice over the threshold to use to test for the signal we are concerned with is made with reference to the nature and extent of the overlap between the two distributions. The areas under each curve to the right of a particular test threshold tell us the likelihoods of a true positive test result and of the false positive test result. The greater the overlap between the two distributions the worse our signal detection problem – the greater the potential for confusion over what is really happening.

The ROC curve is simply a plot of the resulting areas under each distribution to the right of a (varied) test threshold. The ROC curve is plotted by

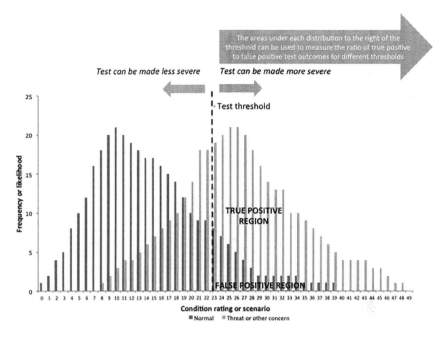

Figure A.2 How test sensitivity thresholds relate to statistical (and assumption) distributions

calculating the size of these areas (each of which gives us a likelihood factor for a false positive test result and for a true positive test result) for a range of different test sensitivity levels. These two likelihood factors are then plotted in a graph with the false positive factor on the horizontal axis and the true positive factor on the vertical axis. The result is a curve that tells us, for a given diagnostic situation (determined by the two distributions) how the much better or worse than random our test results are likely to be. This is illustrated in figure A.3. The higher the diagnostic curve above the diagonal, and the greater its curvature near to the best possible point in the top left hand corner of the diagram the better our diagnostic accuracy. For a given ROC curve, test sensitivity choices must be made in the light of the trade-off between the benefits of an increased true positive rate and the dis-benefits of the higher false positive rate that must also be tolerated. The area under each curve provides a measure of diagnostic accuracy. Hence, random diagnostic performance is indicated by the diagonal line associated with getting it right half the time – below that line our diagnostic abilities are not just severely limited – but potentially damaging and wasteful. The further our diagnostic performance deviates from the best possible point the greater the potential for nasty surprises – and especially so if we exhibit 'worse than random' diagnostic performance. The graph also shows how diagnostic performance can be compromised when the distributions being

200   Appendix

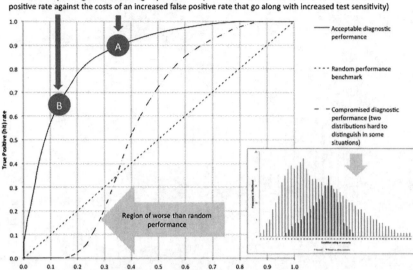

Organisational capability errors can distort the perceived or measured distributions that generate these ROC curves – thus compromising diagnostic performance

Figure A.3 ROC curves as diagnostic capability measures

used to test hypotheses make it hard to work out what is going on. In this case, closely overlapping distributions describing the normal state of affairs and the condition being tested for result in a compromised ROC curve that dips into 'worse than random' territory.

The advantages of adopting this signal detection approach in public policy revolve around the potential that exists for limitations to organisations' capabilities and uncertainty and risk-averse practices and procedures to, in effect, distort the statistical and assumption distributions that are used to derive ROC curves. As the book stresses, in decision-making about the future the uncertainties and risks faced require a significant element of judgment based on tacit knowledge – data based on past experience will be useful but not a sufficient condition for effective decisions. Consequently, assumptions and conjectures are required. It is these assumptions and conjectures, together with weaknesses in the analysis and interpretation of the data that we do have (missed opportunities to learn) that shapes our diagnostic capability curves. In other words, for public policy, the statistical and assumption distributions we base our analyses on (including official statistics) are the outputs of social and political processes that can distort reality via a mix of *a priori* assumptions and deliberate choices over the aspects to prioritise and aspects/issues to downplay.

The result is that this social and political shaping of 'evidence', combined with unavoidable assumptions about the future, can shift ROC curves in ways that push them towards the dangerous 'worse than random' region – in so doing amplifying risks and therefore increasing the potential for nasty surprises. The spurious precision engendered by 'the new public management', an ethos that seeks to govern using 'business like' performance targets and programme management methods, is one example of the way in which how we choose to formulate and deliver public policy can compromise diagnostic capability and the ability of governments to learn and adapt. *Signal detection methods provide us with a tractable means of demonstrating this disadvantage of current modes of governance.*

Finally, and to reinforce the above point, signal detection analysis also provides a potentially useful formula for calculating the optimal point on a given diagnostic curve to aim for given the prevailing cost and benefits associated with the likelihoods of true positive, false positive, true negative and false negative test results, Swets, Dawes, and Monahan (2000). The derivation of this formula in Peterson, Birdsall and Fox (1954) is rather complex in mathematical terms, but it does yield the following using formula. This calculation tells us how the balance of benefits and costs associated with the four different items in the

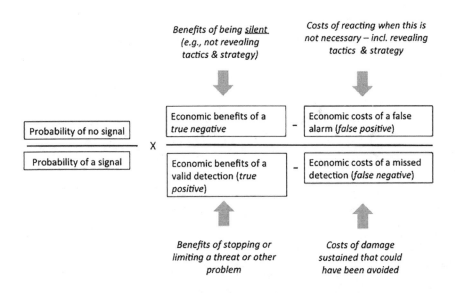

This expected value equation provides a basis for deciding the optimal test sensitivity point to aim for on the ROC (i.e. diagnostic capability) curve associated with specific diagnostic accuracy conditions. Different economic circumstances impact on this test sensitivity threshold.

Figure A.4 The expected value equation used to inform test sensitivity choices

202   *Appendix*

'confusion matrix' net out as an 'expected value' (i.e. a risk-based benefit-cost estimate).

As such, this expected value calculation, when applied in a public policy context, has the potential to help us to evaluate our current diagnostic performance and to inform the choices we make over how much to invest in diagnostic capability for particular situations. The ability of this framework to act as a generic space for measuring how well we cope (or could improve how we cope) with uncertainty and risk in public policy makes in a compelling avenue for further exploration. For example, the regulation of drones around major airports is currently an important issue. Use of this framework would not only help us to assess how effective our current regulatory stance is (via its ability to detect and deal with drone-based threats to aircraft as reflected in an ROC curve) but could also inform the design trade-offs to be made in modifying our regulatory stance. The ability to weigh up the expected value of the combination of the likelihoods of valid detections, false alarms, missed detections and of correctly not intervening (i.e. true negatives) in benefit-cost terms is especially useful in a public policy context. It may also provide a basis (via feedback loops) for dealing with 'learning-by-undoing': the ways in which those people and organisations that an intervention seeks to influence are able to understand and then undermine the efficacy of that intervention.

To sum up, signal detection methods provide a practical framework for implementing subjectivist approaches to public policy that are able to translate the philosophical stance associated with Australian/subjectivist economics into diagnostic tools that can be used within government to deliver a new strategy for coping with uncertainty and risk.

Note

1 This section draws upon a scoping study contributing to the *Regional and Remote Public Policy Initiative* carried out by the author in 2016 for the Northern Institute at Charles Darwin University. This scoping study examined the potential to apply and further develop the ideas proposed in this book in regional and remote contexts.

References

Aitchison, J. and Dunsmore, I.R. 1975, *Statistical Prediction Analysis*. Cambridge University Press, Cambridge.

Gigerenzer, G. (2002) *Reckoning with risk: Learning to live with uncertainty*. Penguin. London.

Gigerenzer, G., Hoffrage, U. 1995, How to Improve Bayesian Reasoning Without Instruction: Frequency Formats. *Psychological Review*. vol 102 no. 4 pp. 684–704.

Kleiter, G.D. 1992, Bayesian diagnosis in expert systems. *Artificial Intelligence*. Vol 54, pp. 1–32.

Kleiter, G.D. 1994, Natural sampling: Rationality without base rates. In Fisher, GH and Laming, D. (eds) *Contributions to mathematical psychology, psychometrics, and methodology*. pp. 357–388. Springer: New York.

Peterson, W.W., Birdsall, T.G., Fox, W.C., 1951, The theory of signal detectability. *IRE Professional Group on Information Theory* PGIT-4, pp. 171–212.

Swets, J.A., Dawes, R.M., Monahan, J. 2000, Psychological science can improve diagnostic decisions. *Psychological Science in the Public Interest.* 1, pp. 1–26.

Tversky, A. and Kahneman, D. 1974, Judgement under Uncertainty: heuristics and biases. *Science.* New Series, vol. 185, no. 4157. (Sep. 27, 1974), pp. 1124–1131.

Index

abductive reasoning 51, 124
academic output 81
academic studies 20–1
accountability 17, 30, 33, 41, 60, 137, 173
achieved potential for surprise 21–3, 25, 91, 112, 115, 118–20, 122, 124, 132, 165, 168, 169
adaptive governance 4; implementation of 95; steps toward 179–85
Admiralty Scale 149
advanced simulation software 83
Apollo space program 43–4
appraisal 6–8, 11; linking to evaluation 159; using updated odds 143, 159
artificial dispersion artillery firing algorithms 96, 115
asset valuations 89
astronomy 103
austerity 164, 169–70; as catalyst for creativity 5–6; and crisis conditions 4; innovation and 4–13
Australian home insulation scheme 115–16, 118–19, 165

bankable feasibility 79–80
banking, government regulation of 117
Bayes factor 146
Bayesian inference: applications of 13, 19, 40, 53, 95, 102–4, 156; in astronomy 103; binary applications of 146, 153; in cognitive processes 51, 53; used in discovery-based interventions 176; history of 97–105, 184; influence on signal processing and machine learning 24, 51, 53, 105–12, 127, 166, 168; linear expression of 100; used by Laplace 3, 184; and the policy learning cycle 156–60; vision as 50

Bayesian learning loop 100
Bayesian updating 156
Bayes Rule 142, 175, 180; conditional probability version 101; Natural Frequency expression of 108–9
benefit–cost trade-offs 153
Berkowitz, Bruce 15–16
beta 78–81
binary frameworks 128, 146, 153
Boolean approach 144, 151–4, 158, 180
brownfield sites 134
budgeting: objectives-based 30; output-outcome 87; public sector 123; risk-aware 145–6
Bureau of Economic Analysis (BEA) 92n3
Bush, Vannavar 69; *see also Science the Endless Frontier*

CAD (Computer Aided Design) 71–2
Capability Maturity Model (CMM) 181
Capital Asset Pricing Model (CAPM) 78, 79, 92n1
CFD (computational fluid dynamics) 83
Challenger space shuttle disaster 116
CIA 152, 154
circularity 184
civil society organisations 161
classical statistical significance 146, 181
climate disruption 84
code breaking 19, 104, 140, 149
code validation 83
cognitive processes 53, 123
Cold War 19, 96, 117
collaboration 77; with academia 167; with civil society 167; cross-sectoral 160–1; government–academic 19, 26, 60, 148
colour perception 50

206　*Index*

commercial activity 81
commercial aviation 10–11
commercialisation 77–8; of research 87
computational fluid dynamics (CFD) 83
Computer Aided Design (CAD) 71–2
Confederation Committee on Science and Technology 90
confidence curves 72, 73, 92n6
Confusion Matrix 107, 108
cooperation, international 171–2
cost overruns 12, 26, 35, 38–40, 42, 79
creativity 51–2, 98, 164, 170
credibility: of evidence 35, 142, 144, 154, 161, 180–1; of government, 76, 91, 168
credibility weightings 144, 180
Crozier, Michael 37

data: analysis of 30; correlation with theory 82; frequency of occurrence 154; generation of 35;
DCP framework *see* Diagnostic Capability Plots
decimal probability coefficients 2–3
decision-making 16, 19, 20, 31, 33–4, 41–2, 61–2, 66, 74–6, 95, 112, 116, 118, 120, 123, 148, 149, 164, 165, 169, 172, 174–5; in public policy 67, 103; risk-averse 37, 67
Defense Technical Information Center 95
Deming, Edwards 6
democracy, as organised uncertainty 27n6
design, de-bugging of 19
design capabilities, as confidence curves 72
developing economies 167–8
diagnostic accuracy 183–5
diagnostic capability, measuring 111
Diagnostic Capability Plots (DCP) 171, 173, 181–2
diagnostic errors 7–8, 17, 60, 142, 144, 154, 178, 180–2; dynamic approach to 158–60
discount rate symmetry 34
Discourse, The (Machiavelli) 1
discovery-based interventions 13, 44, 51, 69–71, 73–4, 146, 160, 176–8, 181–3
disease outbreaks 24
double hermeneutics 12, 19
dynamic learning targets 183

economic perspectives, subjectivist 41
economics: Austrian 26, 47, 76, 113; classical 76; neo-classical 40, 41; subjectivist 26, 41, 46–7, 76, 113
encryption work 23, 24, 106
entropy 14, 47–8, 63n5, 107; decrease in 173; negative 174; *see also* governance entropy; Shannon entropy
equity, inter-generational 85, 89
European Union, national accounts guidelines 86
evaluation 6–8, 11, 18; linking to appraisal 159; marginalisation of 134; parameters for 128
evidence: credibility of 142, 144, 180; weight of 166
evidence assessment, Boolean approach to 144, 151–4, 158, 180
evidence-based policymaking 9, 11, 12, 14–19, 30, 33–4, 98, 129–30, 151, 164, 167, 171, 173, 175, 180
existential threats 37
Expected Value 58–60, 172
experimental development, research and 69–75

FAA (Federal Aviation Administration) 82
'fail early' provisions 135–6
false negatives 118–19, 142, 165, 171, 182, 185
false positives 52, 102, 151, 154, 166, 171, 182, 185
feasibility, bankable 79–80
Federal Aviation Administration (FAA) 82
Federation of Australian Scientific and Technological Societies (FASTS) 84
Federation of Australian Scientific Societies 90
Ferson, Scott 102
Feynman, Richard 2, 102
finance, government regulation of 117
First of a Kind (FOAK) 79, 80–1, 92–3n13
Fisher, Ronald 97
FOAK 79, 80–1, 92–3n13
Ford Motor Company 30
forecast bias methodology 40
'Frascati' manual (OECD) 69
frequentist approaches 9, 13, 97–9, 117, 181
funding agreements 135–6

Index   207

Gaussian copula 117
Giddens, Anthony 19
global financial crisis 37, 85, 116–17, 164
governance: effectiveness of 25;
  experimentalist 37–42; learning in
  61–2; learning deficit in 52; paradigms
  of 32–7; and risk management 42–6;
  signal processing applied to 112–20
governance entropy 21–5, 92, 106, 112,
  165, 169–70, 172–3; *see also* adaptive
  governance
government: privatisation of services 32;
  regulatory role of 67
government–academic collaboration 19,
  26, 60, 148; *see also* collaboration
greenfield sites 134, 179

harm reduction 153
hermeneutics, double 12, 19
heuristics 113, 114–15
hierarchies of evidence 16, 17, 67, 130,
  142
historical experience *see* evidence-based
  policymaking
Hoover Dam 116, 165
horizon scanning 2
human capital 73–4, 92n8
human intelligence 148
hypotheses: competing 157; induction
  of 156; revision of 183
hypothesis testing 135–7, 170; assigning
  odds in 140–7; binary 140; calculating
  odds-based results 147–55; in policy
  and program evaluation 138–40;
  odds-based 141–2

'ideal world' assumptions 40
IMF (International Monetary Fund) 86
individualism, methodological 41
inefficiencies 12
information: actionable 20, 41–2;
  relative importance of 47–8; vs.
  uncertainty 105
information gains, measurement of
  146
information theory 2, 13, 23, 39, 41,
  91, 107, 129; relevance of 47–9
innovation policy, science and 68–9
innovation: and austerity 4–13; and
  expected value 58–9; in hypothesis
  creation 147; and investment risk
  58–61; management of 66; open
  approach to 27, 172–5; in the private

sector 54–8, 66–7; in the public
  sector 57–8, 66; in SMEs 180
institutional failure 75
intellectual property rights 59
intelligence: analysis of 16; assessment
  of 148; security 11, 22, 113–14, 138,
  147–8, 152–5, 160; sources of 148
International Financial Reporting
  Standards (IFRS) 49
International Monetary Fund (IMF),
  national accounts guidelines 86
Internet, technological foundation of 95
intervention(s) 35; discovery-based
  13, 44, 51, 69–71, 73–4, 146, 160,
  176–8, 181–3; as hypothesis tests
  135–7; policy 5, 16, 18, 40, 52, 54,
  87, 96, 98, 100, 101, 110, 135, 137,
  142, 152, 166, 172, 175, 182; target-
  driven 13, 30, 32, 35, 36, 42–4, 46,
  56, 71–2, 96, 98, 100, 146, 176–8
invention *see* innovation
inverse probability 102
investment, risk in 77–84
investment risk trajectory 172–3
ISO 31000: 2009 21, 30, 31, 42, 43,
  112

Key Performance Indicators (KPIs)
  32–3, 100–1
Knight, Frank 76
knowledge acquisition phases 121

learning: adaptive 37–8, 50–1, 53, 105;
  machine 51, 53, 107 110; robotic
  61–2
learning and adaptation 127; analysis
  96; cycle 6–7; heuristics 96
learning-by-doing 2, 12, 31, 32, 36–8,
  42, 48, 127, 160, 168
learning-by-undoing 12, 19, 34, 98
learning curves 56, 79–81
learning loops, Bayesian 100
licensing deals 56
Log Frames 128

M&E frameworks 128
Machiavelli, Niccolò 1
machine learning 51, 53, 107 110
mapping, visual 120–1
Maryland Scientific Methods Scale
  130–1
Mazzucato, Mariana 57
McNamara, Robert 30

208 *Index*

Metric Entropy 23
modernity 14, 27n6
monitoring, evaluation and learning
(MEL) 100–1, 128, 134, 136, 140

NAO (UK National Audit Office) 52
NASA 43–4, 119, 165; Apollo space
program 43–4; *Challenger* disaster
116
national accounts guidelines 86
National Audit Office (NAO) 130
national balance sheets 49, 86
national security 4, 19, 24, 47, 68, 83,
95, 98, 107, 113–14, 120, 152–3
Natural Frequency expression 108–9,
124n4
neoliberalism 36, 41
net domestic product, depletion
adjusted 86
Net Present Value (NPV) 58–9, 78
new public management(s) 20, 30, 62
noise: and entropy 173–4; identifying
48, 106–7; randomness as 14, 23,
48–9, 91, 98, 152–3; signals hidden
in 95, 113, 155; *see also* signal-to-
noise ratio
normal distribution 117
Nowotny, Helga 3, 88

Obamacare (Patient Protection and
Affordable Care Act; ACA) 5
Occam's Razor 103
OECD (Organisation for Economic
Cooperation and Development)
69–70, 77, 86, 171; countries 127,
168
Office of Management and Budget
(OMB) 69, 92n3
OMB (Office of Management and
Budget) 69, 92n3
open innovation approach 27, 172–5
Organisation for Economic Cooperation
and Development *see* OECD
Ostrom, Elinor 4
outlier skills 55–6, 72

Patient Protection and Affordable Care
Act (ACA; Obamacare) 5
patterns: identifying, interpreting, and
reacting to 1–2, 8, 14–15, 20, 51,
70, 76, 123–4, 151–3, 156; random
48–9, 96, 152, 181; in Shannon
entropy 23, 27n9; study of 151–3; of
synergy 182; in test results 171

peer review 73–4
performance targets *see* target-setting
placebo effect 9, 155, 178
plan-do-check-adjust cycle 6
policy interventions 5, 16, 18, 40, 52,
54, 87, 96, 98, 100, 101, 110, 135,
137, 142, 152, 166, 172, 175, 182
policy learning cycle 156–8, 170
policy think tanks 9
policymaking: intelligence-based 33;
see also evidence-based policymaking
Popper, Karl 98
power, theoretical 77–84
preparedness 84, 86
prescience 26; implementation of
as a research outcome 90–2; as
an outcome class 84–5, 146; and
protecting the value of national
balance sheets 86
Prescience Research Portfolios 88–9
Prime Minister's Science, Engineering
and Innovation Council (PMSEIC) 90
probabilities, conditional 102
probability assumption 121
Productivity Commission (Australian
Government) 90
progress: economic 86; monitoring of
22, 35–6, 54, 113, 136, 166; social
98; virtual 80–1
public choice theory 25
public debt 54, 91, 164, 174, 185
public policy 11, 98; cross-sectoral
collaboration over 160–1; decision-
making in 103; integrated approach
to 184; as iterative process 163;
practice of vs. study of 20–1; and risk
3, 26; transformational 134
public science 73, 74–7, 82
public sector problems 17–20, 36–7
public spending 167, 174; rate of return
on 151
Public Value 49

Qualitative Causal Analysis (QCA) 144
Qualitative Causality Analysis (QCA)
180
Qualitative Comparative Analysis (QCA)
151–4, 180
quantifiable risk: avoiding 62; handling
of 2, 97; vs. substantive uncertainty
3, 10–12, 14–15, 27n5, 30, 31,
61; transformation of substantive
uncertainty into 63, 68–9, 84, 87–8,
91, 135, 140, 164

Index 209

Ragin, Charles 151
RAND Corporation 35, 117, 118
Randomised Control Trials (RCTs) 12,
  16–18, 111, 104, 130–1, 142, 160,
  173, 175, 176
range compression 115
Rapid Spiral Development (RSD)
  43–4
Rationale, Objectives, Appraisal,
  Monitoring, Evaluation and Feedback
  (ROAMEF) 129–30
RCTs *see* Randomised Control Trials
Receiver Operating Characteristic curve
  (Receiver Operator Curve; ROC
  curve) 110–11, 173, 174
red teaming 165
regulatory approval 82
research: academic 80; analytical
  methods in 148; blue sky 70–1;
  commercialisation of 77, 87; and
  experimental development 69–75;
  high-tech 71
Research and Experimental Development
  (R&D) 56–7, 69, 120, 70; beta
  outcome 78–9; federally funded 69;
  high technology 83–4; industrial 74–5,
  84; potential for surprise in 120; public
  75–7; SMEs 153
return on investment (ROI) 167;
  calculation of 144; on public
  spending 151
reverse salients 147
*Review of Public Support for Science and
  Innovation* (PC; 2006) 90
Review of the National Innovation
  System (2008) 90
risk: aversion to 135; calculable vs.
  incalculable 39; categories of 151;
  controllable 120, 122; government
  definitions of 42–3; identification of
  45; mitigation of 45; in return-on-
  investment calculations 144;
  socialisation of 25; stochastic 120,
  122; and uncertainty 30; and
  uncertainty and modernity 27n6;
  unmeasurable 76; *see also* quantifiable
  risk; security risks
risk amplification 25, 91–2, 112–14,
  115, 119, 164; factors in 119, 132
risk amplification ratio 21–2, 25, 114,
  118, 120, 165, 166, 168–9
risk curve 150
risk management 2, 4, 35, 45–6, 164,
  165, 184; causing increased risk

42–3; as compliance 42, 114; cycles
  of 7; different perspectives on 132;
  exploiting synergies in 134; and
  governance 42–6; in investment
  banking 117; navigational metaphor
  44–6; nuclear weapons and 117–18;
  in the private sector 57; in the
  public sector 6–8; re-formulating
  131–3; scope for integrating different
  perspectives 133; standards and
  guidelines for 43; and substantive
  uncertainty 87
risk matrices 114, 115, 151
risk–reward relationship 60, 66, 78
ROAMEF policy learning framework
  129–30
robotic learning 61–2; *see also* learning,
  machine
ROC curve *see* Receiver Operating
  Characteristic curve (Receiver
  Operator Curve; ROC curve)

sampling theory 9, 97, 103, 120
science: and innovation policy 68–9;
  public 73, 74–7, 82
Science and Technology Australia 90
Science the Endless Frontier (Bush) 69
Second World War 19, 96, 99, 116,
  149, 164
security intelligence 11, 22, 113–14,
  138, 147–8, 152–5, 160
security risks 114
sensitivity analyses 144
Severity of a Test 104
Shannon, Claude 47, 63n5, 105, 164,
  166
Shannon entropy 23, 27nn8–9, 47, 105,
  106, 107, 166
Shannon error correction model 106
signal detection 24
signal processing 95, 107, 110, 127,
  128, 166; applied to governance
  112–20; methods and techniques 7,
  174, 182
signals intelligence 148
signal-to-noise ratio 10, 13, 23, 39, 47,
  138
simulation modelling 81
simulation technologies 72
SMEs 153, 173, 175, 180
'smoking gun' ethos 77
social rate of discount 85, 86
solid fuel rocket systems 116
source code 82–3

210 Index

speculative thinking 52–3
spin-offs 56
Stage-Gate methods of innovation
  management 66
start-ups 56
statistical significance, tests of 175–9
Stern Report 85
Stirling, Andrew 15
stretch targets 43; *see also* target-setting
subjective contours 123
substantive uncertainty: avoiding 62;
  framing of 3, 31; handling of 2,
  10–12, 14, 19, 31, 33, 36, 41–2,
  84, 87, 89; high levels of 5, 146,
  179; identification of 20, 40, 76;
  vs. information 46; vs. quantifiable
  risk 15, 27n5, 30, 38–9, 61, 67, 87;
  mapping 120–4; vs. statistical 20;
  transformation into quantifiable risk
  63, 68–9, 84, 87–8, 91, 135, 140, 164
surprise(s): avoidance of 37–8;
  minimising potential for 168, 170;
  potential for 22–3, 25, 37, 91, 172,
  185; reducing potential for 113, 118;
  unavoidable potential for 119, 132,
  165, 168–9, 175; *see also* achieved
  potential for surprise
synergies, system of 183
systematic review 125n5, 142, 144,
  148, 161, 171, 173, 180–2

target-driven interventions 13, 30, 32,
  35, 36, 42–4, 46, 56, 71–2, 96, 98,
  100, 146, 176–8
target-setting 9–12, 27n5, 42, 176, 178,
  185
technologies, simulation 72
Teledyne Energy Systems 116
Ternary representations: of the disjuncture
  between theory and practice in risk
  management 123; of knowledge
  acquisition phases 121; of knowledge
  domains 122
terrorism 98–9
theory/theories: applicable 82–3;
  correlation with data 82
Theory (Theories) of Change 128, 136,
  176, 178

threats: elimination of 153; exaggerated
  16; existential 26, 37–8, 123;
  management of 70, 73, 99, 114;
  potential 88; in weak signals 171
'tradecraft' guidance 152
transparency 13, 17, 30, 33, 41, 60,
  137, 140, 173
true negative 108, 110, 135, 166, 174,
  182
true positive 102, 108–10, 135, 142,
  166, 174, 180, 182
truth tables 152
Turing, Alan 3, 104, 106, 140
Turing–Good curve 149

UK: defence intelligence categories
  149–50; National Audit Office
  (NAO) 52; ROAMEF policy learning
  framework in 129–30
unavoidable potential for surprise 119,
  132, 165, 168–9, 175
uncertainty 14, 184; asymmetric 33; as
  even odds 31; vs. information 105;
  'Knightian' 76; limitations of 26;
  management of 2, 4; in return-on-
  investment calculations 144; and risk
  and modernity 27n6; statistical 41–2;
  see also substantive uncertainty
undesirable outcomes 84
unintended consequences 66, 76
United Nations 86
units of output 81
US: Department of Defense 43; Food
  and Drug Administration (FDA) 104

value-for-money measures 140, 167
value trajectory 59
venture capitalism 55, 59
visualisation 26

weak signals 24, 99, 113, 144, 152,
  171; diagnostic errors as 159–60
weapon systems 82–3
Weight of Evidence 104, 156, 166
wicked problems challenge 76
World Bank 30, 86

Xenophon 1